ACID TRIP

TRAVELS IN THE WORLD OF VINEGAR

With Recipes from Leading Chefs,

Insights from Top Producers,

and Step-by-Step Instructions on How to Make Your Own

....

MICHAEL HARLAN TURKELL

ABRAMS, NEW YORK

TO MDK & MASON

Editor: Michael Sand
Designer: Deb Wood
Production Manager:
  Alex Cameron

Library of Congress Control
Number: 2016941953

ISBN: 978-1-4197-2417-6

Copyright © 2017
Michael Harlan Turkell

Vinegar bottle illustrations
by Heesang Lee

Printed and bound in
the United States
10 9 8 7 6 5 4 3 2 1

Abrams books are available
at special discounts when
purchased in quantity for
premiums and promotions
as well as fundraising or
educational use. Special
editions can also be created to
specification. For details, contact
specialsales@abramsbooks.com
or the address below.

ABRAMS The Art of Books
115 West 18th Street, New York, NY 10011
abramsbooks.com

CONTENTS

FOREWORD
BY DANIEL BOULUD

From my office, a small glass-enclosed room dubbed "the skybox" that sits above the kitchen at DANIEL, I notice Michael as he arrives for our meeting. He looks more like one of the farmers who often visit than a renowned professional photographer—with a scruffy beard and red flannel shirt, he stands out like a Christmas light against the starched, ultra-white uniforms of the twenty or so young chefs who make up the bustling kitchen brigade. But Michael looks quite at ease here. No outsider to the culinary world, he's been working in kitchens for the past twenty years, whether holding a camera, a knife, a notepad, or all three, and he chats comfortably with the chefs downstairs.

When he comes up to the skybox and shakes my hand, I immediately recognize him, specifically the expression of total fascination he wears at all times. One day, about ten years ago, I went to speak to my then–*chef boulanger*, Mark Fiorentino, and there was this kid with him (dressed similarly to the way he is today), with the aforementioned notepad and spellbound eyes, scribbling down every word Mark said, totally captivated by Mark's dough-enrobed hands. At the time, Michael was studying bread, as in: bread science, bread art, bread baking, bread sales, bread production, and bread chemistry, literally the world of bread, plus some things you never knew were part of the world of bread.

I wouldn't say I dismissed him, but I was all business and needed to speak with Mark. Still, it was nice to see a young person so interested in the craft, and I wished him the best. Now, as he sits across from me with the same wide-eyed look (though perhaps he's a little under-slept), I have to say that I'm as intrigued by him as he is with me, and it's immediately apparent that he's found a new, unlikely muse in food, leaving planet Earth and setting up camp in the world of *vinegar*.

Many people might wonder what could compel someone to become obsessed with vinegar, but not me. For a chef, acidity is central to the concept of balance of flavor, and the world of vinegar, as Michael illustrates in this book, is vast and complex, much more so than many people, even chefs, realize. For me, growing up on a farm outside of Lyon, where my family made vinegar (we made for ourselves most of the things we ate), I never grasped the depth or the art of fine-tuning vinegar for flavor and sensory enjoyment. We had grapes, wine, and food to preserve, so having vinegar around was just a part of life. But later, as a chef in a wine-rich region of France, I quickly learned the distinct role that white wine vinegar vs. red wine vinegar, for example, plays in a dish, and then moved beyond to choices like tarragon vinegar, rice vinegar, balsamic vinegar, and coconut vinegar—and these are very much just the basics.

At our meeting, Michael opens up his laptop to show me pictures (truly works of art) from his travels while researching the book. They include a field in Kagoshima, in the southwest of Japan, where about 52,000 *tsubo* (jars) are sitting outside turning into *kurozu*, or black vinegar. Also in Japan he captures Akihiro Iio, from Iio Jozo, maker of Fujisu rice vinegar, talking about the importance of vinegar in *shari* (sushi rice) made in a *hangiri* (wooden bowl). Another is the *batteria*, or series of barrels, in Acetaia San Giacomo of Reggio Emilia, Italy, one of only two regions where traditional balsamic can be made. In my home country of France, he visits Martin Pouret in Orléans, the last Orléans-style vinegar maker in an area where at least a hundred producers existed a mere hundred years ago. The expression "This is not your mother's vinegar" comes to mind.

He's also brought his own vinegars for me to try: Triple Berry Vinegar, Dark Beer Vinegar, and his serendipitous Hot Toddy Vinegar. He explains how he met a vinegar maker who had recently dabbled in "cocktail vinegars"—meaning vinegars to use in crafting cocktails, not vinegars flavored like popular cocktails, as Michael had first thought. So, Michael decided to take a stab at it, and created a vinegar built with ingredients such as honey, whiskey, lemon, and cloves, thus tasting like a Hot Toddy. Since, he's made a Posca Sour, a word play on an ancient Greek concoction and reminiscent of the Peruvian cocktail the pisco sour. Maybe it's not the next commercial phenomenon, but it clearly has been some fun for him.

When my assistant offers coffee, Michael proudly announces he's just finished a Maple Coffee Vinegar. I tell him that would be quite the afternoon pick-me-up, and we dive into discussion of vinegar as a health remedy. This isn't news, of course, but it has trended lately as a weight-loss fad, and while the beneficial properties of vinegar are very real, Michael dismisses some of its newfound popularity. To him, it's not a miracle pill to be unpleasantly gulped down in a shot glass; it is an ingredient to be savored that, when done right, is as special and exciting to him as black truffle is to me.

This idea of building vinegar is important to Michael. When he makes vinegar, he treats the potion like a living body, not just throwing liquids together and forgetting about it. It's about nurturing flavors and adjusting, sometimes on a scientific level, and sometimes on the level of pure taste. So when I try his apple vinegar, I'm struck by the complex, authentic taste of apple it has, and then impressed when he confirms it's made from almost a thousand pounds of wild and heirloom apple varieties. The result is no accident, it's something he designed and blended with care. Vinegar can take on the flavor of almost anything, and the options for creativity are near endless, but patience is the most important ingredient.

Meeting Michael again, ten years since our first encounter, I decide that patience is one of his best assets. I don't mean to say that he is calmly twiddling his thumbs while watching wine ferment—over the past ten years he's photographed at least a dozen cookbooks, been nominated for a James Beard award, contributed to countless publications, and he hosts a popular podcast called The Food Seen on Heritage Radio Network—he's a busy guy. Rather, I admire how comfortable he is with his obsession, unapologetically diving in headfirst. He gets ahold of an unsung subject in food and just accepts the fact that it will take over his life for the indefinite future.

Personally, it's something I can relate to: finding a passion, and then engaging it 100 percent, following it wherever it takes you. It's not always an easy thing to do, but Michael does so with a genuine respect for the quality of the ingredients, people, and places in this book, and with a joy that is infectious. His meticulous research for this book took him on a journey seeking out the expertise of not only some of the most authentic producers, but also the important chefs who bring vinegar to life in their cuisine, such as Michel Troisgros, Eric Ripert, Bertrand Auboyneau, Michael Anthony, Massimo Bottura, Sean Brock, April Bloomfield, and so many more. I forgot to ask what his next obsession will be, and I have not on written nearly enough on his incredible talent as a photographer, nor on the striking photos in this book. One thing is certain though, when he lands on whatever is next, he'll dive right in. And it's sure to be one hell of a trip.

INTRODUCTION

A FERMENTED JOURNEY INTO VINEGAR'S SOURED PAST AND BRIGHT FUTURE

We're living in the age of artisan ingredients—even common pantry items are fawned over and refined and sold in elegant little bottles and jars with bespoke labels. And in our favorite condiments, including ketchup, mustard, and mayonnaise; in sauces like hot sauce, mignonette, and chimichurri; and even in some jams and chutneys, there's an unsung hero helping to create flavor and balance: *vinegar*. This sharp, zingy liquid plays a vital role in cooking as well: vinegar livens up vinaigrettes, adds acidity to butter-based and egg-yolk-emulsified mother sauces like beurre blanc and béarnaise, can deglaze a pan of delicious browned flavor bits known as fond, and completes a sweet-and-sour gastrique, which, without vinegar, would simply be sweet.

Of course vinegar is essential to pickling, too, but it's usually the resulting pickle, and rarely the all-important vinegar, that gets the praise and attention. Vinegar is used in baking, braising, and even cocktail making and is essential to virtually every cuisine the world over, and yet despite its versatility and singular nature, this sour wine (from the French *vin aigre*) remains underappreciated and little understood.

My obsession with vinegar came about through an accident, in the clichéd way that most people think vinegar is made: by leaving a bottle of wine out and open. This is a serious faux pas in my house: my wife, Megan, is a wine writer and, in a sense, vinegar is the antithesis to the stuff she studies and adores. Regrettably, for her, that first resulting vinegar was superb. The process was almost effortless and it yielded a far better product than what we had in our cupboard. This impelled me to ask, "Is there more to making vinegar than just forgetfulness?"

I searched for instruction to take the process to the next level, to see what would be involved in making vinegar intentionally. What I found was an abundance of literature on vinegar's restorative health and cleaning powers, but very little on how it's produced for culinary purposes. This got me interested. When I've obsessed over an ingredient in the past, as this certainly wasn't the first time, I've gone out and collected the best of what's on the market, and from there challenged myself to make my own version at home. At this stage, all I knew about vinegar was that with time alcohol turned into it. I had no idea that a small percentage of the acetic acid in water would become my preoccupation and passion.

I filled dozens of glass mason jars with dregs of red and white wines, covering them with cheesecloth to keep flies out, and left them on the counter. After a few weeks, our house smelled like something had spoiled, so I moved my experiments into our Brooklyn backyard. A couple of months later, the weekend after Thanksgiving, I was cleaning up after our annual pizza party and I noticed an unfinished sixtel of Sixpoint Craft Ales' Atlantic Amber. I had also recently acquired a secondhand small wooden barrel used for Tuthilltown whiskey. My initial plan had been to use it for aged cocktails, but instead I filled it with the leftover beer and then waited, impatiently. Every few days I'd draw samples with a turkey baster, but after a couple of months of no discernible change, I grew frustrated with its inertness. Making vinegar worked so perfectly the first time, why not again? Snow fell and coated our patio, and I kind of forgot about the barrel. The mason jars came back inside and had reduced into a slightly tangy liquid, barely reminiscent of vinegar. What I'd eventually discover was that while the key to vinegar making is time, the right amount of time in the right place matters too.

Vinegar takes patience, lots of it, and after experimenting at home on my own, I proposed a project to my friend Patrick Watson, owner of Smith & Vine wine shop in Cobble Hill, Brooklyn. For the past decade, I've been a regular customer for his summer's selection of rosé, celebratory Champagnes, and any shiny new bottles of pét-nat and Beaujolais. Every once in a while, during wine tastings, there's a bad or off bottle (I knew this tidbit from my wife), so I asked him to hold those for me, because, I surmised, maybe bad wine could make good vinegar.

Patrick also owns my favorite cheese shops in the neighborhood, Stinky Bklyn, which I thought would be the perfect place to stock small-batch vinegars. I knew I was getting ahead of myself, but Patrick eagerly agreed to work in partnership, with access to his facilities as my laboratory. We began with trials, and many errors.

I tend to drink higher-acid wines; they're bright, chuggable, and pair well with a wide variety of foods. It seemed logical to test these wines first, if only for their acidic traits, but the results were less than promising; during second fermentation, some of these wines lost their expression, becoming highly astringent, while others didn't quite metamorphose into vinegar. I began reading up on wine making and learned that many high-acid wine grapes grow in cooler climates. Then I stumbled on a game changer: I realized that if these sharp and refreshing wines are dry, they have very little sugar. Wine starts with sugar, of course, before most of it is converted to alcohol. But the sugar that remains can be calculated in degrees of Brix, a measurement of the sugar content of a solution, which can be used to achieve the proper balance of flavor in a batch of vinegar. I learned that 1 degree Brix equals 1 gram of sucrose in 100 grams of liquid mass—the beginning of a string of discoveries that would become my founding principles for future vinegar making.

Years earlier I had been an in-house photographer for Sixpoint Brewery, and I had seen the process of beer making: A hot water mash of cereal grains called wort transforms starches into dissolvable sugars. In home brewing, specific gravity is a similar index to that of Brix; to determine specific gravity you twice measure the density of a liquid, and through comparison between the original gravity during pre-fermentation and the final gravity post, you can get the alcohol by volume (ABV) of said beer. I bought the equipment to take these measurements, including a hydrometer, a funny looking thermometer with one bulbous end. This tool could evaluate prospective alcohol for vinegar-ing. The question now became, "What's the desirable percentage of alcohol that would make the best vinegar?"

Starting a small business is about economics. I thought, "What if I make the alcohol from scratch?" adding yet another level of complexity to a task I'd hardly been successful with so far. "Well, what's cheap to experiment with?" There had recently been a small resurgence of mead, an alcoholic beverage made by fermenting honey with water. "What could be easier? It's only two ingredients!" I got some honey, added some water, and mixed up a few small batches; 1:1, 1:2, 1:3 . . . all the way up to 1:10. I let those sample sets sit for a few days, and, *voilà!* some turned into honey wine! These I allowed to double ferment, and there I had it—a few delicious examples of honey vinegar.

With a bit more experimentation I was able to find the optimal Brix and specific gravity readings. I read a bit more into making mead, and found a handheld refractometer, an instrument that looks like a clarinet, in which you put a sample of sugary liquid onto a slide and look at it backlit by a light source, kind of like a kaleidoscope. It confirmed my earlier readings, that somewhere in what I now call the "Champagne range" (19 to 23 Brix), there was a sweet sugar spot for optimal vinegar making. Now equipped with basic technologies, I was ready to finally make vinegar.

Making alcohol is an essential step in the making of vinegar, but to do so in New York City you have to apply for a brewery, winery, or distilling license, all of which seemed way too pricey just to make vinegar. The New York State Department of Agriculture and Markets Circular 911, Article 17, Section 207, defines vinegars and adulterated vinegars as either "cider or apple cider vinegar," "sugar vinegar," "malt vinegar," "wine or grape vinegar," "glucose vinegar," or "spirit, distilled, grain, white distilled, or white vinegar." Vinegars can be mixed or compounded by two or more of the aforementioned types, compromised of an acetous fermentation or blend of vinegar and raw materials. In a short back-and-forth with the Ag. Department I discovered that there wasn't much of a protocol on regulating vinegars if I were making my own alcohol first, so I asked outright, "Well, which ones can I make?" The response: "glucose, sugar, or store-bought beer and wine."

In 2014 I launched a line of vinegars starting with a honey-based variety. (It's believed that in ancient Egypt, honey may have been the first wine base ever used to make vinegar.) Then, anytime a dark beer was on the growler taps at Stinky Bkyln, I'd fill up a fermenting barrel and it would turn out the best malt vinegar I had ever had. I expanded into other sugar-based starters, like maple syrup. It was all about finding that right dilution, controlling the alcohol output of the first stage of fermentation. At home I began to think more internationally, and played around with regional styles like Vinagre de Piña, or pineapple vinegar from Mexico, Filipino coconut vinegar made from sap (tuba), and a Caribbean mauby, which is a bubbling concoction kind of like root beer syrup.

I drew up plans to make rice vinegars using local grains, maybe even pushing them as far as Chinese black vinegars I had seen in Chinatown. I started talking to breweries about launching a sustainability project that would use their wort and spent grains to make beer vinegars, and consulted with a few chefs and restaurants on starting their own vinegar programs. Here's the thing, I never intended to start a business. Maybe it's my impatient nature, or fear of having to deal with people in a retail space, but this is when my vinegar making began to slow down.

I am not an autodidact; I am more of a collaborator. I work best in groups, brainstorming creative solutions. To do all this alone is, well, lonely. In New York City, there weren't any vinegar makers that I knew of. Most chefs, when asked, had never tried making their own vinegars for their restaurants, nor even knew the first thing about how to start. This was going to have to be a journey of discovery.

When you tell people you're interested in good vinegar, most think of the familiar and peerless example, the storied balsamic. From the cities of Modena and Reggio Emilia in Emilia Romagna, Italy, this *Aceto Tradizionale* has long been prized for its refined flavors, the result of years and even decades of aging. A reduction of Trebbiano and/or Lambrusco grape juice is made into a syrup, or *must* (*mosto cotto* in Italian), then transferred between a series of wooden barrels, descending in size, over a minimum of twelve years. This approach to making balsamic has been consistent since the Middle Ages, and while the process might seem rather extreme for a salad dressing, these time-consuming methods make for elegant and special vinegar.

Today, however, commercial versions are made in large factories using poor quality wines that are colored and thickened to imitate the original and take mere weeks to make. This has diminished the inherent value of a product that was once considered so precious that it was given as a dowry. Balsamic is not the only vinegar to follow this trajectory; the majority of vinegars on the market carry very little of the characteristic attributes once found in the living ferments of centuries before. This trend has affected France, Japan, and the United States; industrial practices have nearly squashed the distinctive personalities of these venerable vinegars.

The art is not lost, however, and after searching far and wide, I've come across a collective of international vinegar producers who've maintained ancient and authentic ideologies while adapting them for our modern times. And there is a community of chefs who support these traditional makers, unwilling to accept mass-produced vinegars and committed to supporting artisan production and the unique flavors that these vinegars provide.

In planning the trip that made this book possible, I chose to go the historical route, plotting a path across the world that would take me to places that have long considered vinegar a key ingredient, not just a condiment. Vinegar being one fermentation process removed from wine, my wife and I have long joked, "Where there's wine, there's vinegar." Traveling in tandem for the majority of this journey, we were a well-matched pair, indeed—each on a parallel fact-finding mission concerning our fermented delicacy of choice. Together we went to Orléans, France, whose traditional and eponymous process makes the most out of bad grapes; to Modena, Italy, where a one-hour meeting with Massimo Bottura, chef of the number one restaurant in the world, Osteria Francescana, reframed my idea of balsamic as a sparsely used specialty item, transforming it instead into something integral to every-day family meals; and to Vienna, Austria, where I finally met the man behind Gegenbauer vinegars, exquisite concoctions I first tasted as a young cook in Boston. To Japan I went alone, reveling in the Japanese appreciation for highly skilled artisans—an appreciation so deeply ingrained that many of Japan's multigenerational businesses span centuries. And finally, here in the United States I've uncovered a breadth of vinegar projects, most of which have grown out of the burgeoning sustainable farming movement—from bumper crops to local foraging.

This grand expedition has taught me that vinegar is so much more than just grapes; in fact, we encountered many eclectic base ingredients, such as honey in Piedmont, Italy; cucumbers in Vienna, Austria; and even purple potatoes in Miyazu, Japan. The biggest takeaway everywhere I went was the importance of using quality seasonal produce—no matter the base—rather than spoiled fruit: the better the input, the better the output. I invite you to join me in this movement toward building a more sustainable pantry and reclaiming our appetite for bright flavors and diverse cuisines. This is a story about a journey, an "acid trip" as it were, that has led me to a new appreciation for acidity and the power of fresh ingredients. It's also a story about patience, and the rewards that await us at the end of a transformative process. This is the story of vinegar.

A VERY BRIEF HISTORY

Vinegar has been present in history since the invention of wine. In ancient Mesopotamia, from 3000 BC to 500 BC, in the city of Babylon, an area presently south of Baghdad, Iraq, bordered by the Euphrates and Tigris Rivers, there were bountiful bushes and trees that produced ripe, sugary fruits like figs, dates, and pomegranates. When their juices were pressed and cooked down, these sweet syrups produced what were possibly the first documented wines; the leftover pulp was then further fermented to make "drinking vinegars." These beverages, now called shrubs, have had a recent renaissance and are suddenly commonplace on many cocktail menus, a way of preserving fruit flavors with vinegar for year-round consumption (see page 281).

Aside from imbibing vinegar, Babylonians may have also been the first to use it as a culinary ingredient for preserving and pickling (though perhaps it was contemporaneously used by some as a condiment in China during the Zhou Dynasty [circa 1000 BC], before spreading to the wider public by the Tang Dynasty of the seventh century). Inscriptions on the walls of Egyptian burial tombs dating back to 1500 BC indicate that some families exchanged jars of vinegar as payment for the embalming services for loved ones. Talk about a preservative! But much of vinegar's early history was indicative of potation; grape growing was a central part of the Fertile Crescent's agriculture, and vinegar was made, intentionally or not, in limited quantities post-winemaking, precipitated by a lack of refrigeration. Vinegar was considered rare and of great value—there's the story of Cleopatra dissolving a pearl in vinegar before imbibing it to prove to Mark Antony her extravagant taste—but this is the opposite of how it was perceived during the rest of Classical antiquity, from the eighth century BC to the Middle Ages, around 1000 AD. During those times vinegar was believed to be the drink of the poor. Wine and beer were much more expensive and were used mainly for celebratory occasions, and vinegar became an affordable, everyday drink, a drink of the people. Some accounts claim that while on the cross, Jesus was offered wine mixed with myrrh, enticing him to partake in an elitist, if not illicit libation; he chose, rather, to drink vinegar as a sign of solidarity.

Vinegar has also been long associated with restorative and healing properties—take Four Thieves Vinegar, also called Marseilles vinegar, for example. Packed with wild sage and rosemary, it was used in the medieval period to combat the bubonic plague in France. Nostradamus survived by it, and Hildegard of Bingen, one of the first noted nutritionists, praised its therapeutic capabilities. You can still find Four Thieves Vinegar sold around Provence. The modern version is steeped with herbs and garlic, which I find tastes great with seafood stew (see page 62). A similar potion may have existed as early as 400 BC in Hippocrates's Greece; called *posca*, water diluted with wine vinegar, woodsy and vegetal, it was considered a cure-all and may have been more potable than water itself. After I made and sampled a sip of this so-called remedy, it resonated with me as a cocktail base. Tempered with honey and oregano (see page 282), it's invigorating and satisfying.

In the fifteenth century the Orléans method was developed after wines that soured en route to Paris were discarded and left on the banks of the Loire River. This non-interventionist technique allowed vinegar to occur naturally, and hundreds of vinegar makers then popped up in the area to capitalize on the growing trend. Now, perhaps due to the slow process of natural fermentation, there is only one remaining *vinaigrier* in the area (see page 38). It wasn't until the eighteenth century, when scientists discovered that acetic acid activity would only occur in the presence of oxygen, that a series of aerobic generators were developed. This led to Boerhaave barrels and the Schützenbach process, both considered trickling-bed systems that relied on filtration (e.g. beech wood shavings, grapevines). Liquid would aerate by use of gravity, dripping down through this substrate, as air would be pumped through the barrels to further usher fermentation along.

There have been barrels that roll and barrels that rotate, agitating any which way to increase airflow, one of the most important factors in vinegar making. These systems aren't without their flaws; without controls in place, you leave bacteria to their whims. In 1865, French biologist Louis Pasteur discovered microorganisms that aid the process of acidification, thus beginning our understanding of microbial fermentation; he even printed a book called *Études sur le Vinaigre* (Studies in Vinegar) soon thereafter.

Scientific insights eventually lead to the Austrian invention of Frings acetators, a highly mechanized, submerged system that doesn't exclusively rely on surface area for alcohol to convert into acetic acid. Most industrial vinegar makers use acetators, if not for consistency then to speed up the process. Though I have seen a few artisan producers embrace them as well, they tend to employ the technology more for finesse than for volume.

The introduction of acetators almost doubled the output of prior methods, which were limited to 10 to 11 percent maximum acidity. Frings acetators can produce upward of 20 percent, and some systems can produce useable 4 to 6 percent vinegar in less than a day, even in thousand-gallon production runs. Using Frings certainly has its efficiencies; for one, they're closed systems, so only a minuscule amount of liquid is lost to evaporation, but you must inoculate your alcohol with a specific yeast strain, losing some of the magic of wild fermentation. What's more, in Europe fermented alcohol is required in vinegar production, so in essence, there is double fermentation. In the United States, large producers are allowed to use synthetic ethanol, which is derived from wood and petroleum, for vinegar making. Where's the purity in that?

We have come a long way since the ancients discovered the uses and pleasures of vinegar, most likely the result of an accidental discovery like my own. Innovations over the centuries have resulted in greater output, but also in the development of exquisite products that deliciously complicate what is, in its purest form, simply an alcohol that has been allowed to ferment yet again. Today, there is a world of flavor to be found in exploring the many iterations of vinegar's magical transformation.

RECIPE INDEX

FRANCE

Bistrot Paul Bert,
Bertrand Auboyneau
at top left

BREAKFAST IN PARIS

There's nothing in the world like waking up to Paris in the morning. For Megan, my wife, it's her happy place. For me, it's where I first felt cosmopolitan. We usually stay steps away from rue du Faubourg Saint-Antoine straddling the 11th and 12th arrondissements, where you can enter any corner patisserie and request, *"Du café crème, s'il vous plaît,"* to start your day. On my first day in Paris to research this book, after enjoying a requisite croissant, Megan went museum hopping, as I set forth to find vinegar's place in French cuisine.

I wouldn't call rue Paul Bert a side street, as most Parisian thoroughfares feel like alleyways. It's more than that. It's a central artery to the heart of bistro culture. Turn off of rue Faidherbe, and 150 meters (500 feet) away, under a neon green bottle that glows as bright as the Pharmacie sign next door, you'll likely see a man named Bertrand Auboyneau. He's often found surveying the scene midblock at Bistrot Paul Bert, dressed the part of a French restaurateur from central casting. He's effortlessly refined and casually hip, an apt description of the ambiance and cuisine in his establishment as well. Short, stocky wine glasses slosh around vins blancs and rouges, as Bertrand greets everyone who enters his restaurant as a neighbor, no matter what distance you traveled to arrive.

From a young age, Auboyneau knew the importance of acidity, eating lemons like apples just for their lip-smacking tartness. French food isn't all butter and cream; it's balanced in its richness. Just thinking about this makes me crave *frisée aux lardons*, a salad with bitter greens and crisp batons of fatty pork that's tied together with bracingly smooth mustard vinaigrette. Fat and bitter needs acid so you can enjoy more than one bite.

Bertrand doesn't like vinegar on his oysters; he thinks it overpowers their creaminess. Just a crack of black pepper for him, though if you do ask, they have a mignonette on hand. He likes a little red wine vinegar in his fruit salads, especially with raspberries. He prefers to drink Loire white wines even if the vinegar used in a dish is red. If you order *lapin á la moutarde* (braised rabbit in mustard sauce), he'll put a crock of Dijon on the table to accompany. Vinegar opens your insides, you feel it, but we're so used to it in starters that we forget it can be used throughout the meal. That said, it was two "breakfast" items that awoke me. A fried egg, a simple egg fried in butter, topped with a creamy "vinaigrette" of sorts, made my heart skip, and it had nothing to do with cholesterol.

FRIED EGG WITH A SPOONFUL OF VINEGAR,
FROM BERTRAND AUBOYNEAU, BISTROT PAUL BERT,
PARIS, FRANCE SERVES 1

1 tablespoon BUTTER	2 tablespoons WHITE WINE VINEGAR
1 EGG	
SALT and PEPPER	CHOPPED HERBS, *such as tarragon or parsley*

Fry an egg as you would, with an ample knob of butter, over medium-high heat. Cook until the edges brown. Place on a warm plate and season with salt and pepper. While the pan is still hot, add the white wine vinegar and allow to reduce by half. Spoon over the egg and garnish with some chopped herbs.

Auboyneau presents me with another way to start the day, and potentially one of the best breakfast-for-dinner dishes I've ever encountered. He asks, "You know the story of beef bourguignon?" I do. It's a dish from the rich wine region of Burgundy, consisting of chunks of beef stewed in red wine, cooked with lardoons and mushrooms, with a stock fortified with garlic, onions, and an aromatic bouquet garni. "Well," he continued, "have you ever tried it with an egg?"

*Fried Egg with a Spoonful
of Vinegar*

Oeufs en Meurette

OEUFS EN MEURETTE, FROM BERTRAND AUBOYNEAU, BISTROT PAUL BERT, PARIS, FRANCE SERVES 4

This dish takes the concept of bourguignon sauce and uses it to poach eggs. What you're left with is the same rich stock, adding the decadence of a creamy egg yolk, with a side of toast to sop it all up. Bertrand, always in need of acidity, uses a portion of red wine vinegar in place of some of the red wine, which gives a much lighter quality to a dish that usually invites a postprandial nap, and instead has you feeling like conquering the day ahead.

¼ pound (115 g) THICK SMOKED BACON, *cut into lardoons*

1 tablespoon BUTTER

¼ pound (115 g) WHITE PEARL ONIONS, *peeled, tops and bottoms trimmed*

1 clove GARLIC, *crushed*

¼ pound (115 g) BUTTON MUSHROOMS, *cleaned, cut into quarters*

3 cups (720 ml) RED WINE, *such as Burgundy, Beaujolais, Cabernet*

1 branch THYME

1 cup (240 ml) RED WINE VINEGAR

4 EGGS, *kept in shell, cold*

BLACK PEPPER

PARSLEY LEAVES, *optional*

TOAST and BUTTER

In a large saucepan over medium heat, render the bacon for 5 to 7 minutes, until it's just browning but not burning. If it's cooking too fast, lower the temperature. Pour out all but about 1 tablespoon of the fat (reserve the excess to cook with another time) and set the bacon aside (you'll add it back in later, so try not to snack on it too much). Add the butter, onions, and garlic and cook for about 1 minute, until aromatic. Lower the heat to medium-low, add the mushrooms and cook for another 2 minutes, stirring occasionally. Add the red wine, scrape the bottom of the pan to release the fond, and add the thyme. Bring back to a simmer and cook for 45 minutes, or until reduced by a third.

recipe continues on page 32

Add the red wine vinegar and continue to cook for another 30 minutes. (If it's too acidic for your taste, add ¼ cup water at a time until it's not.)

To poach the eggs, either in the pot of sauce itself (if you don't mind a few stray pieces of egg white) or in a separate pot of water, bring the liquid to a bare boil. Make a small pinprick on the larger end of each egg, place in the liquid, and cook for 30 seconds (a Julia Child tip); this is just to set the whites. Remove the eggs and crack them into individual small bowls. Slide the eggs back into the pot to poach them. If you like a soft yolk, cook for only a few minutes. Using a slotted spoon, remove the eggs and set aside. In individual serving bowls, evenly distribute the onion and mushroom mixture, then pour a bit of the sauce, enough to cover an egg, into the bowl as well. Place the eggs into the bowls and garnish with the bacon, freshly cracked black pepper, and parsley, if using.

Serve warm with to0uce ahead and simply reheat. *Bon appetit!*

CORNICHONS

Until recently, I'd never really considered the significance of cornichons, the ubiquitous Parisian pickled cucumbers that most of us think of as just small pickles. You probably envision a clear jar, packed with brine, sitting in the back of a refrigerator or tucked away in a dank, dusty basement. But this is a *cornichon*, italicized, and said with an accent and significance. It's more than a fancy garnish at a bistro, it's the definition of what a pickle really is, time and place preserved.

Maille, a French company, now best known for its mustard, was founded by a vinegar maker, and began jarring cornichons for the commercial market back in the 1700s. Now you can find "cornichons" on most supermarket shelves right next to standard-issue gherkins, kosher dill spears, and bread and butters. What I can't understand is why anyone would bring to market something so precious, a tiny little cucumber with a peak season that lasts little more than a month, and not pay equal attention to the quality of the vinegar it's preserved in. I'm not calling these supermarket cornichons bad pickles, but to use distilled white vinegar, well it feels like you're disregarding half of the recipe.

CORNICHONS, FROM BERTRAND GRÉBAUT, SEPTIME AND CLAMATO, PARIS, FRANCE MAKES 2 QUARTS (2 L)

2 pounds (910 g)
SMALL PICKLING
CUCUMBERS

1 bunch FRESH HERBS,
*such as tarragon, thyme,
bay leaf, or dill*

½ cup (144 g) MIXED
SPICES, *such as
peppercorns, fennel seeds,
or coriander seeds*

32 ounces (4 cups / 960 ml)
WHITE WINE VINEGAR

2 quarts (2 L) WATER

⅓ cup (80 g) COARSE SALT

Quickly wash the pickling cucumbers and brine overnight in a 5 percent solution of salt to water. Drain and place in sterilized jars with the fresh herbs and spices. In a large bowl, stir together the vinegar, water, and salt until the salt dissolves. This is approximately a 1-part vinegar, 2-parts water, and 3 percent salt solution, which is a handy rule of thumb for all your pickling needs. Pour just enough of this liquid into jars to cover the cukes, but leave a knuckle's worth of air space on the top. Keep in the refrigerator for a minimum of 2 weeks before using.

J'AIME VINAIGRE

Bertrand Grébaut's food is earnest and honest. Truly one of the best meals of my life was at Septime. With each course I grew to know the chef's point of view in a way I had never experienced before, so intimate and precious, the same way I assume Grébaut regards his ingredients. In my limited French I said, *"J'aime vinaigre."* He nodded and said, "Me too." Carmela Abramowitz-Moreau, a cheery cookbook translator, joined us. At first she apologized for her lack of a lexicon about the science behind vinegar, but as soon as we started chatting, we all realized how simple the concept of acidity really is.

Grébaut grew up in Paris, and though his parents had a wooden vinegar crock doused with the dregs of very good wine, he notes that even in the magnificent repertoire of French cuisine, acid may be the one thing that's slightly underplayed. He then asks the "salad question": when do you use lemon and when do you use vinegar? Bertrand believes if you're having a salad with a cheese platter, then you're best off using vinegar. In the summer, when tomatoes are fresh, and fresh cheese is present, then it's lemon. Yes, this seems counterintuitive, since lemon and tomato seasons don't coincide (Bertrand gets lemons from Sicily at that time), but his cooking style is built around flavor pairings.

BEURRE NOISETTE DRESSING, FROM BERTRAND GRÉBAUT, SEPTIME AND CLAMATO, PARIS, FRANCE
MAKES ABOUT 1/2 CUP (240 ML)

Bertrand Grébaut often makes a salad dressing using the concept of beurre noisette, literally "hazelnut butter," but better known as brown butter. The nutty flavors distinguishable in brown butter are perfectly complemented by the oxidative note of the sherry vinegar. The butter rounds out the cutting edge of the vinegar, making this dressing perfect for a side of salad, something he often serves with the last course of the savory part of the menu. It also goes well with roasted vegetables.

¼ tablespoons (55 g) UNSALTED BUTTER	1 to 2 tablespoons SHERRY VINEGAR
	1 pinch SALT

In a small saucepan, brown the butter over medium heat. While it's still warm, add the sherry vinegar, but stand back, as the vapors will fume. Emulsify with a whisk. Add the salt.

Vinegar isn't just a dressing to coat your greens, it brings out flavors like an exclamation point. It's part of a sentence that also has salt, fat, and bitterness, and that's incomplete without acid. Septime has a tasting menu; next door at Clamato, Grébaut's seafood bar, it's à la carte. If you order oysters, you get a basic mignonette, with really good onions instead of shallots and rancio wine vinegar, and the undressed bivalves. It's a matter of control: depending on your palate, use as much, or little, of the sauce as you please.

Acidity is omnipresent at Septime. With an array of vinegars within reach, Grébaut can be particular about what style of acidity to inflect: chardonnay vinegar d'Orléans (more on this soon), sweet wine vinegar made from vin santo, complex and oxidized sherry vinegar, or cider vinegar from cider maker Cyril Zangs, which goes with everything. Sometimes winemakers give Grébaut wines that didn't quite go right but are gold as vinegar.

As we moved into talking about cooking proteins with vinegar, the approach shifted. Acid cuts fat, but it often needs coaxing, maybe a little extra sugar, to keep the aromatics alive without becoming too acerbic. A perfect example is a gastrique: sugar that's been caramelized, deglazed with vinegar, then reduced to a syrupy consistency. Never waste the fond, those brown bits of flavor left on the bottom of your pan when browning meat. These gems are caused by the Maillard reaction, when amino acids and sugars are reduced together by heat, which can then be transformed into a sweet and sour sauce that refreshes your palate with every bite. Use a stock of that same animal and you will retain the underlying flavors of the cut as well.

DUCK À L'ORANGE, FROM BERTRAND GRÉBAUT, SEPTIME AND CLAMATO, PARIS, FRANCE SERVES 2

Traditionally done as a whole bird, Grébaut's recipe uses only the breasts, cooking them slowly on the bone to a perfect roast. He infuses orange zest and adds orange juice to the base, cooking it down by half. He also prefers using honey to make the caramel for the gastrique, before deglazing with vinegar, but you can also use sugar. The final sauce is then made by balancing the amount of orange gastrique and duck jus. At Septime you will more often find this type of technique used with a salty dairy product (e.g., feta) or a bitter vegetable (e.g., white asparagus), but it's also delicious in its classic context.

2 DUCK BREASTS, BONE-IN, about ¾ pound (340 g) each

SALT and BLACK PEPPER

¼ cup (60 ml) WATER

¼ cup (85 g) HONEY or ¼ cup (50 g) WHITE SUGAR

¼ cup (60 ml) WHITE WINE VINEGAR

1 cup (240 ml) ORANGE JUICE, *freshly squeezed is best*

¼ cup (60 ml) DUCK JUS, *use stock or save some while rendering out the duck fat*

¼ cup (25 g) ORANGE PEELS *cut into 3-inch-long (7.5-cm-long) thin strips*

Season the duck breasts with salt and pepper. In a large heavy skillet, slowly cook the duck skin-side down over medium-low heat, rendering the fat and getting the skin crispy, 15 to 20 minutes. Remove the duck breasts and place them on a roasting pan, skin-side up. Reserve fat to use as jus and save the rest for another recipe.

Preheat the oven to 300°F (150°C).

Scrape the bottom of the skillet, add the water, and stir to release the fond. Add the honey, increase the heat to medium-

recipe continues on page 38

high, and let come to a slow boil. Cook for about 5 minutes, until golden brown. Add the vinegar, but don't lean over the pan, as the vapors will release. Continue to cook until the mixture begins to turn into a caramel, about 1 minute, then add the orange juice, bring back to a boil, and cook for another 10 minutes, or until reduced by half. Add the duck jus and boil for another 1 to 2 minutes. Take off heat and add in orange peels.

Use a bit of this gastrique as a glaze for the duck. Brush on a layer and place the duck breasts in the oven for a few minutes, then brush on some more. Cook for about 20 minutes for medium to medium-rare. Once the duck is cooked to your liking, let rest for a few minutes before serving. Serve it on the bone or slice it for plating.

Make a pool of gastrique on each plate. Place the duck on top. If you pour the sauce on top of the crispy skin, it will get soggy, though I do like adding a few steeped orange peels on top for effect.

OLD ORLÉANS

I woke up on the train to Orléans, one and a half hours southwest of Paris. This city, famously saved by Joan of Arc during the English siege in 1429, sits quietly along the Loire River. It was a foggy ride, mentally and meteorologically, as I had risen before the sun, fighting off an inkling of jetlag. I came to research the sour wine trade, traced as far back as the late fourteenth century, when Loire valley winemakers would ship their bottles by boat, unloading any wine that went bad to avoid being taxed in Paris for what they couldn't even sell. It was like Orléans had been given a gift that no one wanted and only they knew what to do with.

By the sixteenth century, more than three hundred vinegar makers called Orléans home; they were so numerous that King Francis I deemed their vinegar-making process "Orléans style" and designated that the city's artisans could only make it there. French oak barrels held a distinct collection of wine vinegars, from muscadet to Chinon, so coveted that eventually quality wines were being added to the barrels just to keep up with demand.

At 236 Faubourg Bannier, behind a large wooden door painted green like a grape leaf, lives a vinegar maker for the ages: Jean-François Martin, of the sixth generation of the Martins, and his family-owned Martin Pouret, a producer that has taken a pass on industrialization, letting nature transform wine into vinegar, with no additives, no acceleration, only time. Wafting blocks down the street where locals and travelers alike once formed lines, Martin Pouret is now the sole Orléans-style vinegar maker left in Orléans.

All of Martin Pouret's wines are French. Their ingredients have known origins, many grapes from nearby Gâtinais, apples from Normandy, even wasabi from Japan (for their sushi vinegar, a new market product). They are blended from old-vine Bordeaux, Bourgogne, Loire sauvignon, and chardonnay, and nowadays, merlot and Syrah. Unlike industrially produced vinegars, they do not use acetators. What is an acetator? It is a machine that can be manipulated to hasten oxidation through a constant stream of air bubbles. This causes fermentation to happen faster, but vinegars produced in this way lose the innate flavor

Jean-Francois Martin, of Martin Pouret

profiles of the wines from which they are made. Vinegar no longer had terroir; rather, it became a mass-produced product without the inherent characteristics of wine.

Stepping into the fermentation room at Martin Pouret knocked me back on my heels, my eyes welled up, and my breath slowed. It was just above room temperature, but it felt hotter, like a sauna, the fumes almost suffocating. I politely escaped into fresh air, pretending to adjust my camera lens. Is this what vinegar should smell like? So powerful it pushes you away? Jean-François stood still, smirking, immune to the smell, and surveyed his room of Bordeaux wine barrels. "They're maturing," he said. "They have no mothers. But that's no malady." (See page 308, "Mother of Vinegar.")

I made a joke about how that seemed like a dysfunctional family, which Jean-François didn't really get, perhaps because he knows this process has repeated itself for over two centuries, fifty liters at a time, and will turn out right in the end. Fifty liters are removed and fifty more poured on top every three weeks. Where does it all go? A 100,000-liter barrel, the largest of its kind I'd ever seen, stood in an adjoining room. A ladder barely reached halfway up this king of casks. Hundreds of barrels, almost half a million bottles, sat there in that barrel of barrels.

An array of products is displayed in Martin Pouret's offices: Jelly Doucer d'Antan, an ancestral family recipe of wine vinegar mixed with cranberries and beet juice, and a premade béarnaise (see recipe below) that acts like an all-purpose sauce, but it's their limited-edition Coup de Foudre, a nine-year-old, bronze-colored wine vinegar in a squat bottle the shape of a cognac decanter that made me wonder, why is twice-distilled vinegar more highly regarded than twice-fermented?

BÉARNAISE, FROM MARTIN POURET, ORLÉANS, FRANCE
ABOUT 1½ TO 2 CUPS (360 TO 480 ML)

If hollandaise is the mother sauce in French haute cuisine, béarnaise is its natural offspring. And like the mother, it is an emulsification of egg yolks and melted butter, with acidity coming from the vinegar. Traditionally used for topping a steak, it's great with anything that is fatty and needs acid, or just needs both fat and acid to round out a dish, so really, it's pretty damn good on everything from meat to seafood and vegetables, cooked or raw, and great on potatoes, baked and fried.

1 SHALLOT, *minced*

2 tablespoons CHOPPED HERBS, *such as tarragon, basil, or cilantro*

1 teaspoon FRESHLY GROUND BLACK PEPPER

¼ cup (60 ml) WHITE WINE VINEGAR

1 teaspoon WATER

2 EGG YOLKS

12 tablespoons (1½ sticks / 170 g) BUTTER, *melted*

SALT

In a small skillet, combine the shallots, all but 1 teaspoon of the herbs, the black pepper, and the vinegar and bring to a boil over medium-high heat. Lower the heat to a simmer and reduce by half, about 5 minutes. Cool, then strain.

Set up a double boiler. Whisk the vinegar mixture with the water and egg yolks until combined. Reduce the heat to low and cook until thickened, about 5 minutes. Do not overcook the eggs. You can take the bowl off the double boiler if it's getting too

recipe continues on page 42

hot and wait until it cools before you continue. Whisk in about 1 tablespoon of butter at a time; once it incorporates, pour in more until you've used all the butter. Season with salt and add the remaining of chopped herbs. Serve while warm.

NEW FRENCH

Gregory Marchand was given the kitchen nickname "Frenchie" while working in London—and it stuck when he moved to New York City—for the simple reason that he was French. He grew up in Nantes, three and a half hours west of Orléans, near the Atlantic Ocean. Local fish used the Loire River as a passage, which may explain why beurre blanc, or "white butter," is from there, as it pairs so well with fish.

I met Marchand at Gramercy Tavern in New York City during a photo shoot about the restaurant's family meals. Coq au vin came to the pass, deeply hued with red wine, rich and lush, but I swear there was some red wine vinegar in the stock; Marchand cooks with a deft hand, updating classic techniques for a more sophisticated diner without compromising the original recipe. This is what Marchand has done back in France, setting up shop in Paris a few years back, to great acclaim, cooking like a Frenchman who's stayed true to himself but has become more perceptive and precise.

His mise en place is lined with many vinegars: xeres, raspberry, red, white, rancio, cider, fig, a newly discovered pomegranate, white balsamic, rice, and *tosazu*, a Japanese vinegar-based dressing made with sugar, soy sauce, and bonito flakes. He's worldlier now, and uses these flavors to inflect his style of haute cuisine, which is more accessible, and so much more delicious, than the traditional stuff. He even infuses some vinegars with vanilla for an unexpected sweet note, served outside of a dessert context. I spent my Thanksgiving at Frenchie Bar à Vins this year with my wife and another expat friend; we regaled each other with stories of life back in the States and ate nuanced "French food" that felt like home.

SANDRE (WHITE FISH) IN BEURRE BLANC, FROM
GREGORY MARCHAND, FRENCHIE, PARIS, FRANCE SERVES 2

1 pound (455 g) WHITE
FISH, *such as perch,
flounder, or sole, cut into 2
(8-ounce / 225 g) fillets*

SALT and BLACK PEPPER

1 to 2 tablespoons OLIVE OIL

1 cup (240 ml) WHITE WINE

¼ cup (60 ml) WHITE
WINE VINEGAR

1 SHALLOT, *finely chopped*
(about ½ cup / 70 g)

12 tablespoons (1½ sticks /
170 g) UNSALTED
BUTTER

Season the fish with salt and black pepper. Heat the olive oil in a large sauté pan over medium-high heat. Add the fish, skin-side down. After a few minutes they'll be lightly browned and crispy and cooked through. Remove from the pan, set aside on a plate, skin-side up.

In the same pan, over medium heat, combine the wine, vinegar, and shallots and let reduce to a quarter of the original volume, about 3 tablespoons. Add the butter 1 tablespoon at a time, until each knob is fully emulsified. Remove from heat and season with salt and black pepper to taste.

Divide the sauce between two plates, topping the pool of beurre blanc with the cooked fish fillet, skin-side up. Finish with a little salt.

Le Bon Marché, or "the good market," is widely known as the world's first modern department store. In the mid-1800s, entrepreneur Aristide Boucicaut hired Gustave Eiffel, the eponymous engineer behind the Eiffel Tower, to build what would become a most majestic shopping center on the Left Bank. It wasn't until 1978 that La Grande Epicerie, a local supermarket that offered the finest international grocery items, was formed there.

As you take the escalator downstairs, you'll see more than twenty shelves of vinegars from France and afar. Many of Martin Pouret's

Sandre (White Fish) in Beurre Blanc

vinegars are there, as is a Normandy cider variety and a special oyster vinegar that is undoubtedly an ode to mignonette. French classics like Edmond Fallot, a Burgundy mustard company since 1840, see their Provençal herb vinegar sit right next to the centenarian Melfor, an Alsatian brand of vinegars infused with honey.

Le Bon Marché's selection includes white wine vinegars from the Champagne-Ardenne region and vinegars fragranced with truffle juice. You'll find balsamic from Modena and sherry vinegars from Spain, but it's the astounding array of condiments surrounding the vinegar aisle, whose base ingredient is often vinegar, that exhibits the wide-ranging impact that this stuff has in the pantry.

Marche d'Aligre is a neighborhood marketplace, first introduced to me by my friend Claude Cabri, who works under the alias "Miss Lunch." She's a chef and artist whose quirky drawings, and quirkier character, fill a Première Pression Provence olive oil shop location, where her restaurant began as a pop-up and now remains as a study in how to cook without open flame. Cabri crafts meals with microwaves, toasters, and tea kettles, her food seasoned by her journeys to Pantelleria to pick capers (which she sells) and a global appreciation for other people's aesthetic tastes.

For lunch the day I visited, she made an Ethiopian tartare called kitfo, redolent of spices and herbs, usually served with injera bread, but here, instead, it was splashed with date vinegar. A few months later, when I was speaking with chef Renee Erickson from Seattle restaurants The Walrus and the Carpenter and The Whale Wins about her penchant for raw beef (which she now raises, grass fed, for her latest establishments, Bateau and Bar Melusine), she mentioned how much she likes to serve kitfo with date vinegar. Probably no coincidence: date vinegar is dark, rich, and fruity, bringing out those same qualities in the beef itself, the vinegar an elegant stand-in for injera's sour tang. You'll find Erickson's recipe on page 268.

An amalgam of modern bistro and British pub, Au Passage is literally a passage between the thriving 11th arrondissement and the stylish Marais. It also signifies a shift away from the nouvelle cuisine pioneered in the 1960s to the more modern "bistronomy" movement, haute fare at more affordable prices. Edward Delling-Williams is a living union of these concepts. Raised in England, trained under Fergus Henderson at St. John, the offal-forward restaurant, he brought with him the sustainable idea of how to deliver a casual experience at a higher standard. At Au Passage it begins with their beverage program, where natural wines are poured by the glass. The problem is, once they're opened for too long, they can't be sold anymore. Rather than pitching those bottles, Delling-Williams blends them together into a large glass crock, incorporating a good glug of Banyuls vinegar to jump-start the process.

English people know that when you eat fish and chips you need a dash of malt vinegar to balance the fat and salt. (See April Bloomfield's recipe on page 197.) It's so ingrained that you'll find Sarson's on the table of most gastropubs, like Heinz ketchup at an American diner. Every Sunday while growing up in Somerset, Delling-Williams would have roast lamb shoulder at his grandmother's, served with mint sauce that she made from a blend of vinegars with sugar and fresh chopped mint, which grew like weeds in the garden.

For Delling-Williams, it's about utilizing the remains, be it weeds, offal, or the liquid from Opie's Pickled Walnuts, an English delicacy marinating in spiced malt vinegar that is often an accompaniment to charcuterie and cheese. Pour the liquid into a beef braise, Delling-Williams has discovered, and it augments everything around it. Much of the time Delling-Williams thinks of vinegar first when he conceptualizes a dish; pine cone vinegar precedes roasted carrots and pine nuts with a carrot-top pesto; balsamic reduction begets *mi-cuit* langoustine; sherry vinegar gelée brings about a fresh-pea-and-yogurt salad. This is key, because Delling-Williams doesn't really catalog his dishes, they're ephemeral in composition, but he remembers the flavors and uses these cues at inception.

Au Passage,
Edward Delling-Williams at top right

LAMB SHOULDER WITH MINT SAUCE, FROM EDWARD DELLING-WILLIAMS, FORMERLY OF AU PASSAGE, PARIS, FRANCE SERVES 6 TO 8

1 (7-pound / 3.2 kg) LAMB
  SHOULDER, BONE-IN

2 to 3 tablespoons SALT

2 to 3 tablespoons OLIVE
  OIL, *to coat*

½ to 1 cup (120 to 240 ml)
  WATER or LAMB STOCK

Preheat the oven to 300°F (150°C). Rub the lamb shoulder with the salt and oil and place on a rack in a roasting pan, with about ½ inch (12 mm) of water or lamb stock on the bottom. Roast for about 7 hours, basting regularly. It's done when the meat falls away from the bone. Serve with mint sauce on the side.

MINT SAUCE MAKES 1½ TO 2 CUPS (360 TO 480 ML)

1 cup (50 g) MINT LEAVES,
  picked

¼ cup (60 ml) SHERRY
  VINEGAR

¼ cup (60 ml) MALT
  VINEGAR

2 tablespoons WHITE
  BALSAMIC VINEGAR

¼ cup (60 ml) WATER

¼ cup (50 g) SUGAR

Combine the ingredients in a blender and blend until smooth.

*Lamb Shoulder with
Mint Sauce*

MOTHERS OF LYON

At fourteen years old, chef Daniel Boulud learned how to make *poulet au vinaigre á l'estragon* (chicken with tarragon vinegar) as an apprentice at Georges Blanc near his hometown of Lyon. But it wasn't Blanc who taught him the dish, it was Blanc's mother. Lyonnaise cuisine owes a good deal of its heritage to the Mères Lyonnaises (mothers of Lyon), a nickname given to the twentieth-century formerly middle-class women who lost their jobs working in bourgeois kitchens during World War I. Many opened their own businesses, and during interbellum, their regional food defined the culinary identity of the region's restaurants.

As a result, a family style of cooking developed into an international sensation, aided by a spike in automobile tourism, linked to the popularity of the *Guide Michelin*. Famed chef of Lyon Paul Bocuse apprenticed under Mère (Eugénie) Brazier, the first woman to earn three Michelin stars. Acidity was a central component of her repertoire, and the eponymous Sauce Lyonnaise is largely composed of white wine vinegar, scented by sweated onions, and embellished by demi-glace.

Most households in Lyon had a crock with a tap on it, where they'd put their leftover wine. Boulud's family used to make wine, a barrique in the cellar that would go straight to the vinegar jar if they were running low. When Boulud moved to Manhattan, he sensed most vinaigrettes had a pinch of sugar in them, while back in France the degree of acidity and sharpness was far more pronounced. He brought this more intense flavor sensibility to his metropolitan kitchens, establishing himself as one of the city's top French chefs, relying on countryside classics transformed for an urban clientele.

POULET AU VINAIGRE WITH POMMES LYONNAISE AND BOUQUET GARNI VINEGAR, FROM DANIEL BOULUD, DANIEL, NEW YORK CITY SERVES 4

What makes any roast chicken even better? A side of starch to sop up all the juices! This version comes with Lyon-style potatoes, doused in an herb-infused vinegar, to make for a sweet and sour feast that any mother or chef would be proud to serve.

For the chicken:

SALT

12 to 15 CHERRY TOMATOES, about 1 cup (145 g)

½ tablespoon BUTTER

1 tablespoon OLIVE OIL

1 WHOLE CHICKEN, 2 to 3 pounds (910 g to 1.4 kg), *cut into 8 pieces*

FRESHLY GROUND WHITE PEPPER

2 LARGE SHALLOTS, *sliced*

5 ounces (140 g) PEARL ONIONS

1 tablespoon TOMATO PASTE

1½ tablespoons ALL-PURPOSE FLOUR

¼ cup (60 ml) TARRAGON VINEGAR, *try Martin Pouret*

1 cup (240 ml) CHICKEN STOCK

½ bunch TARRAGON

Bring a large pot of salted water to a boil and set a bowl of ice water on the side. Score an X on the bottoms of the tomatoes. Boil the tomatoes for 5 seconds, or until the skins loosen on the bottom. Strain and peel under cold running water; set aside.

In a braising pan, melt the butter with the oil over medium-high heat. Season the chicken on all sides with salt and pepper. Add the chicken to the pan skin-side down and sear until golden brown on both sides, about 10 minutes total. Transfer the chicken to a platter, set aside, and strain all but 1 tablespoon of fat from the pan.

Reduce the heat to medium and add the shallots and onions to the pan. Cook, stirring, until the shallots are softened, about 5 minutes. Add the tomato paste and flour and cook, stirring,

recipe continues on page 53

*Poulet au Vinaigre with Pommes
Lyonnaise and Bouquet Garni Vinegar*

for 1 minute. Add the vinegar, bring to a simmer, then stir in the chicken stock. Bring to a simmer, making sure to scrape the bottom of the pan. Return the chicken to the pan with half of the tomatoes and the tarragon. Cover and simmer for 10 minutes, stirring occasionally. Add the remaining tomatoes, cover, and simmer for another 20 minutes, or until the chicken is cooked through.

For the potatoes:

2 tablespoons OLIVE OIL

3 LARGE YUKON GOLD POTATOES, about 1¼ pounds (570 g), *peeled, and sliced ¼ inch (6 mm) thick*

1 VIDALIA ONION, *halved lengthwise and sliced very thinly crosswise*

KOSHER SALT

BLACK PEPPER

1 tablespoon BOUQUET GARNI VINEGAR, *recipe below*

½ bunch PARSLEY, *leaves chopped, stems reserved*

In a very large nonstick skillet, heat the olive oil over medium-high heat until shimmering. Add the potatoes in a slightly overlapping layer and cook, stirring occasionally, until golden and nearly cooked through, about 8 minutes. Add the onion, season with salt and pepper, and cook, stirring occasionally, until the onions and potatoes are tender, about 5 minutes longer. Add the vinegar and gently toss to combine. Add the parsley just before serving.

For the Bouquet Garni Vinegar:

1 750-ml bottle of good-quality WHITE WINE VINEGAR

3 cloves GARLIC, *cut in half*

3 sprigs FRESH THYME

1 SMALL BAY LEAF

PARSLEY STEMS, *from recipe above*

In a medium saucepan set over medium heat, warm the vinegar to 175°F (80°C). Slide the garlic and herbs into the vinegar bottle, and then use a funnel to pour the warm vinegar back into the bottle. Chill and keep refrigerated. The longer it infuses, the more savory it will be. Serve chicken and potatoes in two separate dishes for family style.

SALMON, TWO WAYS

I was told by Daniel Boulud that if I didn't talk to Michel Troisgros about acidity, I was an idiot. The Troisgros family are famous restaurateurs whose Maison Troisgros in Roanne, France, was awarded three Michelin stars in 1968 and has held them ever since. Multiple chefs have cited that the Troisgros family invented acidity in French cuisine, and no example is more prominent than their Salmon and Sorrel.

It was Michel's father, Pierre, and uncle, Jean, who introduced him to the delight of acidified sauces, highlighted by white or red wine reductions, vermouth, a few drops of Tabasco, mustard, and/or gherkins. Their cuisine was sharp, spirited, and had a temper. Everything had to have a degree of acidity to it, even their eggs, done *à l'assassin* (in the style of the murderer), fried, and sprayed with red wine vinegar (see page 28).

Michel's grandmother came from Frioul, a region north of Venice, Italy. She cooked with heart and plenty of piquancy—tomatoes, oranges, vinegar, capers—and from her he inherited an essential flavor set. When he was a young cook, he traveled to Modena, and inside a small *salumeria* he bought a bottle of Aceto Balsamico, then rare, and expensive. He didn't know what to do with it, so rather than cook with it, he took a spoonful every morning, further training his taste tendencies.

Now, he adds a dash of vinegar in many sauces, at the last moment, with the dexterity to know when enough is enough, never allowing it to dominate the other flavors or compromise the delicacy of a dish. In Michel's mind, vinegar acts in support, and each one has its own personality, from a yellow-tinged wine vinegar from Jura made by Philippe Gonet in Arbois, to a more orange Pineau des Charentes from Françoise Fleuriet in Rouillac.

I hesitated to ask about a core classic dish, but who other than a Troisgros to instruct in the ways of Leeks Vinaigrette? With Roquefort shavings and a mustard and hazelnut oil vinaigrette, you'd be an idiot not to try it. For a postmodern take on Leeks Vinaigrette, see Scott Dolich's interpretation on page 55.

LEEKS VINAIGRETTE, FROM MICHEL TROISGROS, LA MAISON TROISGROS, ROANNE, FRANCE SERVES 4

SALT

1 pound (455 g) LEEKS

¼ cup (60 ml) WHITE WINE VINEGAR, *Orléans style preferred*

2 tablespoons DIJON MUSTARD

BLACK PEPPER

½ cup (60 ml) HAZELNUT OIL, *though walnut oil is great too*

½ cup (70 g) or more ROQUEFORT, *or another high-quality blue cheese*

Trim the green ends and the roots from the leeks. Slice in half lengthwise and rinse well to remove any dirt, keeping the leek halves intact. Cook in boiling salt water, until they are slightly tender, a few minutes, then drain them and put them on a serving platter.

Make the vinaigrette by whisking together the vinegar, salt, pepper, and mustard in a medium bowl, then slowly whisking in the nut oil. Drizzle the leeks with the vinaigrette. Add some Roquefort pieces and eat while the dish is still warm.

What made this and many neoclassical dishes a hallmark of the Troisgros family and, in turn, emblematic of French cooking, was the introduction of an acidic element. And in turn their influence on modern French cuisine would change the course of cooking around the world. Michael Anthony, chef at New York's Gramercy Tavern and Untitled, honeymooned at La Maison Troisgros, and the experience affected him so profoundly that the ideas behind their Escalope de Saumon a l'Oseille (salmon fillet with sorrel) can still be seen in his kitchens.

I've long been a fan of Michael Anthony's cooking and consider him one of the most thoughtful chefs I know. His menus are meditative, a study in simplicity. His years studying in Japan gave him a Zen-like appreciation for how modest touches can effect big change.

Leeks Vinaigrette

The original dish he experienced at Maison Troisgros was very simple, a quarter-inch-thick rectangular slice of salmon, very delicately cooked at a low temperature, placed on the plate without any accompanying garnishes, and nappéd with a creamy beurre blanc steeped with garden fresh sorrel. It had a mouth-watering acidity, with a stunning contrast between the fatty fish and the tart herbs. In Anthony's adaptation, circa 2007, the dish was manipulated into a log of salmon stuffed with sorrel and served with a lighter dashi-based sauce, but with the same bright vinegar tones, likely made with rice vinegar. A global reflection on refinement, and a French classic given a new life. What follows is a more recent fish recipe of his that delivers multiple layers of flavor and acidity. Here Anthony takes cues from the New York City Jewish deli tradition, using brook trout for a metropolitan twist.

SMOKED BROOK TROUT WITH CIPOLLINI PUREE AND PICKLED CIPOLLINI ONIONS, FROM MICHAEL ANTHONY, GRAMERCY TAVERN, NEW YORK CITY SERVES 4

For the pickled cipollini onions:

1 STAR ANISE

2 RED BEETS, *diced large, reserve 1 tablespoon for beet juice*

2 tablespoons RED WINE VINEGAR

1 cup (240 ml) WHITE WINE VINEGAR

½ cup (120 ml) WATER

1 tablespoon SUGAR

1 teaspoon SALT

4 CIPOLLINI ONIONS, *sliced into thin rings*

In a medium saucepan over medium heat, toast the star anise until fragrant, about a minute. Add the beets, red and white wine vinegars, water, sugar, and salt, bring to a simmer, then strain into a heatproof bowl, reserving the liquid and discarding the solids. Add the onion rings to the liquid and let chill.

recipe continues on page 58

For the vinaigrette:

2 tablespoons RED WINE

1 MINCED MEDIUM
  ONION

1 tablespoon BEET JUICE,
  *squeezed by hand from
  grated beet*

1 tablespoon RASPBERRY
  VINEGAR

1 tablespoon RED WINE
  VINEGAR

1 tablespoon PORT

½ cup (120 ml) OLIVE OIL

1 drop of LEMON JUICE

In a saucepan over low heat, reduce the red wine by half, a few minutes, then combine all the other ingredients except the olive oil and lemon juice. Bring to a simmer and let the liquid reduce until almost dry, a few minutes. Remove from the heat and whisk in the olive oil and lemon juice.

For the onion puree:

4 cups (440 g) PEELED AND
  SLICED CIPOLLINI
  ONIONS

½ cup (120 ml)
  GRAPESEED OIL

SALT and BLACK PEPPER

In a large sauté pan over medium-low heat, sweat the onions in 2 tablespoons of the grapeseed oil until softened, a couple of minutes, stirring often. Transfer the onions to a blender while slowly streaming in the remaining oil. Strain the puree through a fine-mesh sieve and season with salt and pepper.

For the fish:

1½ pounds (680 g) TROUT,
  cut into 6-ounce (170-g) fillets

Using a grill or smoker with apple chips, smoke the trout fillets over low heat for 7 minutes.

To serve, spoon the cipollini puree onto the center of 4 plates. Streak one side of the plate with the pickled cipollini onions and the other side of the plate with the onion vinaigrette. Place the smoked trout fillets on top of the puree.

I can't write of French-influenced seafood in New York City without mentioning Le Bernardin. Eric Ripert has been at the helm of this seafood mecca since 1994. In the past couple of decades, he's developed a cult following of *poissonniers* (fish cooks) who want to work with him. Originally from Antibes, a Mediterranean resort area near Cannes and Nice that sits on the seas of the Côte d'Azur, Ripert comes from a land esteemed for its fishing industry. His grandfather would make his own vinegars, in large glass containers, used to deglaze tuna steaks for dinner. Here, Ripert shows that not all fish has to have a light touch; deeper, darker flavors can bring out wonderfully surprising attributes in delicate seafood.

RED SNAPPER AND MUSHROOMS IN A PORT REDUCTION, FROM ERIC RIPERT, LE BERNARDIN, NEW YORK CITY SERVES 4

2 cups (480 ml) 10-YEAR-OLD EXCELLENT-QUALITY PORT

2 cups (480 ml) GOOD-QUALITY SHERRY VINEGAR

3 tablespoons VEGETABLE OIL

1 pound (455 g) FRESH WILD MUSHROOMS, *cleaned and cut into bite-size pieces*

1 bunch ASPARAGUS, TIPS ONLY, *cut 2 inches (5 cm) long and blanched*

2 branches FRESH THYME

5 tablespoons (70 g) BUTTER

4 (6-ounce / 170-g) RED SNAPPER FILLETS

FINE SEA SALT

FRESHLY GROUND WHITE PEPPER

¼ teaspoon CHINESE FIVE SPICE POWDER

4 teaspoons MINCED FRESH CHIVES

Bring the port to a boil in a medium saucepan over medium-high heat. Lower the heat slightly and simmer until reduced to 1 cup (240 ml) (if using a gas stove, never let the flames extend above the bottom edge of the pan). Add the vinegar and simmer until reduced to an almost syrup-like consistency, lowering the heat as

recipe continues on page 60

necessary and watching carefully to keep it from burning around the edges—you should have about 7 tablespoons (105 ml). (The sauce can be made to this point up to 1 week ahead; cover and refrigerate until ready to use.)

Divide 1 tablespoon of the vegetable oil in each of two 10-inch (25-cm) nonstick skillets and place over high heat until just smoking. Divide the mushrooms between the pans, lower the heat to medium, and sauté until browned, about 4 minutes. Reduce the heat to low and divide the asparagus tips, thyme, and 2 tablespoons of the butter between the skillets. Cook until the mushrooms are tender, about 1 minute more. Discard the thyme and combine the contents of the two skillets.

Season the snapper on both sides with salt and pepper. Sprinkle the five spice powder over the skin and rub it in. Clean the skillets and divide the remaining 2 tablespoons vegetable oil between them. Place both over high heat until just smoking. Add the snapper to the skillets skin-side down and briefly hold the fillets down with a spatula to prevent the skin from shrinking. Sear until the bottom is dark and crusted, about 5 minutes. Turn and cook until a metal skewer inserted into the fish for 5 seconds is met with medium resistance and feels warm when touched to your lip, about 5 minutes longer. Keep warm.

Meanwhile, reheat the mushrooms. Bring the sauce to a boil over high heat. Cut the remaining 3 tablespoons butter into ½-inch (1.25-cm) pieces. Lift the saucepan a few inches above the heat and add the butter. Shake the pan back and forth until the butter is melted and incorporated into the sauce; this will take about 3 minutes. Do not stir or whisk the butter into the sauce. When ready, the sauce will be very shiny and clear.

To serve, stir the chives into the mushrooms and asparagus and arrange them in the center of 4 large plates. Top with the snapper. Drizzle the sauce around the mushrooms and serve immediately.

Red Snapper and Mushrooms in
a Port Reduction

With a nod of reverence in the direction of Chef Ripert, I'd be remiss if I didn't mention one of my favorite French seafood dishes, bouillabaisse. This seafood stew is thought to have originated in ancient Greece, but the dish we know today emerged in Provence, when Marseille fishermen simmered their unsellable fish at day's end. It's a soupy stew, but I like mine a little thicker, so rather than using fresh tomatoes in the base, I use crushed. Also, instead of submerging the fish fillets, I float them on top of the mussel shells and let them steam delicately. It's a slight twist on the classic, gently infused with floral saffron and enlivened by herbal Four Thieves Vinegar, but I promise it retains plenty of fishiness to make it seaworthy fare.

FOUR THIEVES BOUILLABAISSE SERVES 4

2 tablespoons OLIVE OIL, *plus more to garnish*

5 cloves MINCED GARLIC

1 CHOPPED MEDIUM ONION

1 CHOPPED BULB FENNEL, *fronds reserved for garnish*

1 pinch SALT

¼ cup (60 ml) FOUR THIEVES VINEGAR, *see page 314*

1 MEDIUM POTATO, *cut into 1-inch-square (2.5-cm-square) pieces*

1 cup (240 ml) FISH STOCK

⅛ teaspoon SAFFRON (125-gram packet)

32 ounces (960 ml) CRUSHED TOMATOES

4 cups (906 ml) WATER

1 pound (455 g) MUSSELS *in the shell, rinsed*

1 pound (455 g) BLACK SEA BASS, *cut into 4 (4-ounce / 115-g) pieces*

2 teaspoons CHOPPED LEMON THYME

CRACKED BLACK PEPPER

In a large saucepan over medium heat, combine the olive oil, garlic, onion, and fennel, and a pinch of salt and cook until fragrant, 2 to 3 minutes. Deglaze with the vinegar and let reduce down to almost dry, 1 to 2 minutes. Add the potatoes, stock, and saffron, and bring to a boil. Reduce the heat to a simmer and cook for 5 minutes so that the flavors come together. Add the tomatoes and water (use the crushed tomato can to measure the water—that way you'll get all the tomatoes that were left in the can), stir, and cook for another 10 minutes.

Taste the broth and see if it needs some salt; adjust the seasoning so it tastes faintly like the sea. Add the mussels, leaving some with their tops sticking out a bit (for the next step), then cook, covered, for about 5 minutes, until they've barely opened. Lay the fish pieces on top of the protruding mussel shells so they sit on top of the broth, not submerged, then cover and cook for another 5 minutes, or until the mussels have completely opened and the fish is cooked through.

recipe continues on page 64

Four Thieves Bouillabaisse

To serve, fill bowls with the stew and provide a side bowl to discard the shells. Garnish with a bit of lemon thyme and cracked black pepper.

Traditional bouillabaisse is served with toast and a garlicky red pepper *rouille*, which is kind of like an aioli, but I usually eat this version without. If you're missing these elements, grill some bread and try some Malt Aioli from page 175.

ITALY

Acetaia San Giacomo,
Andrea Bezzecchi

BALSAMIC CO.

On my second day in Modena I sat in a coffee shop, next door to Hosteria Giusti, a famous *salumeria* (delicatessen). Both the coffee shop and the deli were established by the Acetaia Giusti family, who claim to have been making balsamic vinegar in Modena since 1605. Even within the city limits, there's contention, and rather than embrace one another's uniqueness, balsamic makers continue to clash over ownership of the vinegar's origin and identity.

Whatever the real story may be, balsamic vinegar has become many Westerners' first introduction to vinegar. The industrial production of *Aceto Balsamico di Modena* began in 1967, flooding the global economy with one million bottles. Today, the *Balsamico Tradizionale*, which is protected by its DOP (*Denominazione di Origine Protetta*) status, accounts for less than 0.01 percent of the balsamic vinegar produced annually. What once was made in the attics of a family's home and reserved as a daughter's dowry for marriage has become one of the most commercially successful—though some might say abused—pantry items in history.

Andrea Bezzecchi is the president of Reggio Emilia's traditional balsamic vinegar consortium. In the mid-1990s when his father passed, his family possessed more than one hundred barrels of balsamic vinegar. His family's vinegar-making legacy could have died too, but later that decade, he decided to reopen the family's *acetaia* (vinegar factory). Fortunately, their land was still farmland and flush with Lambrusco grapes.

Bezzecchi and I met in the hallowed streets of Modena, an ancient city known for its fast cars and slow food. There's no arguing that Ferrari, Lamborghini, and Maserati are all Modenese, but balsamic vinegar, well, that's another story. It was a forty-five-minute drive out to Acetaia San Giacomo in Novellara, on the outskirts of Reggio Emilia, or just Reggio, as the local Reggiani call it. Reggio and Modena are the only two consortia that can produce traditional balsamic vinegar.

We arrived at his acetaia at dusk. I could sense fields around us, and as we approached, the whiff of fermentation greeted us from the front of the building. An exterior staircase led us up to the top floor, to the barrel room; the first thing we saw were Bezzecchi's grandfather's *batteria* (barrels), which were in such good condition that they might have been display or still in operation.

Bezzecchi quoted one of Virgil's minor poems that mentions grape mosto, and also cited balsamic vinegar's inclusion in Apicius's magnum opus, considered the first cookbook, but these fragmented suppositions led me to believe that no one really knows the provenance of balsamic vinegar. Fortunately, Bezzecchi is a vinegar pioneer of sorts; he's looking to change the consortia rule, while respecting the past. He thinks tradition can be a hindrance; that's not to say that Bezzecchi doesn't abide by tradition—he does—but he sees room for more creative expression.

The process for making balsamic vinegar begins with boiling down the juice of either Trebbiano or Lambrusco grapes, the two varieties allowed by the consortium, to 30 percent of its original volume. Trebbiano is used more prevalently, and happens to be a low-acid white grape, a fact that often surprises people. Likely due to a higher yield, Trebbiano makes up a third of all white wine in Italy, whereas Lambrusco, grown primarily in Emilia-Romagna and southern Lombardy, makes up significantly less by comparison. Starting from either grape, the resulting syrup, which is called *mosto cotto* ("cooked must," or freshly pressed grape juice), is then aged in a series of batteria. These batteria descend in size, and are made from a variety of woods: chestnut, cherry, oak, ash, mulberry, and juniper.

A minimum of twelve years of aging is a required for any *Aceto Balsamico Tradizionale*, which is designated by a red or *aragosta*-colored label (*aragosta* means "lobster"). Silver signifies eighteen years, and gold means twenty-five or more. Modena, however, uses a white cap for its twelve year and a gold cap for its *extravecchio*, or "extra old" twenty-five year plus. These two DOP products are the only true balsamic vinegars—by definition.

Condimento-grade balsamic vinegars, on the other hand, are made by the same process with the same grapes, but are aged for less than twelve years—usually between three and seven years. *Condimento* can also be made outside of these two cities. Some are even sold by reputable DOP makers—it's just a matter of checking their integrity. *Condimento* is not a protected designation and it's not well-supervised, thus it can be used on balsamic-like products, so proceed with caution.

Then there's Balsamic Vinegar of Modena, which has IGP (*Indication géographique protégée*) status. This is the least bona fide of the three kinds of balsamic vinegar. Marked by a blue and yellow label certifying that the balsamic vinegar was "either manufactured, processed, or prepared at its place of origin," this vinegar only has to be "aged" a minimum of two months, though no real fermentation has to happen, and wooden barrels are optional. This vinegar does not have to contain cooked must—it truly does not resemble anything near traditional balsamic vinegar, other than maybe the 6 percent acidity. It will often contain up to 50 percent wine vinegar base, with artificial sugars, caramel coloring, and thickening agents added.

And last, there's imitation balsamic, which is a complete imposter; it can be made with any kind of vinegar base (e.g., white distilled), and it is industrially manipulated to seem like balsamic. But what this "balsamic" vinegar lacks in quality, it more than makes up for in quantity; its ubiquitousness means most people have experienced fake balsamic at one time or another. That's not to say there aren't any good balsamic-style vinegars made around the world (e.g., George Paul's Emilia from Nebraska and Traditional Aceto Balsamico of Monticello, New Mexico), but authenticity is something makers of *Aceto Balsamico Tradizionale* pride themselves on.

There are differing accounts of the early history of balsamic. (I will skip past the likelihood that the Egyptians cooked date must circa

1000 BC and the *cella defrutaria* of Roman times, when wine was boiled in basement cellars.) What's often brought up as the decisive moment in balsamic's past is the year 1046, when monk and poet Donizo refers to Matilda of Tuscany, one of the most powerful feudal leaders of the Middle Ages, as having made a "balm" in her castle of Canossa, just south of Reggio. She presented that concoction to Henry III, who was to become the king of the Roman Empire. Though the word "balsamic" wasn't officially used in the printing, its essence was implied, though this is still part of folklore, unverified hearsay.

Rumor has it that in 1629, when Francesco I d'Este succeeded his father as Duke of Modena and Reggio (the provinces comprised a single state at the time), he finished building what is arguably his legacy, the construction of the Ducal Palace of Modena, a Baroque masterpiece that still stands today. Perhaps an even greater accomplishment, however, originated deep within the walls of the palace: it is alleged that the west tower was specifically designated for balsamic vinegar production by Francesco himself. The word "balsamic" supposedly did not appear until 1747, when it was written on a list intended to track the movement of goods throughout the palace. Every balsamic vinegar maker has their own version of the story, and there are plenty of families who beg to differ with the above account.

Today, Bezzecchi sells a diverse array of balsamic blends, from *condimento*, to *saba*, an intentional overcooking of grape must to one-third its original volume, also known as *vin cotto* or cooked wine. Bezzechi's blends challenge the antiquated notion that it's DOP or nothing. He also makes an excellent line of wine vinegars, a well-rounded Timorasso made from a Piedmontese grape variety, a Tinto da Ânfora acetified in amphora ceramic containers, a lovely Lambrusco Viadanese of grapes grown between the rivers Po and Oglio, and a Riserva 6 Anni aged to show that even non-balsamic vinegars can mature.

Tradizionale bottles look more like an eau de toilette or cologne than a condiment—perhaps a bit too precious and pricey for those who don't understand the nuances of how to use it. I still believe it's worth the price tag, but age-old ways of fermentation are an investment in time that may no longer be worth the cost of production. Remember, balsamic was originally a small, regional—if not exclusively community-based—product. To scale up was an outlandish idea to say the least.

After we finished touring the acetaia, Bezzecchi, my wife, and I went out for aperitivos at his brother's Antico Bar Roma in town, then dinner at Antica Trattoria Cognento, where plentiful bowls of *ciccoli* (pork rinds done right) and *tortelli*, enhanced by a liberal shower of Parmesan and a splash of balsamic, were trumped only by dessert. The largest piece of cheese (yes, more Parmesan!) I've ever seen on a dinner table appeared, with an "eat what you want" invitation.

Bezzecchi asked the waiter for small ceramic spoons, an option that was printed on the menu right under dessert but before coffee. He then filled three spoons up with generous pours of gold label, and we slurped them down. The taste of balsamic vinegar may inspire nostalgia for its rich past, but in Bezzecchi's case, his gratification was tinged with a palpable enthusiasm for the pleasures and innovations to come.

I was wildly excited about re-creating this experience for friends back home. Instead of serving dessert, I gave them spoons of DOP balsamic; I thought they'd savor it in the same way I did. Some appreciated the idea but others yearned for something sweeter. To accommodate both desires at once, I called up Jeni Britton Bauer of Jeni's Splendid Ice Creams, whose Ohio-based creamery has a cult-like following for her grass-fed milk and her fanciful flavor medleys like Roasted Strawberry Buttermilk and Whiskey and Pecans. Jeni also had the ingenuity to rehydrate dried cherries to make a shrub, or fruit syrup, with balsamic vinegar, which now may be one of my new favorite ice cream toppings. A triumphant dessert to end the meal!

PARMESAN ICE CREAM WITH BALSAMIC CHERRY SHRUB, FROM JENI BRITTON BAUER, JENI'S SPLENDID ICE CREAMS, COLUMBUS, OHIO

For the cherry shrub:

MAKES ABOUT 1½ CUPS (360 ML)

1 cup (145 g) DRIED SWEET CHERRIES

½ cup (100 g) SUGAR

½ cup (120 ml) WATER

⅓ cup (75 ml) BALSAMIC VINEGAR

Put the fruit in a heatproof bowl. Combine the sugar, water, and vinegar in a small saucepan and bring to a boil, stirring to dissolve the sugar. Pour the syrup over the fruit and let cool to room temperature. Refrigerate until chilled. To produce an ice cream with scattered individual cherries, simply strain the cherries and reserve. For a finished product with swirled cherry sauce, begin by straining the cherries, then put them in a food processor. Pulse the cherries lightly, slowly adding the reserved vinegar syrup until the sauce has the consistency of a loose jam.

For the ice cream:

MAKES 1 QUART (960 ML)

1 tablespoon plus 2 teaspoons CORNSTARCH

2⅔ cups (645 ml) WHOLE MILK

4 tablespoons (60 g) CREAM CHEESE, *softened*

⅛ teaspoon SALT

1½ cups (360 ml) HEAVY CREAM

¾ cup (150 g) SUGAR

¼ cup (60 ml) LIGHT CORN SYRUP

1 cup (100 g) SHREDDED PARMESAN CHEESE

Mix the cornstarch with 2 tablespoons of the milk in a small bowl to make a smooth slurry. In a heatproof bowl, mix the cream cheese and salt until smooth. Fill a large bowl with ice and water.

recipe continues on page 74

*Parmesan Ice Cream with
Balsamic Cherry Shrub*

Combine the remaining milk with the cream, sugar, and corn syrup in a 4-quart (4 L) saucepan over medium-high heat. Bring to a rolling boil and boil for 4 minutes, keeping an eye on it so it doesn't boil over. Remove from the heat and gradually whisk in the cornstarch slurry and Parmesan cheese. Return the mixture to a boil over medium-high heat and cook, stirring with a heatproof spatula, until slightly thickened, about 1 minute. Gradually whisk the hot milk mixture into the cream cheese mixture until smooth. Let cool a bit before pouring it into a 1-gallon (3.8-L) zip-top freezer bag (if you don't have an extra set of hands, use a quart container or bowl to hold the bag, folding the edges over the rim to stabilize it) and submerge the sealed bag in the ice bath. Let stand, adding more ice as necessary, until cold, about 30 minutes.

Pour the ice cream base into a frozen canister of an ice cream maker and spin until thick and creamy. Pack the ice cream into a storage container, adding in the cherry shrub as you go. Press a sheet of parchment paper directly against the surface, seal with an airtight lid, and freeze in the coldest part of your freezer until firm at least 4 hours.

Serve with a Parmesan *frico* (crisp), or tuile, to garnish.

AMICI ACIDI

I was first introduced to the five Amici Acidi, or "vinegar friends," when I sampled a 100-ml spray bottle of grape vinegar from Friuli-Venezia Giulia, a region in northeast Italy near the Slovenian border. There, nestled in the hills at the base of the Dolomites, Joško Sirk and his son Mitja operate their vinegar factory, Sirk Della Subida, in conjunction with a hotel called La Subida—a first-rate gastronomic getaway.

Although they do make wine, they are better known for their vinegar, whose labels boldly name the grapes responsible for the contents of each bottle. Identifying the grapes is more than pride of product: it is to dispel the myth that all vinegars are mere by-products of bad vinification. Sirk's method is simple yet precise: vibrantly aromatic Ribolla Gialla grape juice is aged five years in oak. The result? A spectacularly idiosyncratic vinegar, undeniably evocative of the grapes themselves. Sirk believes that by using top quality, unadulterated, raw ingredients— in no way manipulated by mechanization (e.g., acetators)—the grapes' natural flavor and aroma is preserved and, better yet, showcased.

His philosophy is shared by his four fellow Amici Acidi: Baron Andreas Widmann in Alto Adige; Mario Pojer of Pojer e Sandri and Andrea Paternoster of Mieli Thun, both in Trentino; and Andrea Bezzecchi. Any one of these friends would have been a great exemplar of their shared vinegar philosophy, but since I was headed to Modena, I had decided to reach out to Bezzecchi, in the hope that he could act as the group's ambassador.

I thought we'd discuss their different approaches, flavor profiles, and points of view about vinegar, so it was quite unexpected when Bezzecchi wanted to talk about barbecue—perhaps his attempt to relate the Italian palate to the American. He told me there are two warring factions regarding smoked meat in Emilia-Romagna, the large region of northern Italy that includes Modena and Reggio Emilia. (This led me to ask, obtusely, "Wait—you put balsamic vinegar in your barbecue sauce?")

Following the tenets of good barbecue (generally speaking: "slow and low," i.e., a long time on a low temperature) guarantees the meat's tenderness and thorough flavor absorption. Similarly, the slow and steady methods of well-crafted vinegar maximize the flavor and quality of each batch. Vinegar, like meat, also shows signs of its progress on the surface: While smoking a brisket, you're aiming for a crusty bark and a well-defined smoke ring just beneath it; in vinegar you're watching for the formation of a mother, a substance made of cellulose and living acetobacter (acetic acid bacteria), which floats at the top of fermenting liquids.

The second I got back to the United States, I began a hunt for the perfect vinegar-rich barbecue sauce. As serendipity would have it, Jon & Vinny's, an Italian-inspired restaurant in Los Angeles known for creative yet casual pizza and pasta, proved to be just the place for what I was seeking. They in fact have a house-made tomato vinegar, established with verjus and white wine vinegar, heirloom tomato scraps, and some sugar, but it's an ode to old school balsamic that's the mark of distinction.

BALSAMIC BARBECUED RIBS, FROM JON SHOOK AND VINNY DOTOLO, ANIMAL, SON OF A GUN, AND JON & VINNY'S, LOS ANGELES, CALIFORNIA SERVES 4 TO 6

For the barbecue sauce:

1 cup (240 ml) KETCHUP

1 (12-ounce / 360 ml) bottle of BEER, LAGER STYLE, about 1½ cups

½ cup (120 ml) BALSAMIC VINEGAR

1 MEDIUM RED ONION, *diced*

1 clove GARLIC, *finely chopped*

½ cup (110 g) BROWN SUGAR

3 tablespoons HONEY

1½ tablespoons GRAINY MUSTARD

1 to 2 teaspoons TABASCO SAUCE, *depending on how hot and tangy you like your ribs*

1 teaspoon WORCESTERSHIRE SAUCE

¼ cup (60 ml) WATER

To make the barbecue sauce, whisk all of the ingredients together in a medium saucepan and bring to a boil over medium-high heat. Reduce the heat to medium-low, keeping the sauce at a low simmer, and cook uncovered until it's thick, at least 1 hour, stirring occasionally (you can cook it for up to 3 hours, partially covered, for an intensely deep flavor). This can be made days ahead and brought up to room temperature before being applied to the ribs as follows.

recipe continues on page 78

Balsamic Barbecued Ribs

For the ribs:

2 racks ST. LOUIS PORK
RIBS, about 2½ pounds
(1.2 kg) each, *membrane
removed*

CANOLA or
GRAPESEED OIL

SALT

4 sprigs FLAT-LEAF
PARSLEY

4 sprigs THYME

4 cloves GARLIC, *smashed*

Preheat the oven to 500°F (260°C).

Place each half rack of ribs on a 2-foot-long sheet of foil, shiny side up. Rub each half rack with enough oil to coat, then sprinkle with salt and divide the herbs and garlic among the packets. Wrap the foil around the ribs tightly and place them in a roasting pan. Roast the ribs for 30 minutes, then reduce the oven temperature to 250°F (120°C) and cook until the ribs are fork-tender, about another 1 ½ hours. Remove from the oven, carefully open the foil till the ribs are cool enough to handle, 15 to 20 minutes. Remove herb sprigs and discard.

Turn the oven to broil. Liberally brush the meaty side of the ribs with half of the barbecue sauce and broil until caramelized, 2 to 3 minutes. If you don't have a built-in broiling element in your oven, then crank the oven to 500°F (260°C) and roast the ribs until the sauce is hot and bubbling. Transfer to a platter and serve with the rest of the barbecue sauce on the side.

BLOOD IN MY VEINS

One hour with Massimo Bottura is all I needed to understand the clout he has in the Italian food scene. He's a dynamic thinker, whose restaurant Osteria Francescana, located on a residential side street near the Duomo di Modena, was recently named number one by San Pellegrino's World's 50 Best Restaurants. Bottura is Modenese in every sense of the word, representing his heritage on every plate, but his contemporary style of cooking, as seen in dishes like Five Ages of Parmigiano, which could be described as a deconstruction of Parmesan cheese done by varying texture and temperature—now treasured—was once misconstrued.

I have heard it said that in the mid-sixteenth century Catherine de' Medici of Florence often sent for bottles of balsamic vinegar from Modena; after eating, she'd swallow a spoonful or two to ward off morning sickness. Balsamic, however, was seen as not so much a miracle drug to be exploited, but rather a practical and honored tradition to be shared and perpetuated; rarely sold for retail, a batteria would be kept in the family, passed down from mother to daughter.

Modena's star chef does not have a barrel of his own in the Museo del Balsamico Tradizionale di Spilamberto, where donated barrels from many prominent Modenese families are displayed; instead, the barrel representing his family belongs to his daughter Alexa. Bottura does make balsamic; however, in 1999 he founded Villa Manodori, which produces Aceto Balsamico di Modena. He also bottles an Aceto Balsamico Tradizionale di Modena DOP Extravecchio, which he calls "black gold"—it's acidic, sweet, and bitter all at once. But (like a chef) he tinkers, using cherry wood barrels to bring out the red fruit, chestnut for intensity and a bit of darkness, juniper for depth and more interesting notes, and oak for body. His experimenting proves balsamic vinegar has personality and can adapt. "Balsamic is the blood in my veins, and Parmigiano, the protein in my muscles," he told me.

Bottura's sense of tradition is playful—an endearing quality. He recounted for me a memory of receiving a bottle of balsamic vintage for Christmas as a child (a traditional gift in his family) and hurrying outside to pour it over packed snow to make a snow cone. This creative idea undoubtedly inspired his Croccantino, a dessert kindred to a Good Humor Toasted Almond ice cream bar, except with foie gras from Torino as the ice cream, hazelnuts from Piedmont, and almonds from Noto as the crunchy exterior, and, of course, a balsamic heart.

Osteria Francescana's pantry does include non-balsamic vinegars. At dinner one can taste a twenty-seven element Caesar salad, composed

of a bouquet of petals from flowers in bloom, almond milk yogurt, a concentration of chamomile, and aromatic chlorophyll, all sprayed with a house-made elderflower vinegar right before it is served. This extraordinary salad would be impossible to replicate at home, but the takeaway for me was this simple rule: when you dress your greens, use vinegar first. This way, the vinegar penetrates the leaves before any oil is added; the acidity permeates rather than sliding off into a pool at the bottom of the bowl. Olive oil should be added *à la minute*. Though this technique may seem obvious to those with a chef's acumen, it has had a huge influence on how I prepare my salads now.

Another classic chef's trick Bottura introduced me to was his quick and easy frittata—one that he often serves for Sunday lunches with his family, or sometimes for a staff meal. Made with sweated onions deglazed in balsamic, topped with Parmesan, and finished with more balsamic, this recipe is illustrative of Modena's modesty. Massimo spoke of the recipe with such esteem that I felt I had to try it for myself. Whereas Massimo makes a fluffy crust of scrambled egg in the pan before adding the fillings, I pour my eggs over the balsamic onions for a lightly crisp top. *Mangia!*

FRITTATA WITH BALSAMIC ONIONS AND PARMESAN,
MY RECIPE, INSPIRED BY MASSIMO BOTTURA SERVES 4

1 WHITE ONION

SALT

1 tablespoon OLIVE OIL

2 tablespoons BALSAMIC
VINEGAR, IGP,
the cheaper stuff

8 EGGS

1 cup (100 g) SHAVED
PARMESAN, *plus more
to garnish*

BALSAMIC VINEGAR,
DOP, *the good stuff,
to garnish*

*recipe continues
on page 82*

*Frittata with Balsamic
Onions and Parmesan*

Cut the onion in half at the core. Slice into thin half circles, salting slightly to separate.

Heat a nonstick pan over medium. Sauté the onions until translucent, 5 to 7 minutes, then deglaze with the IGP balsamic and reduce until it's almost dry, 2 to 3 minutes. Crack the eggs into a bowl and whisk until combined. Drop the pan to medium-low heat, add the eggs, wait about 30 seconds, then add the Parmesan and put a plate on top of the pan to cover and steam the frittata. Cook for 10 minutes untouched. Remove the plate, but caution, it will be hot, so use pot holders, then give a jiggle to the pan to see if the frittata is cooked through. If not, put the plate back on for a couple of minutes.

When done, release the sides of the frittata from the edge of the pan with a spatula, then invert it back on the plate that was used for steaming (so it stays warm when served). To do so, take the pan off the heat and put the plate back on top. For this next step, it's best to work over a counter or table. In one quick motion, while still holding the pan and plate together, flip the frittata and slide the plate onto the surface. You can serve it immediately, let cool, or even refrigerate overnight.

To finish, drizzle with the DOP balsamic and, while it may seem overindulgent, you can shave more Parmesan on top as well.

TUTTO IN FAMIGLIA

I visited Hosteria Giusti—which I'd been hankering to do ever since I passed it en route to the Giusti café a few days earlier in my trip—to meet up with Alberto Medici, winemaker for Medici Ermete, whom my wife introduced me to as the person largely responsible for the resurgence of the drinkable Lambrusco we usually have at our house back in Brooklyn. We shared some snacks and Champagne before heading back to Reggio Emilia, whose reputation for sticky-sweet sparkling wine peaked in the 1970s and 1980s. Whereas the Lambrusco of old was like drinking bubbling balsamic before it becomes acetified, today the wine has found a drier, more tasteful effervescence. Medici and I mused on the curious symbiosis of wine and vinegar—the paradoxical ways in which they both can and cannot develop simultaneously.

Alberto's sister, Alessandra, tends *sotto tetto*, or "under the roof," where her batteria lie. Following the matriarchal tradition, she is in charge of the balsamic production of what Alberto calls *mezzo vino*, or "half wine." An illustration of Pavarotti, the famous tenor from Modena, hangs on the wall near the entrance of the acetaia. The caption reads, *Do Di Petto*, or "From the Chest." This signifies the deep bodily resonance of a lower-toned voice, in contrast with *falsetto*, which is higher and sharper, resonating more in the head and sinuses.

I see the analogy, but can't with certainty figure out which one sings more truly, the winemaker or the vinegar maker. This is not to say there isn't a harmony to be found between these two disciplines; however, as far as I can tell it's either illegal or just strongly discouraged to have an acetaia on the same grounds as a winery in Italy. Is it a fear of cross-contamination? Or concern for clarity of intent, perhaps? Nevertheless, this was the first time I had ever seen both wine and vinegar alive and well in the same place. We headed into the tasting room, Alberto collected bottles, and Alessandra assembled *dosatore*, little glass vinegar pourers.

Alberto and Alessandra Medici,　**83**
Medici Ermete

While my wife sat with Alberto, comparing notes on past vintages, Alessandra and I tasted flights of balsamic and discussed pairings, each bottle an almanac of that year's harvest. Red label goes great with fresh fish, fresh cheese, and raw or lightly cooked vegetables. Silver is for cooked fish, meat, twenty-four-month-old Parmesan, and frittata. Gold is what she likes to call "meditation vinegar," best with strong cheeses (e.g., blue vein), thirty-month Parmesan, and desserts like panna cotta with strawberries, or, alternatively, by itself on a spoon.

What I didn't ask, and still wonder, is how their crop is allocated—which grapes become Lambrusco wine, and which become balsamic vinegar? This intersection interests me, because whenever I've asked a wine or vinegar maker what quality grape they use in their product, the answer is always "the best possible." So who wins this family fight?

The next morning I took the 740 bus from Modena to an acetaia in Castelvetro, about forty minutes southwest. After driving through flat countryside, I was dropped off along SP17, and the bus driver pointed up a hill to a piazza. Zigzagging across the Guerro River and up a steep-incline drive, I arrived at the base of a clock tower. Across from it was a building with a marquee on the facade that read *La Vecchia Dispensa*, which translates to "The Old Pantry." There, Simone Tintori warmly greeted me.

He seemed to me to be more of an emissary than a salesman. Often, when you're meeting with someone about their commercial product, you get swept up in their scripted banter. In contrast, Tintori is very open to having a dialogue. He's fourth generation, his sister isn't in the business, and he doesn't even have his own batteria; only one barrel bears his name, but it's for personal use. We gossiped over Ponti, a company that used to be in pharmaceuticals but is now part of "big vinegar," and Acetum, probably the biggest balsamic supplier in Modena, if not the world. Because of these IGP monopolies, a need has arisen for better middle-market products.

The production of higher-quality balsamic is increasing markedly, while, at the same time, production of lower-quality balsamic is decreasing—a good thing, because it indicates a more informed customer base, but it should be noted that this trend creates a much more competitive market for vinegar producers. This doesn't discredit how good (and economical) a midrange bottle can be. La Vecchia Dispensa's eight-year aged balsamic is a great everyday balsamic. It strikes that balance between affordability and quality. Their vinegar sings a signature high-end note of cherry wood; the wood for their barrels comes from Vignola, the cherry capital of Italy.

At our meeting, Tintori brought out what looked like an apothecary box containing half a dozen vinegar bottles labeled in handwritten cursive. It felt like a reformist, even slightly steampunk, way to display balsamic, but does making it look old-timey make it more authentic? Tintori doesn't produce the newly trendy balsamic glazes or balsamic creams, but he does call those products balsamic in deference. At this point, trying to re-educate consumers on what is and isn't true balsamic would be too much of an uphill battle, in his view; Tintori is trying to change the balsamic frame of reference.

The city of Reggio Emilia is like a brother to him, one with whom he has a love-hate relationship, but at the end of the day, they're still

La Vecchia Dispensa,
Simone Tintori

family. The word *campanilismo*, which translates to "parochialism" in English, illustrates the sentiment. The sense of community in each town is strong, but in some ways made stronger by the competiveness with neighboring towns over petty debates, such as who has the tallest building or the best wine. In fact, I have found that while abroad Italians are likely to mention the town they're from, believing it's too broad to say "I'm Italian."

However, Simone says they're not competing against a neighboring city anymore; rather, they are facing a global market. For him this means regions have to stick together to promote their shared traditions. It's like Champagne: while there are *méthode champenoise* wines, like crémants, that are delicious, superb Cavas from Spain, and other popular sparkling wines on the market, people know that real Champagne is from the Champagne region of France, and "champagne" from anywhere else is a con. Simone's goal is to unite a class of balsamic vinegar makers that care more about credibility with an emblem of authenticity, trusting the market will follow.

A 100 ml bottle of DOP balsamic in the 1970s used to cost one-third of an average monthly salary in Italy. With inflation, it would cost about 350 euros on the shelf today. Even once the market was flooded with IGP, the demand for DOP balsamic remained inelastic. Over time, though, the on-sale price of DOP decreased but the cost of production didn't, and people didn't know the difference, so what's the value of paying for tradition? During a recent business trip to Germany, none of Tintori's clients asked for DOP, or even IGP, they just wanted to taste "*balsamico.*" That's like asking for "wine" without stating what kind. Calling balsamic a "vinegar" may even be considered a misnomer, since it starts from cooked wine, which is distinctly different from any other vinegar.

We left Tontori's tasting room to ascend a winding staircase—one as seemingly steep as the clock tower I'd passed in town—to a nondescript room where the barrels are stored. The unobstructed, panoramic

view of leas and distant villages from the open windows was breathtaking in its splendor—completely worth the strenuous climb to reach it. I next had the pleasure of meeting Mariangela Montanari. At La Cà dal Nôn, which means "The House of the Grandfather," in the Modenese dialect, there's a century-old vine waving visitors in from the courtyard. Montanari insisted on first stopping by their vineyard in Savignano sul Panaro, a small village a few minutes from the acetaia in Vignola. Her five hectares of vines, where grapes like Trebbiano, Lambrusco, Sauvignon, and Pignoletto grow side by side, is an unusually substantial plot of land for a balsamic maker. However, the integrity of Montanari's vinegars comes from her holistic involvement in their production process.

The four seasons dictate the activity inside the barrels of developing vinegar. When it's hot in the summer, the microorganisms are alive and working; during the winter, they're dormant. Spring and fall are mild in both temperature and activity. The largest barrel is topped with grape must at the end of the winter, and racking down (removing liquid from a larger barrel then adding it to the next smallest one) descending barrels happens once a year when necessary. It's a "feel" thing, and Montanari believes observation is the best way to attend to balsamic. Yes, science can help with creative control, but good old-fashioned instinct goes a long way too.

La Cà dal Nôn

Musk of mulberry wood from Bologna perfumed the air as I stepped into Montanari's batteria room. The presence of Montanari's grandmother Demetria, who passed only a year and a half prior at age ninety-eight, could still be felt. Montanari described her grandmother as delicate yet incredibly witty; it was clear to me that Demetria's signature levity lives on in Montanari and in every drop of La Cà dal Nôn's balsamic vinegar. We sat for lunch with the whole family in a sprawling house with at least one hundred windows; it took everything in me not to excuse myself from the table just to take myself on a tour. I was told by Montanari, "A drop of DOP balsamic on grissini wrapped in prosciutto may just be an appetizer, but it's entrée into what family is all about in Modena."

The Coterie of the Traditional Balsamic Vinegar of Modena was established in 1969 as a way to protect and promote balsamic vinegar. With over fifteen hundred members, they hold meetings and organize tastings, and once a year a panel of judges comes to assess the top bottles from the area, this, in a town of 11,500 residents. There's even a systematic organoleptic test that quantifies the taste of each vinegar.

The Coterie meetings are hosted by the Museo del Balsamico Tradizionale di Spilamberto on Via F. Roncati. I had arranged to tour the museum, and when I arrived, I was warmly greeted by a woman named Elena, who promptly asked that I sit and watch the obligatory film about the origins and production of balsamic vinegar. I obliged, sitting alone in a small theater, really half watching as I snuck glances toward the adjoining rooms. On the walls were *alzavini*, or wine thieves, skinny long cylindrical tubes used to draw samples from active barrels. There was an impressive display of Renzi barrels, wooden casks said to produce the best balsamic—and did I mention the display is inside a room that looks like the inside of a barrel? A shadowbox on the wall in another room held a framed letter with the first recipe for balsamic vinegar from the nineteenth century, and next to it was an encased bottle of vinegar from even earlier than that. At the conclusion of the film, Elena led me upstairs to view the many donated barrels, Massimo Bottura's daughter Alexa's among them.

In addition to these priceless heirloom barrels, the museum maintains a collection for tastings; in a side room I was shown a cabinet filled with samples of all sizes, predominantly DOP. So much balsamic, and I hadn't yet experienced palate fatigue in the slightest—if anything, my craving for vinegar had only heightened. I took the 731 bus back to Modena, where I met my wife for some *gnocco fritto* and tortellini *in brodo*, and for dessert, a piece of Parmesan and, of course, a spoonful of balsamic.

Back in New York City, I was eager to share my Emilia-Romagna experience with a trusted authority (or two) on Italian cuisine. I consider Sara Jenkins my top Italian advisor in the United States. Her mother, Nancy Harmon Jenkins, who happens to be a very experienced cookbook writer, only occasionally surpasses Sara's adept knowledge of Italian cooking. The summer before, I had spent a week with them both at their house in Camden, Maine, where we photographed *The Four Seasons of Pasta* cookbook. As they prepared their dishes for the shoot, I witnessed Sara, a chef with Tuscan bias (whose first impulse would usually be to reach for lemons when a dish needs acidity), adeptly use vinegar to embellish a beautiful summer salad.

I didn't think anything of it then, but now more attuned to the uses of vinegar, I asked her about it. Sara said that as a steadfast rule she doesn't pair lemon with cheese, so any salad or pasta that might have some gratings will require a vinegar component for acidity. And furthermore, she believes the more authentic choice is straight vinegar, not vinaigrette (which is more French, she says), because in Italy the table traditionally comes equipped with bottles of oil and vinegar for diners to dress their salads themselves.

I recall that after that week of heavy carbs, Sara treated us to a restorative *pinzimonio* (Italian style crudités) with red wine vinegar. The secret to Sara's food is straightforwardness; she uses the best ingredients at their peak freshness and pairs them such that each flavor shines through.

PINZIMONIO: SALAD WITH GREEN BEANS, FENNEL, CELERY HEARTS, CUCUMBERS, FRIED ALMONDS, AND RED WINE VINEGAR, FROM SARA JENKINS, PORSENA, NEW YORK CITY SERVES 2 TO 4

1 FENNEL BULB, *cut into bite-size pieces*

½ pound (225 g) HARICOTS VERTS, *blanched*

1 CELERY HEART, *cut into ¼-inch (6-mm) slices*

2 PERSIAN CUCUMBERS, *peeled, cut in half lengthwise, then sliced into ¼-inch (6-mm) half moons*

¼ cup (35 g) OLIVE-OIL FRIED ALMONDS, *roughly chopped*

SALT and BLACK PEPPER

¼ cup (60 ml) EXTRA VIRGIN OLIVE OIL, *estate bottled preferred*

2 tablespoons ITALIAN RED WINE VINEGAR

In a large bowl, toss all the vegetables and the almonds together. Season with salt and black pepper. Drizzle with the olive oil first, and toss, then add the vinegar and toss again. Serve as dressed crudités.

Back when Sara lived in Italy, she didn't even know what balsamic was; balsamic didn't really exist yet outside of Modena. Nowadays, she uses it to make a special snack that takes pancetta (cured pork belly rolled with spices) to a supernatural level. The cured meat transforms into a crunchy antipasto with a bite of acidity that's best enjoyed as is, on grilled bread, or as a complement to the salad before.

PANCETTA COOKED IN BALSAMIC VINEGAR,
FROM SARA JENKINS, PORSENA, NEW YORK CITY SERVES 1

4 slices of ROLLED PANCETTA, 3 to 4 inches (7.5 to 10 cm) in width, *cut about ⅛ inch (3 mm) thick*

2 tablespoons BALSAMIC VINEGAR, 2 YEAR

In a dry sauté pan, over medium heat, cook the pancetta on one side until slightly crispy, 1 to 2 minutes, then turn and repeat on the other side. Add the vinegar and cook briskly until the vinegar is reduced by half, 20 to 30 seconds. Serve and eat immediately, as is, or on grilled bread.

In Venice, there's a style of preparation known as *en saor* ("in flavor" in the Venetian dialect) in which fish (usually sardines) is soaked in a sweet-and-sour marinade that serves to temper the fishiness while preserving the flesh. First you dredge and fry the fish, then you add it to a vinegar-based solution sweetened by plumped raisins, and finally you cover the fish with sizzled onions and toasted pine nuts. It's versatile because it can either be served cold as an *antipasto* or warm as a *secondo*. For the impatient, Sara shares a dish her mother used to make in Tuscany, a similarly structured marinade that is poured over the top of the cooked fish but can be eaten right away. There is still the option to let the fish sit and soak up more of the sauce, but either way the result will be full of flavor.

BROILED MACKEREL WITH CHILE, ROSEMARY, GARLIC, AND VINEGAR, FROM SARA JENKINS, PORSENA, NEW YORK CITY SERVES 4

2 cloves GARLIC

2 sprigs (about 2 tablespoons) ROSEMARY

1 SMALL DRIED CALABRIAN CHILE

4 (6- to 8-ounce / 170- to 225-g) FILLETS BOSTON or SPANISH MACKEREL, *skin on*

SALT and BLACK PEPPER

4 tablespoons (60 ml) OLIVE OIL

½ cup (120 ml) ITALIAN RED WINE VINEGAR

Fine chop the garlic, rosemary, and chile together and set aside.

Lay the fish fillets skin-side up on a rimmed baking sheet and rub salt, pepper, and 3 tablespoons of the olive oil over them.

Turn on your broiler.

In a small pan, over medium heat, sauté the garlic, rosemary, and chile in the remaining 1 tablespoon olive oil until the garlic is just golden, 2 to 3 minutes. Add the vinegar and reduce by a little more than half, 2 to 3 minutes.

Meanwhile, broil the mackerel skin-side up, until the skin is crisp and bubbly and the flesh is just cooked all the way through, 3 to 5 minutes, depending on the thickness of the fillets.

Remove to a serving platter and drizzle the garlic-rosemary-chile vinegar over the fillets. Serve immediately or let marinate for 30 minutes or so and eat at room temperature.

PIEDMONTESE BEES

A nomadic apiary is hard to find. Detouring from Milan (where my wife had been dying to order a Negroni Sbagliato at Bar Basso—the chalice is as big as your head!), we made our way to Piedmont so she could dig into Barolo country. I knew it was time for wine, but I had seen a bottle of honey vinegar at Renee Erickson's The Whale Wins in Seattle, Washington, and logged it to memory. When something like this occurs, I often solicit a taste at a restaurant, or procure some for my home collection, and such was the case with Acetum Mellis Italian honey vinegar: After one sip, I knew I had to visit the vinegar maker himself. The Acetum Mellis bottle is clad in a yellow honeycomb design, and the glass glows like the honey that made its contents. It stands tall, like its founder, Michele Gaido, who, when we first met, excitedly buzzed about the office procuring samples, like a bee in its hive.

There aren't many bees where the vinegar is actually made, a large barn that looks like a cedar closet. This is because the part of Piedmont that Gaido calls home is highly agricultural, which means drifting pesticides from neighbors are a serious threat; at one point, Michele's bees began displaying Alzheimer's-like symptoms as a result of the pollution. His solution was to relocate his hives to the nature preserve, a protected wildlife refuge where he regularly rotates their location in the fields and forests.

Acetum Mellis

Since 1989, Gaido has been making his signature *miele millefiori* (mixed flower honey), as well as dozens of other varieties of honey, including a rich *melata* (honeydew), a creamy *tarassaco* (dandelion), a dark *castagno* (chestnut), and a floral acacia. The *millefiori* is the type Michele uses to make mead (honey wine) vinegar: First the honey is diluted with water and then it is inoculated with natural yeast to jump-start the fermentation process. After mead is made, it is aged for a year in stainless steel vats, where it develops a saison-like farmhouse profile. Though most of that funk dissipates by the time it's all acetic acid, the taste remains sharp but not overly assertive. Gaido also has a line of barrique-aged mead vinegars, which are a bit mellower but still inherently honey flavored. That's the enduring and endearing thing about these vinegars; they're made like a fine wine, even when turned into vinegar.

I must add that in Barolo, Italy, where your table wine is Barolo more often than not, there's a great prestige surrounding the village's namesake export. However, when we visited wineries for tasting and I asked if they also made vinegar, most scoffed at the idea of allowing their superior grapes to turn into something so foul. There were a few, though (who asked not to be mentioned), who do make their own Barolo vinegar, the taste of which still sings of tar and roses. The stigma of vinegar's supposed inferiority may be alive and well, but I am certain vinegar is approaching its defining moment, finally gaining the widespread respect it deserves.

AUSTRIA

Erwin Gegenbauer,
Gegenbauer Vinegar Brewery

GEGENBAUER

Megan and I woke up as the train was approaching in Vienna. After eating breakfast in our sleeping car, we disembarked at Wien Hauptbahnhof. It was only upon stepping into the bustling capital city that we remembered that this was Austria and the sorry extent of our German was *Hallo, guten Tag, Auf Wiedersehen*, and *Danke schoen*.

Because Viennese coffee houses are considered to be of "intangible cultural heritage" (ICH) by UNESCO, we spent the day patronizing the various establishments along the Ringstraße (ring road) of the inner district. We stopped in Café Hawelka for coffee and apple strudel, had a slice of Sacher torte at Café Central, then munched on Krampus cookies from Demel, the legendary bakery. We sipped *Gluhwein* at the Christmas markets and mingled with bonneted horses—it felt as though we were inside a Yuletide snow globe. As we sat in the famous Blue Bar at the Hotel Sacher soaking in the culture of the city, I couldn't help but reflect on—or psychoanalyze, if you will—the reasons I found myself there in Vienna. It is the city of Freud after all!

Fifteen years prior, my aspirations lay somewhere between chef and documentary photographer. I used to sling a camera around my neck and head into Boston's top kitchens during the dinner rush, hoping to capture a few frames—and pick up some cooking tips along the way. One of my favorite kitchens from that time is still in full swing today: Barbara Lynch's Beacon Hill restaurant, No. 9 Park, whose essence could be summed up as "French bistro meets politico chic." Its rise signified a new golden age for Boston's food scene.

Though it was her only restaurant at the time, and is still her principal address, Lynch now owns more than half a dozen storefronts around town, from a butcher shop to an oyster bar, a pasta counter to a cocktail den. I remember the night she handed me a capful of liquid and said, "Drink this." Feeling a bit like Alice in Wonderland, I obeyed. "What is it?" I asked, completely bewildered. The gulp had been incredibly lively and juicy, yet also contained a hint of raisin. As it turns out, this was my first kiss with Noble Sour P.X. vinegar, whose taste sparked the most intense flavor memory I would have for a long time. I came to Vienna to meet its maker: Erwin Gegenbauer.

Made with Pedro Ximénez grapes—the same kind used to make sherry, the Spanish wine customarily oxidized through the solera method (a blending method that involves mixed vintages, such that the average age gradually increases over a prolonged period of time)—I'd later find out this was an atypical example of his product line, and unique in its methodology (it does not abide by solera). The vinegar came potion-like, in a dark, ridged glass bottle, and after that first taste I was captivated; I continued to seek it out, all the while brewing a plan to meet the man behind the magic. In fact, I have Erwin Gegenbauer to thank for inspiring this "acid trip" of mine. Before my travels began, I told my wife innumerable times that Gegenbauer is quite possibly the best vinegar maker in the world, and I stand by that statement. I have now tasted other vinegars that rival it, but the effect of Gegenbauer's vinegar on the palate is undeniable, its taste not quite sweet, not quite salty, not quite bitter. The acid is almost cathartic in its richness.

I often pictured Erwin Gegenbauer as a kind of vinegar-making Willy Wonka: an eccentric middle-aged man, living in a lavish funhouse laboratory, concocting unforgettable flavors. However, the man who answered the door of the Wiener Essig Brauerei (Viennese Vinegar Brewery), while certainly passionate about his craft, was a great deal less fanciful than I imagined he'd be. He struck me as a somber, occasionally sardonic man, and was at times quite dismissive of the current apathetic state of the industry in which he works.

In 1929, Ignaz Gegenbauer (the original Gegenbauer) established a sauerkraut and gherkin factory—one whose competition numbered more than six hundred companies in Vienna alone. That same year the Great Depression spread like wildfire across the Western world. Although Gegenbauer's family business managed to survive (few other sauerkraut makers did), his descendants' interest shifted in the early

1990s toward the pickling liquid itself. That's when Erwin founded his family's new vinegar enterprise.

Erwin Gegenbauer told me that today his company produces dozens of varieties of vinegar, including beer, malt, and wine vinegars (I recommend the sweet white *Trockenbeerenauslese* and red *Zweigelt Spätlese*); fruit- and vegetable-flavored vinegars made from such ingredients as handpicked aronia berries, ripe cucumbers, quince sap, and gently pressed tomatoes; and even a few balsamic vinegars, including a nine-year muscat grape and a five-year Golden Delicious apple. The Gegenbauer website features hundreds of recipes that utilize their unrivaled vinegars, as well as videos that discuss and celebrate both the vinegar-making process and the Gegenbauer family legacy.

Gegenbauer produces tens of thousands of liters of *Essig*, or house vinegar (which is made of pure alcohol) each day. This vinegar is then transferred from the brew house to a gargantuan wooden vat outside. Once inside the barrel, the vinegar drips down through a series of wood chips, with air being pumped in from below. It's a method called Schützenbach, and it was invented in Southern Germany circa 1820. By the mid 1900s, however, this process was widely replaced by industrial acetators, which use submersion techniques to ferment the vinegar more rapidly.

Gegenbauer is one of the few European vinegar makers to still use the Schützenbach method (O-Med in Spain does as well); the commitment to a long, traditional fermentation process produces a highly aromatic, deep-flavored vinegar with character. It's a bit like moonshine—which makes sense, since both are made from wheat. Unlike Gegenbauer's other vinegars, this one is more utilitarian. It helps carry flavors in marinades and sauces, but may be too assertive to use alone.

The flavorful Gegenbauer showstoppers that most pique my appetite were actually conceived as alternatives to a very Austrian tradition. Schnapps, the local liqueur, which can be distilled from apples, pears, plums, and other orchard and stone fruits, is often quite high-proofed.

Gegenbauer

Instead of partaking in the customary schnapps before and after each meal, Erwin Gegenbauer decided to create similarly sweet virgin alternatives (e.g., Noble Sour P.X., Noble Sour Traminer) with a playful, acidic kick.

Gegenbauer utilizes both old and new techniques, cultivating bacteria with a Frings acetator system, controlling oxygen and temperature to a tenth of a degree (Celsius). This gives his vinegars empirical life, creating an environment wherein each special product can thrive. Only wine vinegars go in barrels, which include dozens of balsamic casks on the rim of the roof. In the cellar there are countless rows of demijohns (teardrop-shaped glass jugs) filled with fruit and vegetable vinegars. These are carefully aged until they find their way to his shop in the busy Naschmarkt, a marketplace with more than one hundred stalls of food vendors and restaurants, stretching for nearly a mile down Wienzeile (Vienna Row), which runs parallel to the Wien River.

When Erwin Gegenbauer first started his vinegar company, he began by studying wine and balsamic vinegars, with guidance from Professor Paolo Giudici of the Università degli Studi di Modena e Reggio Emilia, a top scholar in the field of acetic acid. His expansion into other base ingredients would come later. Whatever the ingredient, however, Gegenbauer insists on quality. "Only a good wine is a base for a good vinegar; you only get what you put in," Gegenbauer quipped. "We pay twenty-five euros for a good wine, and vinegar is one more fermentation past that. The worth [of vinegar] needs a new definition." Wine is often described as being expressive, as having clear aromas and flavors. Vinegar, not so much, but Gegenbauer begs to differ with those who would overlook the complexities of his vinegar, and I wholeheartedly agree; a single drop can encapsulate an entire season, a specific terroir, a ripened fruit.

We stayed in Erwin's modest, rentable guest room, where there are no drawers and the light switches dangle from metal chains hanging from the ceiling. It's unadorned, to say the least—no television or art on the brick walls, the bathroom partitioned by curtains on an overhead track, with conservationist quirks such as bowls without drains in the place of sinks, to minimize water consumption. He likens the architecture to his product: "Our bottle is transparent; everything is evident, even the vinegar." When we woke up, Gegenbauer was already in the kitchen making scrambled eggs that had been laid by his rooftop chickens. With our eggs he served us bread and butter, both homemade, on a skillfully handcrafted table. He is a self-sufficient essentialist, his home and business stripped down in an almost Swiss Family Robinson way. He has an oil mill, roasts his own coffee beans, and brews his own beer—all sold around town, to top chefs and neighbors alike. It's likely a bit of pushback against his family's pickling days. "I don't want to have a uniform product. I used to be told how many gherkins were in a jar," Gegenbauer said to us. "I hate to be perfect. If you want to eat the same thing over and over, then you're losing your intellectual taste. It's like a painter making prints, where's the endeavor in that?"

STYRIAN GOALS

I was introduced to Konstantin Filippou through Lotta and Per-Anders Jörgensen of the authoritative food magazine *Fool*, from Sweden. Part of the Jorgensens' job is to traverse the globe in search of talented and innovative chefs, and Filippou is a prime example. A city that's largely gone unchanged since World War II, Vienna relies heavily on wavy pork schnitzel and spreadable Liptauer cheese as the standard cuisine (though I was delighted to find that their Viennese potato salad is actually cooked in a tangy vinegar-based broth).

Filippou, who is of Greek heritage, hails from Graz, the second largest city in Austria after Vienna. Graz is located in the southeastern state of Styria, in a region also known as Thermenland because of its many thermal hot springs. The "spa food" there is mainly salad based and often saturated with a Styrian specialty called *Kernöl* or *Kürbiskernöl*, a dark forest-green pumpkin seed oil. The need for acidity to complement this oil is apparent; the salads are often generously doused in apple vinegar. At O Boufés, Filippou's natural wine bar in Vienna, however, Filippou likes to mix things up. For his *Käferbohnen*, a simple Styrian salad traditionally composed of scarlet runner beans dressed with nothing more than oil and vinegar, Filippou uses Gegenbauer's elderberry vinegar as a sweet twist on the usual apple vinegar. Truthfully, any dark berry vinegar can work—I've even used younger traditional balsamic vinegars, which have the necessary sweetness to stand up to the dense pumpkin seed oil.

STYRIAN KÄFERBOHNEN (SCARLET RUNNER BEAN) SALAD, FROM KONSTANTIN FILIPPOU, VIENNA, AUSTRIA
SERVES 2 TO 4

1½ cups SCARLET RUNNER BEANS, approximately ½ pound (225 g)

SALT and BLACK PEPPER

1 to 2 tablespoons STYRIAN PUMPKIN SEED OIL, *try Stony Brook Oils*

1 to 2 tablespoons ELDERBERRY VINEGAR

1 to 2 tablespoons GRATED FRESH HORSERADISH

Soak the beans overnight in cold water.

The next day, drain, put them in a saucepan with plenty of water, and bring to a boil over high heat. Reduce the heat and simmer until tender, about 1 hour, then drain and rinse with cold water. Note: Do not salt the cooking water, because the proteins of the beans will coagulate and they won't attain the softness you desire.

Put the warm, soft beans in 1 bowl and season with salt and black pepper. Add 1 tablespoon each of the pumpkin seed oil and elderberry vinegar. Taste and add more of each to your liking. You want the beans coated but not swimming in the vinaigrette, though a small pool at the bottom of the bowl is a delicious dipping sauce.

Grate some horseradish on top, eyeballing about 1 tablespoon, increasing by teaspoons to taste. Serve warm, or let sit and soak up all the goodness, as the dish can be enjoyed cold as well.

Styrian Käferbohnen
(Scarlet Runner Bean) Salad

Cabbage is still a fixture in the Austrian diet, but not all of it is served as sauerkraut. Konstantin makes a warm variation that soaks in a syrupy mixture of cooked onions deglazed with apple vinegar. The cabbage retains its crunch but tastes like it's been marinating for ages.

WARMER SPECKKRAUTSALAT (MARINATED CABBAGE), FROM KONSTANTIN FILIPPOU, VIENNA, AUSTRIA MAKES ABOUT 1 QUART (1 L)

1 LARGE CABBAGE, about 2 pounds (910 g)

1 tablespoon SALT

½ cup (115 g) PANCETTA, *cut into small dice, reserving the rind of the pancetta to marinate with the cabbage (subbing thick smoked bacon is more than acceptable)*

2 tablespoons GROUND CUMIN

5 BAY LEAVES

4 tablespoons (60 ml) APPLE VINEGAR

1 tablespoon SUGAR

1 LARGE WHITE ONION, *cut into thin strips*

2 cloves GARLIC, *finely chopped*

FRESHLY GROUND BLACK PEPPER

Cut the cabbage in quarters, removing the core. Slice the cabbage into ¼-inch (6-mm) pieces widthwise, which will produce strips approximately 3 inches (7.5 cm) long. Put the cabbage in a large bowl or pot and add the salt. Add the pancetta rind, cumin, and bay leaves and let the cabbage marinate, covered, for 24 hours.

After it has finished marinating, press the cabbage through a sieve, or squeeze in cheesecloth get out all the liquid from the cabbage. Pick out the pancetta rind and bay leaves and discard.

In a sauté pan over medium heat, fry the diced pancetta until crispy, 4 to 5 minutes, and deglaze with half of the vinegar. Pour the cooked pancetta and vinegar over the cabbage, along with the sugar. Set aside, reserving the fat in the pan. In the same pan, sauté the onion and garlic until translucent. Deglaze with the remaining vinegar, then pour in a little water, about 2

**tablespoons, and briefly boil for about 1 minute, until the liquid
is reduced by half.**

**Pour the liquid over the cabbage mixture and season with
black pepper and, if desired, salt. Serve immediately. This dish
goes well with crispy pork belly or just warm bread.**

I finished my meal at O Boufés with a quick kitchen tour, then a scoop
of balsamic banana ice cream while standing next to the radiant wine
fridges. The next day I planned to travel through Filippou's old stomping
ground to visit Gölles, a schnapps and vinegar producer in Riegersburg,
Styria. My wife would not be joining me. Instead she headed to Gols, a
town in the Burgenland wine region, to taste grüner veltliner with a few
producers that piqued her interest and whom she hoped to research.
Because of our poor pronunciation of "Gols" and "Gölles," we encountered quite a bit of confusion when soliciting directions, as people
thought we were talking about the same place. Nevertheless, we each
found our way to our respective destinations. I arrived after a six-plus-
hour bus-train combination, tired, but soon thoroughly energized by
the sight of Gölles's spectacular, ten-hectare orchard. To discover a
large-scale operation devoted to the symbiotic production of schnapps
and vinegar was like having your dissertation's closing argument handed
to you on a silver platter.

Gölles's visitors' center looks like a modern church, palatial, lots of
glass and light. Upon walking through the door, I heard "Spannenlanger
Hansel" playing overhead—a jolly children's song about the pear harvest
that sounds oddly similar to "Itsy Bitsy Spider." Gölles harvests Williams
pears and *Kriecherl* (damson plums)—both handpicked. They also grow a
myriad of berries: including shiny clusters of red currants, rowan berries
(which taste like marzipan), and, of course, plenty of native elderberries.
I was first introduced to their vinegars when a friend gave me a gift of
Gölles raspberry vinegar. Thinking it was schnapps—not yet knowing
Gölles made vinegar—I took a shot, and rather than being repulsed, I
was pleasantly surprised to find how smooth and balanced it was.

The Gölles cellar holds fourteen hundred oak barrels, some more than sixty years old. The founder of Gölles, Alois Gölles, first began growing apple trees in 1950. In 1979, the company began to brew schnapps, and by the mid-1980s they had amassed a batteria of twenty-plus-year apple balsamic vinegar. Today they also produce jars of jelly made of 20 percent vinegar, fruit juice, and pectin. The overall impression that every one of their products gives is that of "fresh fruit"; nothing tastes cooked, double distilled, or even fermented. Rather, it tastes as though it was just picked. Twenty-five thousand people come annually to their visitors' center, with peak visitation occurring in the spring, for blossoms, and the autumn, for harvest.

To end on a sweet note, I stopped by Zotter Chocolates, a popular bean-to-bar confections shop in Riegersburg, a ten-minute drive from Gölles. Before becoming a chocolate maker, Josef Zotter owned a pastry shop that unfortunately went bankrupt in the 1990s. Luckily, his switch to chocolate has garnered him great success; his company now boasts almost one thousand tons of chocolate and 250,000 visitors annually! The shop features a view of the chocolate-making process; large glass windows reveal the raw ingredients' complete transformation into the decadent treats available for purchase in the shop (there's a chocolate bar made with Gölles vinegar, and there are unlimited free samples as well!).

My fellow visitors exclaimed in awe over having access to a chocolate factory's inner workings. "You know it's good because you can see where it comes from," I heard one woman remark. I refrained from pointing out that the cocoa beans weren't homegrown, but was happy to hear people taking an interest in where their food is made. It's the kind of spirit that could help launch quality, artisanal vinegar to new heights of appreciation and respect.

Gölles, Riegersburg

JAPAN

SHOKUNIN 職人

The word *shokunin* describes a class of craftsmen in Japan: highly skilled and highly respected, focused on a single subject, vinegar artisans are among these ranks. It may sound myopic, focusing on one product for generations, mastering a specific craft through repetition and refinement, all to fill a tiny niche. Well, that niche is bigger than you'd think in Japan. And once you've become highly accomplished in your field, others don't dare meddle or try to compete, and you become known as the one—the only one—people go to, the one their children and grand-children go to, for a given artisanal product.

With such deep-rooted devotion, brand loyalty is hereditary. In a country dominated by big vinegar houses like Mizkan, Marukan, Kikkoman, and even Kewpie (yes, that squeezable mayonnaise with the cute baby logo), there's limited room for any other vinegar makers, so only the best can succeed. And although there are about five hundred vinegar makers in Japan (of mainly rice-based vinegar, widely known as *komezu*), two-thirds of these businesses actually buy and rebottle vinegar from the aforementioned larger companies. Then there are the Uchibori brothers, who brew both as a large company and a small one with a mighty heart.

Mitsuyasu Uchibori is singlehandedly establishing a culture of drinking vinegars in Japan. The concept exists in Korea and Taiwan, and can even be found in the United States, most prominently embraced by Andy Ricker, a chef with northern Thai–inspired Pok Pok restaurants in Portland, Oregon; New York City; and Los Angeles. Ricker was inspired by Korean drinking vinegar to launch his own line of Pok Pok Som drinking vinegars in 2005. Growing interest in drinking vinegar has also inspired mixologists to incorporate the shrub, a colonial American favorite comprised of vinegar-based syrup and soda water, into their cocktails in recent years. For Uchibori, however, drinking vinegars are a natural extension of his genealogy; he belongs to the fourth generation of a vinegar business born in the Gifu prefecture around 1876.

Uchibori is a self-proclaimed "su-mmelier," a riff on the traditional *sommelier*, or wine service specialist; *su* means vinegar in Japanese, which you can spot in kanji on all of his bottles: 酢. We planned to meet for dinner a couple of days after my arrival in Tokyo, but having not yet had a taste of his vinegars, I set out to find and sample of his Oaks Heart product line in advance (found in Takashimaya department stores throughout Japan). I was so excited to try a sip that I woke up early to beat the morning rush at Mitsukoshi, another department store, where in Ginza they have a much-heralded *depachika*, or basement-level food market.

As I descended the escalator down two flights to level B2F, I saw on my left a luminous array of rainbow bottles that looked like splits of champagne and two tasting stations marked by black floor mats contrasting the glowing white of the rest of the interior. Osuya is a small boutique shop within Mitsukoshi, in many of its locations, where employees serve sweet samples of Uchibori's "dessert vinegar" in little plastic shot glasses. If you ask, you can try the yellow yuzu citrus concoction whirring in the slush machine dispenser on the counter. If you didn't know what you were getting into, you wouldn't realize until you were a few samples deep that you'd been drinking and enjoying vinegar. It's bright; it feels effervescent without having bubbles; it enlivens your taste buds. Uchibori's Expre-su Bar in Tokyo Station sees people on their way to work line up every morning as if it was for their daily dose of caffeine. In the afternoons, workers come on their lunch hours for soft serve topped with vinegar as if it were raspberry sauce, cutting through the cream's fattiness, refreshing the palate for the next bite.

Until 2003, Uchibori vinegars were used mainly for sushi, sauces, and pickles. In Japanese cooking, vinegar is usually blended into a more complex mixture for balance; it rarely stands alone. Most rice vinegar, if tasted straight, would be a bit milder than white wine vinegar in flavor, but still pretty acidic, upward of 6 percent. It needs to be softened with shoyu (soy sauce), mirin (sweet rice wine), dashi (stock made of kombu seaweed), or a combination thereof, as seen in the very popular and versatile *nanbansu* (you can tell if a sauce has vinegar in it by its -*su*, or sometimes -*zu*, suffix), which can be used as a marinade, dipping sauce, or dressing.

NANBANSU, INSPIRED BY UCHIBORI VINEGARS
MAKES 1 CUP (240 ML)

½ cup (120 ml) RICE VINEGAR

½ cup (120 ml) MIRIN

¼ cup (60 ml) SOY SAUCE

¼ cup (50 g) SUGAR

Combine all ingredients in a small saucepan and cook over medium heat, stirring until the sugar is dissolved. It will keep, covered, in the refrigerator for up to a month.

Nanbanzuke (see page 126), a fried fish dish that is marinated in this sweet vinegar sauce, isn't even Japanese in origin. Rather, it was likely inspired by Portuguese missionaries in the sixteenth century, whom the Japanese people called *Nanban*.

You might be surprised to learn that the purpose of many vinegar sauces is not primarily flavor; rather, these sauces' fundamental function lies in their power to preserve. But Mitsuyasu Uchibori isn't about the sauce. While his brother runs the more industrial part of the business, making volume vinegars for use in the commodity market, Mitsuyasu spends time cultivating vinegars that are particular and precious.

My visit to Japan began at the start of Sakura Matsuri season, a week or so before the cherry blossoms would open. That morning at Osuya, there was cherry blossom vinegar, which blooms in your mouth like a spring awakening; a very expensive, dark honey vinegar, buzzing of buckwheat grain; and even vinegar hot-chocolate heart pops meant to be dissolved in warm milk as an invigorating after-meal sipper. Osuya's inventory changes with the seasons, reflecting which produce is freshest, similar to Atelier du Soleil Sun Fruits, the vendor in the stall next to them, which, that day, was selling three-hundred-dollar musk melons and boxes of perfect strawberries. Unlike their perishable counterparts, however, Uchibori's dessert vinegars are shelf stable and won't go bad, extending those ephemeral flavors far past the spring.

FOOD & COMPANY

Product design is a triumph in Tokyo—even the washi tape that seals each envelope is a bow to this compulsion. I assumed that the product inside every package would be similarly exquisite. To test my theory, I stopped by a gourmet retail store in the Meguro ward of Tokyo called Food & Company. The owner, Bing Bai, carries Uchibori's pure rice vinegar, as well as balsamic from Italy. The reason a store like this is important is that most Japanese home cooks don't deviate from mass-market labels when it comes to vinegar, yet are very particular with their other pantry items.

During my tour of Food & Company, Bai paused to pick up a bottle of sesame oil that he was proud to have recently acquired. He described with great detail the oil's place of origin and the process by which it was made. But when it came to vinegar, his stories were far briefer. He knew of the ubiquitous Uchibori and told me he carries another vinegar maker called Iio Jozo, whose facilities I also planned to visit on my trip, but then he pivoted to tell other products' lengthier back stories. Bai was not at fault here; if anything, his understanding and care for his products was far beyond any other specialty food store of its kind that I visited. It's part of the culture he's trying to promote, in which every ingredient—even pantry staples—is as thoughtfully sourced as the fish one eats and the sake one drinks.

SHOJIN RYORI

Daisuke Nomura is one of three sons of Satoko Nomura, the matriarch behind Daigo, a two-Michelin-star vegetarian restaurant in Tokyo. Daisuke learned to cook, whereas his brothers worked in managerial roles, but it wasn't until the family decided to open Sougo in Roppongi (an area known for its nightlife, home to many foreign embassies, and populated by a diverse group of active eaters) that rules were broken.

Daisuke, along with translator Yoko Goto, a cooking instructor in her own right, are both well versed in *shojin ryori*, the cuisine of Buddhist monks; it is, in fact, Daisuke's specialty and widely considered to be the basis of most Japanese cooking. Unlike its vegetarian sister restaurant, Sougo is a bit more modern, adding bonito to its dashi, fabricating foams, and using newer equipment like Pacojets—all of which deviate markedly from his family's culinary philosophies. And though Daisuke uses unusual ingredients in *kaiseki*, the sequenced multi-course meal format to which shojin ryori subscribes, the foundation is still based around the five tastes: sweet, bitter, sour, salty, and hot (though recently hot has been replaced by umami, the savory taste). There are five colors—white, black, red, blue, and yellow—and five methods: raw, simmer, grill/roast, fry, and steam. The common thread throughout each meal is vinegar.

Sunomono, also known as "vinegared dishes," are a subset of Japanese food, often served to begin a meal and/or to complement the main dishes. They are not to be confused with *tsukemono,* however, which are traditional pickles not always made with vinegar. Goto and I had a laugh about this confusion. I explained to her that, in the United States, it's almost imperative for pickles to be "in vinegar," even though favorites like sauerkraut actually go through a "pickling" process that involves lactic acid fermentation and doesn't involve vinegar.

Daisuke then served me Chinese cabbage (a tsukemono), salted, pressed, and aged, but he poured in a bit of *amazu* (sweet vinegar) to wash away some of the salinity and add a little liveliness. He spoke of iterations of vinegar-based sauces, like *tosazu,* made with *katsuobushi* (bonito flakes), dashi, vinegar, and soy sauce; and *tadezu,* an herbed vinegar that utilizes *tade* (water pepper) and sake, and is served on *ayu,* a small freshwater sweet fish only found on menus in the summertime.

AMAZU (SWEET VINEGAR SAUCE),
INSPIRED BY DAISUKE NOMURA, SOUGO, TOKYO, JAPAN
MAKES ABOUT 1½ CUPS (360 ML)

1 cup (240 ml) RICE VINEGAR	½ cup (120 ml) WATER
	2 tablespoons SUGAR

Put all ingredients in a small saucepan, place over medium heat and cook until the sugar has dissolved. Cool and serve. It will keep, covered, in the refrigerator for a couple weeks.

Daisuke Nomura,
Sougo

TOSAZU (KATSUOBUSHI VINEGAR SAUCE),
INSPIRED BY DAISUKE NOMURA, SOUGO, TOKYO, JAPAN
MAKES ABOUT 1 CUP (240 ML)

⅓ cup (75 ml)
 RICE VINEGAR

2 tablespoons SUGAR

½ cup (120 ml) SOY SAUCE

1 cup (12 g) BONITO
 FLAKES
 (*KATSUOBUSHI*)

Combine all ingredients in a saucepan, bring to a boil, then turn off heat and let cool. Strain. It will keep in the refrigerator for a week or so.

Pictured above is a small bowl of *tokoroten*, which are clear noodles made from *kanten*, the gelatin extracted from seaweed. These are doused in a syrup called *kuromitsu*, which in the Kanto region is made with vinegar and soy sauce, while in Kansai black sugar and sweet vinegar are used. Either iteration can double as a dessert. Next to the tokoroten is *mozuku*, a type of seaweed from Okinawa, mixed with dashi, soy sauce, vinegar, and mirin, with a small plate of pickled cabbage served alongside. Later I'm served a riff on *goma dofu*, tofu made from sesame paste and kudzu starch topped with a sweet tomato-basil–infused soy sauce, and a simple cheese made by combining milk and vinegar until it coagulates, forming something between a ricotta and a mozzarella. It certainly nods to the components of an Italian Caprese salad, but it also reminds me of the creaminess of a roasted sesame dressing made with mayonnaise called *goma*, the base of which is called *gomazu*.

GOMAZU (ROASTED SESAME VINEGAR SAUCE),
INSPIRED BY DAISUKE NOMURA, SOUGO, TOKYO, JAPAN
MAKES ABOUT 3/4 CUP (180 ML)

2 tablespoons RICE
 VINEGAR

2 tablespoons SOY SAUCE

1 tablespoon SUGAR

½ teaspoon SALT

2 tablespoons ROASTED
 SESAME SEEDS, *ground*

Mix or blend all ingredients together. It will keep, covered, in the refrigerator for up to a week.

To make goma dressing, add 2 tablespoons mayonnaise (Kewpie brand if you can find it) and 2 tablespoons sesame oil. You can play with the amounts of vinegar and mayonnaise to make it a looser or thicker sauce.

Hiroyuki Sato, Yokoi Vinegar Brewing

Daisuke noted that while vinegar may seem omnipresent at his restaurant, he believes in the doctrine of *koro-su*, or "kill the vinegar," which declares too much acidity to be no good. Thus, he practices—and preaches—moderation.

EDO PERIOD

It was my third lap around the Seiwa Silver Building, and I was close to quitting. Google Maps had given up, so I was on my own to try to find Sushi Tokami. In Tokyo, sometimes your best directions come by way of intuition. I entered a vacant building, climbed down a flight of stairs, and came to some closed sliding doors, behind which I could hear either the clangs of an elevator room or the bustle of the eight-seat sushi bar I was seeking. I found a *noren*, a fabric divider hung between rooms, and walked through. The wood in the room was ocher; the rice on the plates was umber. "Do you make your sushi with brown rice?" I later asked. "No, it's *akasu*," proud owner Hiroyuki Sato told me.

Before I explain what akasu is, let me tell you a little about *Edomaezushi*. During the Edo period in Japan, which lasted until the mid-1800s, raw fish was a luxury. Edo, the old name for Tokyo, was fast paced and growing exponentially, and many food vendors, from *izakaya* (gastropubs) to *yatai* (street carts), had little to no refrigeration. Ice was expensive, and spoilage was a serious concern, so much of the fish was cured. Some was simmered in broth; some employed the *zuke* method of immersing fish in soy to retain texture; and fattier fish, like mackerel (*saba*), spent time in a vinegar-and-salt solution, which its stronger flavors could withstand, in order to prolong its lifespan. This vinegar practice began even earlier, in the Muromachi period, which lasted from the mid 1300s to the late 1500s.

It wasn't until the late 1800s that a fast-food chain in Tokyo capitalized on modern industrialization and transportation to begin propagating the raw version of sushi we know now. At the time it was called *Edomae*, meaning "from Tokyo Bay," where most of the fish was caught, but today, this type of sushi is more commonly known as *nigrizushi*, or hand-pressed sushi.

Akasu, the near-forgotten red vinegar of the Edo period, is made from sake lees, or the solids leftover from the sake brewing process. These solids are held in wooden boxes and aged for a few years or more until they are black. Then they are pressed, and drips of dark maroon vinegar result.

Hiroyuki Sato's gaze was steady and wise, a sliver of a smile on his boyish face. As with many sushi chefs, he displayed an aweinspiring ease as he moved about his open kitchen, utterly unfazed by his audience. A few patrons sat to my right, and I watched as they ritualistically accepted Sato's offerings with their bare hands. His menu is pared down during lunch, focusing mainly on bluefin tunas (*maguro, toro*) and gizzard shad (*kohada*), two fish rich enough to stand up to his assertively vinegared sushi rice.

Yokoi Vinegar Brewing, akasu

Every sushi chef has their own special ratio of rice to vinegar, built into the chemistry of how they like their sushi served. For Sato, the rice is slightly warm, the tuna just under room temperature. Controlling these constants happens while preparing the fish as well. Kohada can't be eaten raw; it's too fishy and has lots of bones. It's first salt cured, which softens the skeleton, then "washed" in white rice vinegar. I tried samples of one-day and two-day trials to see which was more toothsome. I found that they both had their virtues: the less aged piece was firmer, luscious, while at two days the fish proteins markedly break down and become softer, the vinegar more noticeable. Sato told me that akasu has allowed him to find his unique character, or *kara*. The red vinegar is sour up front before fading into a soupy sweetness, and white rice vinegar, though much thinner, is more prominently acidic, like sour milk. Combining these two together makes for a proprietary mixture, at once a nod to the Old World and a modern twist.

Sato-san directed me to Yokoi Vinegar Brewing, a forty-five-minute train ride to Shin-Kiba Station. Founded in 1937, it's the only vinegar company to set up shop in Tokyo in the past seventy years. Their akasu is aged for ten years. When I visited, Yasuka Sakamoto and her associates offered to show me just how black the *moromi* (fermentation mash from sake) becomes over time. When we opened the box, it was like looking into a deep, dark night. My nostrils immediately captured and identified its scent as antique, a value that only maturation can give.

When the mash is maturing, it's treated like grapes: stomping is required. But when it is aged this long, the mash becomes too hard for machinery designed to macerate grapes. Instead it must be shoveled by hand into an *assakuki* (a heavy-duty press machine). Yokoi has seventeen tanks, ten tons apiece, for this process, and still it's a small percentage of their total production; they also pump out twenty-thousand liters of *awasezu* (their standard mixed-grain vinegar) every day. Yokoi has a few New York City clients, including Nobu, the celebrated restaurant in TriBeCa, and 70 percent of the Michelin-starred chefs in Tokyo.

Yokoi's success relies on more than the company's long legacy—there's ingenuity too. The *shokuzensu*, a shot of vinegar served before a meal, is heavily promoted, and so is sushi cider, which uses rice vinegar as the acidic base for a sparkling bottled refreshment meant to pair with sushi. It is clear that the Edo period lives on in Tokyo as vinegar makers work to both honor and reinvent their traditions of yore.

LOCAL CITRUS

To say that Shinobu Namae is worldly is an understatement. Namae was trained in the kitchens of Michel Bras, a contemporary master, first in Laguiole, France, before becoming Bras's sous chef in Hokkaido, Japan. He then took a position in Heston Blumenthal's The Fat Duck in Bray, England, which is known for its innovative approach to classical dishes. In 2010, Namae opened his own restaurant in Tokyo: L'Effervescence, which he calls European in style and technique, yet Japanese in terroir. He refers to his approach as "I'm just one man on the globe," which for him means there is no rigid, culturally enforced protocol for how he develops his cuisine; rather, he finds that the world offers many perspectives from which to take inspiration.

When I visited the kitchen of L'Effervescence, the staff was eating taco rice, which, as I was later told, was a recipe Okinawan in origin (although to me, the flavors were more reminiscent of an Old El Paso seasoning packet). Adjacent to the line is a room that houses a rack of translucent containers of fruits, herbs, and spices, all suspended in liquid. Many of these medleys are vinegars, some made from over-fermenting kombucha, and a few are infusions, but the chef d'oeuvre, in my opinion, is a small square tin filled with Day-Glo orange *mikan* (citrus fruit) juice, a local citrus closely resembling a mandarin orange. A fish bubbler accelerates the airflow, converting juice into acetic acid before it sours—a technique Namae learned while touring the avant-garde kitchen of Noma in Copenhagen.

For Namae, mikan is a centerpiece, a familiar flavor for the Japanese palate; in the winter, families gather daily to converse over green tea and rice crackers, all while peeling away layers of the cit-rus's skin. Balsamic is too specialized for L'Effervescence, reminding a diner of something Italian, but mikan is recognizable—homespun enough that it can be used to enhance the foods it accompanies. This is best illustrated in a salad; most of a salad's elements don't have fat, salt, or acidity, so you have to add those things to bring out otherwise unrealized flavors. Yes, he could use rice vinegar, but for him it reads as too traditionally Japanese. Instead, Namae prefers kombucha vin-egars for savory dishes and rice vinegars for desserts. A signature dish in this regard is his rice-vinegar ice cream, which he serves in place of the steamed rice that would customarily follow a meal.

Juice cannot live forever. Citrus season starts in November and ends around April. To save the sweetness in these fruits, especially when you're craving their refreshing flavor in the summer, making them into vinegar is a perfect solution. Not to say fresh citrus doesn't have its place, but when I mentioned a recent meal at Maisen, a legendary *tonkatsu* (fried pork cutlet) mini-chain in Tokyo, Namae questioned why they served it with a lemon wedge, when the tonkatsu sauce (whose taste could be described as Worcestershire meets barbecue) is already perfectly balanced to complement the fat and salt of the cutlet. He was right: Lemon with tonkatsu is overkill, and best relegated to the cabbage slaw on the side. You have to ask yourself, "Why *this* acid?" rather than assume that they're all the same.

MIKAN VINEGAR, ADAPTED FROM SHINOBU NAMAE, L'EFFERVESCENCE, TOKYO, JAPAN MAKES ABOUT 6 CUPS (1.4 L)

4 cups (960 ml) MIKAN JUICE, *mandarin orange can be substituted*

2 cups (480 ml) SHOCHU, 45% ALCOHOL

1 cup (240 ml) RAW RICE VINEGAR, UNPASTEURIZED, *white wine vinegar can be substituted*

SUGAR, *optional*

Mix all ingredients together.

Using a refractometer, check to see if the Brix is above 20 percent. If it's below, add some sugar to make it higher.

In an uncovered nonreactive container, add a fish tank pump so there's a constant flow of bubbles from the bottom up and aerate for 10 days. Check the pH level to make sure it's below 3.2; if not, aerate for another day or two.

See Making Vinegar, page 300, for further information.

DEN

How should we relate to tradition today? Is it traditional to follow tradition or to challenge it? Perhaps there's a union, wherein two doctrines can be followed in tandem. Kaiseki restaurants are traditionally quiet and serious. Zaiyu Hasegawa's food, on the other hand, is loud and resolute. The first time I ate at Jimbocho Den was also, as it happens, my very first dinner in Japan. This was a few years ago. I sat down having no criteria or expectations for kaiseki cuisine, but I soon found my experience was like taking a political history lesson from Jon Stewart—someone so informed that despite being a satirical pundit he is still considered one of our smartest commentators.

Jimbocho, a neighborhood teeming with used bookstores, is where Hasegawa is working to rewrite history; history is quite literally penned on the walls of his restaurant. Influential chefs from across the globe have visited Jimbocho Den and have partaken in its living history. As I understand it, *den* is a root word in Chinese, used to make words like "electricity" and "electron"; Hasegawa himself is a ball of energy who likes to keep recontextualizing. For example, he serves his foie gras *monaka* with a surprising scoop of plum jam—a Japanese sweet usually reserved for the traditional adzuki bean–paste dessert—an idiosyncratic move that undoubtedly inspires delightful confusion in the taste buds of his guests.

Hasegawa admitted to me that, like many Japanese today, he does not like a strong taste of vinegar in his food, that many Japanese palates have evolved toward sweet, which in turn may be traced to the fact that vinegar's preservation properties are no longer as crucial to food preparation as they once were. I've been told many children have an aversion to sunomono dishes nowadays, because they didn't grow up experiencing the assertive acidic tastes their grandparents did.

Hasegawa served me his mozuku, the same seaweed dish I had had at Sougo, but with a twist: Typically mozuku has quite a bite to it, so to adjust, Hasegawa adds a puree of cucumber and ginger and a side of *sujime*, which is a little pickled ceviche of sorts. He uses *sawara* (Spanish mackerel), a fattier fish, to tone down the acid even further, and, as is done in many sushi bars and izakaya, suggests sake to temper the tang. His nanbanzuke, a deep-fry of fish and vegetables then permeated by a broth, is mitigated by dashi, mirin, soy, and citrus, before vinegar is even introduced. Even his *kimizu*, a dressing made with egg yolk and rice vinegar, has a decent amount of sugar to soften its piquancy. I worried that the future might just be more saccharine, but Hasegawa reassured me that you need both acid and sweet to have balance; by coexisting, each taste offers context for the other.

SUJIME (JAPANESE CEVICHE), FROM ZAIYU HASEGAWA, DEN, TOKYO, JAPAN SERVES 4

3 SARDINES, about 1½ pounds (680 g), *filleted*

¼ cup (33 g) SALT

½ cup (120 ml) CITRUS JUICE, *from a tart orange, or a mix of orange and lemon*

½ cup (120 ml) GRAIN VINEGAR

In a container or bowl, sprinkle the sardines with the salt, cover, and let sit in the refrigerator for 40 minutes.

Make a citrus vinegar by combining the citrus juice with the vinegar.

Wash off the salt from the sardines and marinate the sardines in the citrus vinegar for 20 minutes. Slice and serve.

Zaiyu Hasegawa, Sujime (Japanese Ceviche)

NANBANZUKE (DEEP-FRIED FISH IN MARINADE),
FROM ZAIYU HASEGAWA, JIMBOCHO DEN, TOKYO, JAPAN
SERVES 2 TO 4

3 cups (720 ml) DASHI

½ cup (120 ml) MIRIN

½ cup (120 ml) SOY SAUCE

⅓ cup (75 ml) CITRUS
  VINEGAR, *see Sujime,*
  page 125

1 tablespoon SUGAR, *optional*

1 pound (455 g) MACKEREL
  or SMELT, *cut in 16*
  1-ounce (28-g) pieces

¼ cup (60 ml) OLIVE OIL

Mix all liquids except the olive oil together in a small pot and bring to a gentle boil. Once boiling, turn off the heat.

If you want to sweeten up the marinade, add the sugar. Transfer to a container large enough to hold the fish.

Quickly panfry the fish in the olive oil for a few minutes, then place directly into the marinade. Let the fish sit in the mixture, covered in the refrigerator for at least 1 day. Serve at room temperature.

You can try this technique with bluefish or chicken as well as eggplant, peppers, and onions.

GETTING SCHOOLED

Naoyuki Yanagihara's grandfather started a cooking school in the Akasaka district of Tokyo just after World War II. The Yanagihara family comes from a long line of chefs who, over two hundred years ago, operated various *ryokan* (traditional Japanese inns) in Ueno and Atami. Presently, Yanagihara doesn't train aspiring chefs but, rather, laymen and -women who hope to employ at home traditional Japanese cooking techniques: how to hold a knife, how to cut a fish, and other essential skills.

While visiting the kitchen of the Yanagihara School of Traditional Japanese Cuisine, I was fortunate enough to be joined by Yukari Sakamoto, author of *Food Sake Tokyo* (as well as the blog by the same name), who is one of the top gastronomic guides in the city. I welcomed her expertise, eager to learn how much overlap there might be between Yanagihara's curriculum and her own culinary routine.

Preserving tradition is of utmost importance to the Yanagiharas, yet Naoyuki did not hesitate to acknowledge the marked shift away from Japan's prevailing sweet tooth in recent years. Both he and Sakamoto agreed that food products like Benmatsu bento boxes, which are sold at most department stores, are far too sugary for their tastes. If you went to a depachika and ordered one, the women at the counter might readily describe it as a taste of old Tokyo.

But it's true—Japan's eating habits are changing. Sakamoto tells me, "Japan is a country whose citizens used to eat three cups of rice a day on average but now eat only one." Rice itself doesn't have a huge amount of a taste, which is why flavor enhancers like vinegar were added in the first place. Now that there's a reduced palette of rice to play with, acids have been replaced with small doses of rich umami—the savory tastes of glutamic acids found in ingredients like soy sauce, green tea, and seaweed.

Children are now less accepting of sourness, a taste that causes them to recoil as if what's been put in their mouth is rotting. Yanagihara told us, "When children grow up, they're first fed dashi, maybe a little bonito, some kombu . . . " A Japanese child's palate seems to owe its development to the same tastes simmering in Yanagihara's students' soup stocks downstairs.

By the nineteenth century, large companies like Kikkoman were producing shoyu (soy sauce) for mass-market consumption as an inexpensive all-purpose condiment. There are many varieties, but broadly speaking, soy sauce is rich in lactic acid and contains a lot of sodium. As a flavor enhancer, it functions similarly to table salt, whereas vinegar cleanses your mouth. Soy coats your tongue, while vinegar helps oil spread across it, produces digestively beneficial *daeki* (saliva), and invigorates the metabolic system. Yanagihara wanted to be clear, however: not all vinegars are for flavor—some have too acetone an odor, and vinegars like *kokumotsu* (grain vinegar), for example, are used primarily for cleaning fish and are rarely ingested.

Another pantry staple is miso; to put it simply, it's the paste form of soy sauce. I know this definition isn't technically accurate, but the soybeans for both are fermented with the same fungus, *kōji* (*Aspergillus oryzae*), so I believe the comparison is a useful one. Miso is widely used as a soup base; its earthy aroma is too powerful on its own, so it is usually combined with dashi or sugar.

Sakamoto asked me if I knew hollandaise. I do, of course, know the iconic French sauce served over eggs Benedict, steamed asparagus, and other dishes. We watched closely as Yanagihara began to prepare a Japanese version of sorts, the versatile dressing *sumiso*, which was comprised of, in this case, Yamabuki miso—a sweeter rice miso, classified in the *shiro* (white miso) realm. He then mixed it with sugar and rice vinegar, slowly stirring in the saucepan over low heat to keep the blend from burning. Then he took the pan off the burner and finished it by adding an egg yolk.

It's a quick recipe, made with ingredients that take a long time to produce—a truism of much Japanese cooking. What you're left with is a beautifully round, complex, and creamy sauce, a step up from kimizu. It's so multidimensional, it can really be served with everything, and even though at Yanagihara's school we enjoyed it with hyper-seasonal *hotaru-ika* (firefly squid), *wakegi* (green onion), and *wakame* (seaweed) from Miyagi, I found myself dreaming of bringing the recipe back to America to crown a steaming platter of fresh asparagus.

SUMISO, FROM YANAGIHARA SCHOOL OF TRADITIONAL JAPANESE CUISINE, TOKYO, JAPAN MAKES ¹/₂ CUP (120 ML)

¼ cup plus 1 tablespoon (75 ml) SHIRO (WHITE) MISO

2 teaspoons SUGAR

2 tablespoons RICE VINEGAR

1 EGG YOLK

Combine the miso, sugar, and vinegar in a small saucepan, and gently warm it over low heat, stirring constantly for 1 to 2 minutes, until the miso is shiny. Take off the heat and stir in the egg yolk. Serve warm or cold over fish and vegetables.

Naoyuki Yanagihara making Sumiso

THE MAN WITH THE BOW TIE

On my last night in Tokyo, I was supposed to meet a man with a bow tie. That's all the information I received—that and instructions to be in the lobby of my hotel at eight o'clock, and then we'd go for dinner together. I felt how others might feel at the prospect of meeting a famous athlete, actor, or rock star; that night I would be meeting a vinegar celebrity, and I couldn't wait. When I arrived in the lobby I saw a modest-looking man with impeccable posture sitting patiently on a cozy leather couch, a medium-size piece of wheeled luggage next to him. One look at his collar and I knew it must be Uchibori.

We sat, along with his daughter Kana, in the dark corner of an izakaya, where he is surely a regular based on the warm welcome he received from the staff. Curiously, Uchibori's suitcase was still by his side rather than checked; I couldn't help but wonder at its contents. I soon found out: After we ordered beers, he instructed me to first take a sip before our *kanpai* (cheers); then, from his mysterious suitcase, he produced a small bottle of what seemed to me to be an apple vinegar and gave me a hearty pour on top of my Asahi. Ninety percent beer, 10 percent vinegar, that's how Uchibori likes to drink.

Everything that graced our table got a glug; beef katsu with cherry blossom vinegar, his favorite honey vinegar over something else—the night grew blurry, and if I didn't know any better, I would have thought it to be a lucid dream. At some point he gave me a bottle of chardonnay dessert vinegar, which I rolled around in my hands, attempting to decipher the kanji. At the conclusion of our meal he offered a firm handshake and posed for a photo of the two of us, his daughter taking the shot. I have the photo somewhere, but, truthfully, the perfect evening lives on even more vividly in my mind.

52,000 JARS

It was not my first time in Kyushu, the southwestern-most island of mainland Japan. The last time I had visited had been for a day of live sumo wrestling in Fukuoka—but that's another story. In a bay near Mount Sakurajima, the active volcano that looms over the subtropical landscape, there's a valley of *kurozu*, or black vinegar—a coveted condiment and supplement that is said to have restorative health properties, among other benefits.

After seven hours on the train from Tokyo, I disembarked at Kagoshima-Chūō Station to transfer for the final leg of my journey to Kirishima, which is where the majority of kurozu makers are. Before I boarded, I decided to take a quick detour to Kurozu Farm, a café and market owned by Akihiro Sakamoto of Sakamoto Kurozu, a straight ten-to-fifteen-minute walk from the station. A metropolitan showcase for his company's vinegars, Sakamoto's shop in Kagoshima welcomes customers with a polychromatic collection of vinegars in a well-designed aseptic space, serving soft-serve and salad. Twenty-five miles from the nearest fermentation plant, I didn't stay long—I was eager to make it to black vinegar country.

Upon arriving in Kirishima, I was struck by the small-town remoteness of the place. Whereas the city of Kagoshima has the bustling population of Boston or Washington, DC, Kirishima felt like less of a suburb than a hamlet of a town, oddly occupied by big tech companies like Sony and Kyocera. I walked from the train to my hotel, stopping at the local Lawson, a 7-Eleven competitor, where the clerk told me that *Godzilla vs. SpaceGodzilla* had once fought just across the bay. I smiled, nodded, gave a half-hearted *azasu* (a very informal thank you), and purchased my nightly *onigiri* (filled rice ball) and Suntory highball. The next morning, I opened the blinds from the seventeenth floor of Hotel Kyocera to find a solitary cloud hovering over the lip of Sakurajima. Even from a distance, I could sense the vitality percolating in the air.

Akihiro Sakamoto picked me up and we drove for twenty-five minutes along the northeastern side of the bay, my eyes affixed on Sakurajima. Off highway 220, Sakamoto Kurozu stands a few blocks inland, a small percentage grade up from sea level, but not like you'd see in wine country. There are no rolling hills, but instead, a flat plot of land facing the sun, with over fifty-two thousand black ceramic jars called *tsubo*, leisurely becoming vinegar—one million liters of kurozu made by the same method that originated more than two hundred years ago.

Sakamoto Kurozu,
Akihiro Sakamoto at right

The term "black vinegar" wasn't coined until Sakamoto's father—of the fifth generation—named it so. In reality, kurozu isn't as dark as its name implies. Out in the field, Sakamoto pulled samples of one-, three-, five-, and seven-year vinegar to show me. Together the vinegars formed a spectrum ranging from shades of whiskey, to moonshine, to a nice deep maple. Instead of the char of the barrel, it's actually amino acids that tint the vinegar.

Before touring the grounds, I was shown a video called "Listen to the Sound of Kurozu." When fermentation begins, the tsubo emit what sounds like a Rice Krispies ad—"snap, crackle, and pop"—rice doused in sunshine instead of milk to catalyze the transformation. The process begins with a layer of rice koji in the bottom of each fifty-four-liter tsubo. The koji is then covered with steamed rice and spring water, which is finished with floating rice koji, or *furi kōji*, in reference to how it's thrown or spread across the top. In one week there's glucose. Two to three months later, alcohol fermentation yields the necessary amount of ethanol. In three to six months the solution is completely acetic. After that, the vinegar is aged at least a few years, until it's ready for sale.

Many of the tsubo themselves were originally made in Kagoshima; now the majority are made in Shiga, if not imported from Taiwan, which

is exactly where the throngs of tourists seem to be bussed in from, their caravans crisscrossing seemingly nonstop between visitors' centers of the dozen or so kurozu makers in the area. Droves stop at Sakamoto Kurozu to buy its famed vinegar, but they also stay for the food. Sweet and sour pork headlines the Chinese menu, highlighting the famous Kagoshima *kurobuta* (black pig) in many preparations. Sakamoto pulled a torso's length of noodles high above his head before offering me a bowl of sweet and sour noodles. The food is Chinese, I was told, because kurozu's flavor profile lends itself better to the tastes of Chinese cuisine, said without admitting black vinegar likely began in China. There were no complaints on my end as I slurped up my meal. Being served Chinese food was certainly unexpected—but so was stumbling upon a thriving vinegar-based agritourism empire.

Kurozu making is a lo-fi operation that seems to rely more on intuition than scientific method. To agitate the vinegar solution every so often, Sakamoto's workers use hand-carved bamboo stirring sticks, notched at one end, and splayed into three prongs. These, plus a tool that looks like a wooden cup fastened to the end of a long stick, are really the only pieces of equipment you'll see on the field.

A lab was started about twenty-five years ago, headed by long-time employee Kazunori Hashiguchi. There they use spectrometers and HPLC (High Performance Liquid Chromatography) to analyze everything from proteins to saccharides, which are inherent parts of kurozu's color and flavor. In the spring and fall, Sakamoto cultivates their own koji, which is mainly made at Akihiro's grandfather's house. In Kaizo Sakamoto's backyard, there are six hundred jars, some more than two hundred years old.

Today, more than fifty products are made by Sakamoto, with such health benefits as controlling cholesterol and providing supplemental calcium and vitamin C support. There's even Su'Witch, a beauty supplement for younger-looking skin. With its proliferation into other markets, kurozu now has GI status (Japan Geographical Indication), a protection similar to the European AOC (*Appellation d'origine contrôlée*) and DOC (*Denominazione di origine controllata*), joining other Japanese products like Kobe beef, Yubari melon, Yame green tea, and cassis from Aomori.

RINGO-KUROZU MIRUKU (APPLE BLACK VINEGAR WITH MILK), FROM SAKAMOTO KUROZU, KIRISHIMA, JAPAN
MAKES 1 DRINK

1 ounce RINGO-KUROZU   4 ounces (120 ml) MILK

Mix ringo-kurozu and milk in a glass, shake or stir, and let set. Drink immediately or keep in the fridge for later use. Usually ringo-kurozu is mixed one part vinegar to five parts water for a refreshing drink, but in Sakamoto's tasting room you can try their "breakfast smoothie," which combines a shot of vinegar with milk, forming small curd, with a silky texture and sweet flavor—part lactic, part acetic, all tang.

The tourist marketing of black vinegar isn't over the top, but when I stopped by Kakuida, another kurozu maker in Fukuyama-cho, easily identified by its golden jar logo, I couldn't help but feel that it's essentially Chinese Chinkiang vinegar being sold at an amusement park. Green mats that look like mini-golf turf guide visitors through the grounds. Tsubochan (Jar Baby), Kakuida's official mascot, greets visitors as they enter. Tsubochan looks a little like an anime version of McDonald's Grimace character. (And if you have to ask, yes, I did take a photo with Tsubochan.) I'm not going to start a discussion about authenticity here.

Chen-Ho, an employee of Kakuida, explained to me that the area was originally settled by samurais who grew rice, but hid their crop from the government in order to evade taxes. They fittingly named their land Kakuida, which loosely means "hidden field," although nowadays with its bright signage and bustling welcome center, it has become, ironically, very conspicuous.

The first floor of the center is a veritable marketplace for all things kurozu. I spied every fruit flavor imaginable: blueberry, strawberry, peach, *ume* (plum), and apple, many of which took a form akin to the colonial shrubs (fruit syrups preserved with vinegar). I saw kurozu jams, kurozu pound cakes in the shape of a volcano, kurozu health doughnuts, and even kurozu hard candies made with moromi, all of which were available to sample.

I asked a woman what she likes about kurozu, and she told me it's good for her diabetes. Another woman vowed it helps with her blood pressure. Both women carried baskets full of salad dressings and Cross Water sports drink, the regional Gatorade, which sponsors Cannondale biking teams all across Kyushu. Upstairs, there's a four-hundred-seat restaurant with a Japanese, Chinese, and Western menu. On the tables are many of the condiments found downstairs. The synergy of Kakuida's brand is big, and they only hope to grow. Were it a wine region, it would still be in its infancy, but in its marketing, it's fully matured.

KYO RYORI

If you ask multigenerational Kyotoans what the capital of Japan is, many will still say Kyoto. It had quite a run; from 794 to 1869, the emperor lived in the imperial palace there, making it the de facto capital

Matsuo Taisha Shrine

for centuries. Kyoto belongs to the Keihanshin region, as do the cities of Osaka and Kobe. Collectively the three form the second most populous zone of Japan after Tokyo. Of the three, however, Kyoto is the only one that has a specific cuisine named after it, *Kyo ryori*.

My gracious guide, Chika Yoshida, the media coordinator for Kyoto's Visitors Bureau, suggested we first visit the Matsuo Taisha Shrine, located on the outskirts of the famed Arashiyama bamboo forest. Both the Matsuo Taisha Shrine and the Fushimi Inari Shrine—known for its thousands of vermilion torii gates—were built by the Hata clan, who first brought sake-brewing techniques from Korea more than two thousand years ago. At Matsuo, a single torii marks the entrance. As I stood at the gate, it began to rain—a fitting touch: Kyoto is split by the banks of the Katsuragawa River, topography that has greatly influenced both the spiritual and practical role that water plays in Kyoto's culture. Though I knew very well that sake is only one fermentation process away from being vinegar, I was impatient to leave the shrine. It felt like ordering grape juice when what I really wanted was wine.

Nearby is Kame-no-I, a well of spring water said to have magical properties. Reverent sake brewers regularly visit the well, filling up bottles to bring back to their breweries; they believe the special water imbues their sake with the gift of longevity. Water as a preservative? I was mystified. Nevertheless, I paid ten yen, bowed and clapped twice, said a prayer, bowed once more, and rang the bell (as instructed by

Yoshida). I can't tell you exactly what I wished for, but it certainly involved vinegar. On our drive back into town, we used the Togetsukyo Bridge to cross the Katsura River, which feeds into Osaka Bay sixty kilometers away. I couldn't quite put my finger on it, but something about my encounters with Kyoto's waterways had started to take on greater significance. I had a vague sense that the Shinto gods were watching over me.

I had arrived in Kyoto a day before meeting Yoshida. My friend Nori Akashi back home told me to check out a service called the Good Samaritan Club, in which university students will guide you around the city for the price of a meal and a conversation. Local student Ryosuke Kizaki responded to my email, and I told him that all I wanted to do was walk around—get my bearings, as it were. What I secretly hoped to do, however, was to sneak by Murayama Zosu, the highly respected maker of Chidori-su vinegar. Their factory is on Sanjo-dori, between Sanjo Keihan and Higashiyama train stations. It looks like a three-story factory, but I wouldn't know—I wasn't allowed in. Murayama-san had turned down my request for an interview or tour. I respect their right to decline, but having heard so much about the company, I had hoped to at least see the facade.

As Kizaki and I approached the address, there was a faint waft of acetic acid in the air, stronger with every step. Navigating by olfactory instinct, we arrived at our destination. It was closed, but I lingered in its unseen aroma, almost drunk on the fumes. Later I learned that *chidori* are the plover birds lining the embankments, and those with "*chidori* leg" were often drunk businessmen hopping their way home. As disappointed as I was not to meet Murayama-san, in a way I feel like I did, and I even found a bottle of Chidori-su at a neighboring store to take home with me. Little did I know, it wouldn't be the first time I was denied entrance at the door, or *noren*, the Japanese doorway curtain.

Fast-forward to my expedition with Yoshida. We set out with a map and a plan: we would visit a handful of vinegar makers in Kyoto, including Saito Zosu and Hayashi Kotaro Zosu. First, in the Sakyo ward, we walked by the Daishogun Hachi Shrine (in Kyoto, it's sometimes easier to locate something by the shrine it's near, as opposed to the physical address) on Yokai (or "monster") Street, a moniker for Ichijo-dori, which is lined with storefronts displaying monster statues. It's a thoroughfare of ghosts and demons, some in the form of humans, some animals—figures used to impart lessons from Japanese folklore.

On the exterior of a black-slatted building, I spotted a sign with an image of a tsubo on it. Inside I encountered an elaborate display of the vinegar wares of Saito Zosu. Tamahime-su is the name of their classic vinegar, though they also sell *ponzu*, a shoyu-and-citrus-based sauce. (As I later found out, vinegar is a major balancing component in ponzu.) The wife of Saito-san greeted us with the same quizzical face that many do when I say I'm writing a book about vinegar. What begins as bewilderment soon unfolds into inquiry. I believe it's because many of these artisans take it for granted; it's a trade they've plied for generations. As pertinent as it is to many dishes and sauces, it's still just vinegar.

When I began this project, I thought my challenge would be to change the minds of consumers, not the producers! I hoped that by expressing my fondness for this wonderful (if commonplace) pantry item, I could ward away the demons that were diluting its relevance.

A 170-year-old business, Hayashi Kotaro's branch store in the Nishijin district of Kyoto is understated in appearance, until you walk through the sliding door and the architecture opens up into a lofted space. It's large, yet still feels intimate enough to conduct small ponzu blending classes, in which students are taught to mix shoyu, vinegar, and dashi, with an array of citrus (yuzu, *sudachi, daidai*).

Shop manager Mr. Nakae told me they sell to Nijiya Market in Hartsdale, New York, much to my surprise. Sometimes they even export their raisins in vinegar, classified as their "morning" version, whereas when rum is added it becomes their "evening" version, perfect for topping ice cream. There are black vinegars, fruit vinegars, and even little single-serving packets for a one-cup bowl of sushi rice. Modestly, Nakae-san said his branch is only in its fourth generation—the company's headquarters is in its seventh—but they hope to have a long legacy someday.

Next Yoshida and I visited Gion, Kyoto's famous geisha district. Sitting catty-corner to the Yasaka shrine is a little restaurant called Izuju. Although *hako-sushi* (boxed sushi) originated in Osaka, it has been playfully reinvented by Izuju, where guests are treated to a special version—sans soy. There is no sauce on the table, unless you ask—but don't. You won't need it. There's *sabazushi* (pickled mackerel cured in kelp), *inarizushi* (fried tofu stuffed with sushi rice and vegetables), and *sasazushi* (fish and rice wrapped in a bamboo leaf). All are treated with a good dose of vinegar, which is used to help preserve rice and fish alike for its journey from Osaka Bay. The owner and chef, Kitamura-san, carefully hand-paints his dishware to match the flora of each season. Centuries ago, simply due to heat and lack of refrigeration, many sushi restaurants were closed during the summers, but now you can enjoy hako-sushi year-round and on the road; it was truly made to travel.

One of the happiest accidents was stumbling upon a vinegar maker I hadn't even heard of. While at Izuju, I asked the hostess which vinegar the restaurant uses, fully assuming they were going to say Chidori-su, which is made a few blocks away. Nope. They use—and have for years—Itsuki's hanabishi vinegar, bought from a storefront only a quick cab ride

away. I finished my lunch and hailed a taxi, off to visit this ninth-generation maker. Like most vinegar houses, Itsuki makes a 1.8-liter bottle. Behind the counter, a middle-aged woman rattled off a list of local restaurants that use their vinegar: Kinobu, Hyoki, and others. She was justifiably proud of their reach. In such a competitive vinegar-making city, an enduring enterprise is greatly esteemed.

Chika and I made our way to Nishiki Market, an assemblage of all things food related, set along a six-block stretch, east of the Teramachi Street arcade. Filled with over a hundred shops and restaurants, Kyoto's Kitchen has been serving the city for more than four hundred years. Though open seven days a week, many stalls are closed on Wednesdays, so plan accordingly. Between the hours of 9:00 AM and 6:00 PM there is no busier confluence of culinary delights—from *shichimi* spice blends to Kyoto-style *tsukemono* like *senmaizuke* (Shogoin turnip) and *shibazuke* (cucumber and eggplant with red shiso), and there's also Aritsugu, a cash-only knife maker known to chefs the world around.

I was there to explore Inoue, a deli of sorts that sells *obanzai*, or daily specials, based off the seasonal and sustainable premise of *mottainai*, in which no part of any ingredient is wasted. They sell more than eighty kinds, and my favorites, as expected, were the ones with vinegar in them. I searched each label for one of the few kanji characters I knew, loading up my basket with *ika myoga su* (squid ribbons and ginger in vinegar) and cucumber with eel. I even found they have their

own vinegar, sold in pint-size bottles, as opposed to the larger ones I'd been finding at most other vinegar makers. Most tourists go straight for the deep-fried chocolate croquette, but they're missing out on the delicacies that the locals eat.

A few blocks away from Nishiki Market, Motokazu Nakamura greeted us at his self-titled restaurant, Nakamura, with the maxim "Mochi should be made by the mochi maker," and I took this to mean that he would leave vinegar-making to the experts. His astuteness was apparent to me even before he spoke; the moment I stepped into his restaurant I was deeply impressed by his minimalist décor, shades of beige like a tranquil beach. Shoes removed, I made my way to a private tatami room in the back. Tea was served—fitting, when you consider how kaiseki cuisine came to be: In the 1500s, tea master Sen no Rikyū decided green tea was too strong to drink on an empty stomach, so he recommended that miso soup and three sides accompany a cup. Nakamura serves *kyo ryori*. In some of the restaurant's printed matter I've seen a mantra: "*Ichigo ichie*," or "Treasure every encounter, for it will never recur." But it did recur, time and time again, in the form of a thoughtful and superbly executed meal, one thoroughly deserving of Nakamura's three Michelin stars.

Nakamura's opening comment echoed in my head. From the glut of vinegar makers within a few miles, Chidori-su rice vinegar is used for Nakamura's sushi; a more generic kokumotsu grain vinegar is reserved

Amanohashidate

for sauces; and kurozu black vinegar is paired with shrimp (which gives the crustacean the body it needs).

Nakamura is often tapped by vinegar companies to help educate the public about their products. He also offers classes in kaiseki cooking, although his lessons may not resonate with everyone: at home, the Japanese more often prefer amazu (the sweet and sour sauce that is equal parts sugar, vinegar, and soy sauce; see page 115) to straight vinegar. Nakamura told me that when vinegar interacts with umami flavors, its acidity is softened, complemented, but not negated. A sauce like amazu, however, is designed to mask the acidity with sugar. But Nakamura knows that straight vinegar is more regularly used to dissolve the collagen and bones in fish, and that many people think of vinegar as something to be tempered or overcome, as opposed to something that can activate the flavors of a dish. Nevertheless, as a chef, he focuses on the food and lets the vinegar maker worry about the acid.

THE KING OF TEMAKI

Amanohashidate, a sandbar grown thick with pines, is one of Japan's three most celebrated scenic sights. This "bridge to heaven" extends through Miyazu Bay, just off the Sea of Japan, in northern Kyoto prefecture. I sat on the terrace of Genmyoan, a hilltop ryokan, with Akihiro Iio and his wife, sipping coffee and admiring the "flying dragon view," as they call it. The Iio Jozo vinegar brewery is five generations old, and when Akihiro took over only five years ago, he became the bridge connecting rice vinegar's past to its future.

In 1893, Akihiro Iio's great grandfather Chozo began making Fujisu, their house brand; Iio's father, Tsuyoshi, and mother, Satomi, carried on this tradition, fermenting rice, apples, figs, black beans, and even purple potatoes, all for the sake of making vinegar. I was struck by Akihiro's quiet confidence; he carried himself with a seriousness and a deeply rooted commitment to the craft—we're talking about someone who grows his own rice in order to brew his own sake in order to make vinegar. From April to October he tends to the rice paddies, all located within the region. Between April and the following January he makes sake, and though vinegar is made year round, it's this regimented cycle that sets him apart and gives Fujisu the deserving title of "premium" vinegar. There's even a small quantity of vinegar made from rice grown merely a few miles away from the brewery in Miyazu.

In the 1960s, Akihiro's grandfather, Terunosuke, stopped using chemical pesticides. The yields lowered at first, but the resulting quality of their product ultimately launched Iio Jozo as a significant player in the vinegar scene. This same investment in value also extended to their touching hospitality—known in Japan as *omotenashi*. When I first arrived at his parents' house, I was received with such sincerity that I felt a sense of *déjà visite*; despite never having visited before, it felt like being welcomed back. A grill was smoking in the backyard, lit with dried rice straw (they truly utilize every part of their crop). A piece of mackerel was lightly marked on one side, touched with just enough heat to bring out its tenderness.

A buffet followed: soulful dishes with pork, chives, and daikon; another of salmon, onions, and *sansho*; but describing these dishes doesn't begin to capture the peace and enjoyment I felt eating Akihiro's food.

In particular, I found myself enraptured by a bowl of rice—who would've thought? I breathed *"itadakimasu,"* which loosely means, "I humbly receive," a common benediction before a meal. Rice vinegar, poured over a fanned wooden spoon, seasoned the *shari* (sushi rice), embracing every single grain. It sat in a *hangiri* (a wooden bowl) as it continued to cool, absorbing all the flavor of the vinegar.

Some people call Akihiro the "Temaki King." He even has it in gold lettering on a second business card. *Temaki* are sushi hand rolls, a meal that many Japanese families delightedly feast on with rice and all the fixings, as if it were Taco Tuesday in the United States. The grilled mackerel reappeared: with palm-size squares of seaweed, beef, and sesame and a side of *myoga* ginger and *perilla* and *shiso*.

SUSHI RICE MAKES ABOUT 1½ CUPS (276 G)

⅔ cup (135 g) SUSHI RICE

2 to 2 ½ tablespoons SUSHI RICE VINEGAR

Wash the rice with cold water, rinsing it off a few times. Let the rice sit in water for 1 hour.

Steam the rice, then add to a hangiri bowl (a heat-resistant glass bowl works too). Add the vinegar, folding it into the rice, then keep covered until ready to serve. Place bowl in center of table to serve family style.

Iio Jozo, shari, temaki

Akihiro Iio,
shabu-shabu

"Oishii, oishii," I chanted with a mouthful of temaki. "So delicious, I can barely eat any more." "Okay, only one more thing," said Akihiro. He placed a portable burner on the table and raised the lid on a boiling *donabe* (clay pot). A cloud of steam drifted toward me, like that come-hither finger you see in cartoons.

Shabu-shabu, which I consider "Japanese fondue," is a close cousin of the "hot pot," and a wonderful onomatopoeic phrase that refers to the sound the ingredients make when they are stirred in a pot. First, meat and vegetables are dipped into a boiling donabe filled with water or dashi that becomes flavored by all the ingredients plunged into it, and when they're cooked to your liking, you add them to your own personal bowl, with a splash of ponzu as you please. Akihiro's shabu-shabu was fantastic—but we weren't finished yet. The grand finale: vanilla ice cream topped with a drizzle of *benimosu*, Akihiro's prized purple potato vinegar. I practiced a few times in my head, saying *"gochiso sama deshita!"* ("It was quite a feast!"), and the instant the table was cleared and before another course materialized, I murmured it out, fuller than I've ever been in my life.

Akihiro led me a short car ride away to sample freshly pressed sake at the brewery, a space buzzing with palpable energy in the air. It was the off-season for sake making, so most of the employees were peeling green apples (the ones Yoko Ono made famous) for cider (and inevitably vinegar). What's important to note is vinegar must move

through several key and precise stages in order to reach its desired form. Accordingly, Iio Jozo knows to leave nothing to chance.

More than 90 percent of Japan's vinegar comes from ethyl alcohol that was made commercially in anywhere from eight to forty-eight hours. Iio Jozo's takes from forty to one hundred days. Add the 180 days to grow the rice, and we're already at two-thirds of a year without starting on acetic acid. Most of their vinegars take about one hundred days to convert, and then more than 250 days of aging. In total, from grain to bottle, we're looking at about two years' time, and that's just for baseline vinegar. Their akasu takes twelve years!

Wallpapering the vinegar factory are infographics explaining things like the degree to which *koshihikari* rice is polished, and why that matters; why it's important to steam the potatoes first (to help break down and covert the carbohydrates into sugar), but only after cutting off the fibrous ends that can impede the process; and how Iio Jozo initiates the course of fermentation with exactly 10 percent koji. There's a poster that states one of their rarer vinegars, black bean, has higher polyphenol levels than many red wines, and three times the amino acid. It ages nine years until it reaches it maturity, and every step of the way Akihiro stays attuned to its biorhythms, its transformation slow but sure.

In the fermentation room, a smell like that of Beaujolais's gamay grapes—a favorite variety of mine—filled my nose, yet I was quite a distance away from the Loire Valley in France, where gamay grapes are grown. Gripping the top rung of a ladder, I leaned over an open vat to discover not grapes but pretty violet tubers fermenting before my very eyes.

HAKO vs. HAKKO

I admit, I did not travel to Osaka in pursuit of vinegar—but every trip must take a detour at one point or another. So I decided to attend the March 2016 sumo *basho* (tournament) and got tickets for a couple of the matches. I was curious to see if Kotoshogiku, the first Japanese-born wrestler in a decade (prior to him, most wrestlers hailed from Mongolia), could defend his title. At sumo matches, many people bring their own bento boxes, because although food is sold at the stadiums, most of the refrigeration space is reserved for beer. Here in Osaka, *hakozushi* (box sushi) thrives. All the ingredients are either cured or cooked, then pressed into a square or rectangular box.

Before I headed to the Osaka Prefectural Gymnasium for the day, I met my friend Nobuko at Hankyu's bustling basement food hall in Umeda. There we bought a couple of boxes of sushi at Sushiman, with bite-size pieces of *anago* (saltwater eel), *tai* (red snapper), and *tamago* (egg omelet)—function meets form in a cubic to-go box!

After all that sporting (Kotoshigoku lost that day, as he did the three prior) and beer, sake is the only cure. We went to Utsutsuyo ("Sake Reality"), an izakaya with more than one hundred dishes on the menu, most of which use Chidori-su vinegar from Kyoto. Mr. Fujii, the affable chef, has a proclivity for acid in his food: he believes it's a great foil for sake's smooth tendencies and general lack of acidity. Even though Tamanoi, a one-hundred-plus-year-old manufacturer of vinegar,

Shime Saba

is located in Osaka, Fujii prefers Chidori-su's milder taste, reserving Tamanoi for home cooking. The real showpiece, however, was a jar of plums, or *ume*, macerating in vinegar. *Umesu* (plum vinegar) is one step removed from *umeshu*, the Japanese liquor made from steeping these specific plums in alcohol. Umeshu is more of a cordial, sweet and sour, while umesu has uniformity to it, imperceptibly sharp, with the plush undertones of ripe stone fruit.

Countless Japanese make their own version of plum vinegar, but here, Fujii steeps the fruit with brown sugar, letting the ume infuse for nine months. Add some sparkling water and it's an invigorating tonic. At Utsutsuyo, plum vinegar is used for *shime saba*, the ubiquitous pickled mackerel found in most professional and home kitchens in Japan. Here, Fujii uses umesu as the pickling liquid. What that does is morph the fattier, fuller flavored fish into mouthwatering morsels that you'll want more of the second you finish a plate.

SHIME SABA SERVES 1-2

1 (1-pound / 455-g) MACKEREL, *scaled, separated into 2 skin-on fillets, pin bones removed*

1 cup (240 g) COARSE SALT

½ cup (120 ml) UMESU (PLUM VINEGAR)

SOY SAUCE

FRESHLY GRATED WASABI

Salt the fish by rubbing the salt into the flesh, then allow the fish to sit in the refrigerator for about an hour.

Remove the fish from the refrigerator and rinse in cold water. Pat dry with a paper towel, then place the fish and vinegar in a container (or zip-top bag) that can hold the fish in the liquid. Let marinate for a few hours or overnight.

Remove the fish from the the marinade; pat dry again. You can either remove the skin or keep it on and slice it into ¼-inch-thick (6-mm-thick) pieces. Serve with soy sauce and wasabi.

With sixty to seventy sakes, all served by the glass, it's easy to find a pairing that complements your fare. Utsutsuyo's aim is to bring out the singularity of the ingredients, whereas much of Western cooking focuses on layering, emulsifying, masking the fundamental flavors. The essential power of vinegar lies in the structure it brings to a dish; when used right, it becomes a building block to a better meal.

En route back to Tokyo via bullet train, I had my conventional onboard train snack, *ekiben*, which is nothing more than a bento box meant for consumption on the go. I found the *saba oshizushi* (pressed mackerel sushi) soused in vinegar. Although exceeding my expectations, I know I have since had a superior taste of what shime saba should be: my last meal in Japan was at Shiojiri Jozojo, a restaurant serving *hakko-ryori*, fermentation-based cuisine on the Shibuya district. The chef, Nobuaki Fushiki, is an authority on all things microbial.

At his counter, diners can sit facing a row of translucent jars burbling away with a colorful composition of his live pantry. Fushiki serves *amazake*, the sweet rice drink, which is aged two years and comes in flavors of pineapple and strawberry. Then there's a soy sauce and a mirin, both three years aged, chili paste upward of four, and his prized six-year shoyu, which he presses through a miniature sieve to order. When I asked him where the vinegar was, he said, "Making vinegar is very delicate," and then showed me a bottle of Fujisu from Iio Jozo. I remarked that I'd been there, and that I agree—it's an art—but Fushiki-san's retort was, "It's more than that; it's a practice."

All of Fushiki's products are rich in glutamic acid (which is responsible for umami), though he did admit, too much umami is too much! "You get used to or bored if you rely on umami too much, and most Japanese tend to not use much acetic acid nowadays," he told me. But he still uses it—with care. This was evidenced by one of the most intriguing tasting menus I've ever experienced. One dish—or should I say platter—in particular, called The History of Sushi, is a five-part series that begins with Tohoku-style shime saba, a piece of *kohada* (gizzard shad) over rice, yellowtail marinated in *hishio* (a soybean-based sauce that may predate soy sauce as we know it), tuna in hishio with an avocado fermented in chili oil, and *chawanmushi* (egg custard) with *unagi* (eel) liver, fermented three days in amazuke, with a slick of kombu (seaweed) soup on top. Centuries of Japanese culture are expressed in these five small bites—an indescribable feat—and vinegar is present throughout.

ASHKENAZI NOSHES

If you're an American returning home from Japan, you're either desperate for the taste of pizza or you're desperately craving more sunomono. Personally, I fell in the latter category. Luckily, it's not difficult to locate havens for Japanese cuisine in America. One of my favorite noodle joints in New York City is Ivan Ramen. The owner, Ivan Orkin, is a self-proclaimed half-sour (pickle) guy, whose favorite sandwich in the whole world is corned beef, pastrami, and tongue on rye with coleslaw and Russian dressing.

Born to a Jewish family on Long Island, Orkin's current status as a highly respected chef in the contemporary Japanese food movement in America would seem unlikely on paper, to say the least. However, Orkin reflects fondly and often on his decades living in Tokyo, where he established the first of his many Ivan Ramen shops. He told me he misses the ripening plums in April and the Japanese supermarkets, with their shelves of rock sugar and where barrels abound for home brewing umeshu, or umesu.

The recipe that follows is a perfect amalgamation of Orkin's Jewish roots and his passion for Japanese cuisine. It calls for the fish and brine from Acme Smoked Fish, a New York City institution in Williamsburg, Brooklyn, that specializes in appetizing seafood, and which on Friday mornings is open to the public. Note: A *battera* is a sushi box, named after the Portuguese word for "little boat."

PICKLED HERRING BATTERA WITH ACME SMOKED FISH, FROM IVAN ORKIN, IVAN RAMEN, NEW YORK CITY
SERVES 2

2 cups (368 g) COOKED SUSHI RICE, *warm*

1 tablespoon RICE VINEGAR

1 tablespoon PICKLED HERRING BRINE, *use Acme Smoked Fish pickled herring if you can find it, either home-style or in wine, not in cream, but any pickled herring brand will do*

1 tablespoon FINELY CHOPPED ONIONS, *from the pickled herring jar*

6 to 9 pieces PICKLED HERRING, *to cover the battera*

WASABI-COATED SESAME SEEDS, *or plain roasted sesame seeds*

In a large bowl, mix the rice with the vinegar, brine, and chopped onions.

Gently press into a battera mold, or as an alternative method, wrap sections of the mixture in plastic wrap, spinning the ends like you would to make sausage. You can form a long "link" that resembles the shapes of the battera.

Top with the herring fillets, skin-side up for presentation. Press into the mold, not too firmly, but just enough to be able to slice the finished mold. This takes a couple of times to do perfectly, but luckily it's tasty practice.

Pop out of the mold and cut into bite-size pieces. Top with a sprinkling of the sesame seeds.

TSUKEMONO (SPICY DILLED CUCUMBER PICKLES),
FROM IVAN ORKIN, IVAN RAMEN, NEW YORK CITY   SERVES 2
TO 4 AS A SIDE

8 SMALL PERSIAN CUCUMBERS, about 1 pound (455 g)

2 teaspoons KOSHER SALT

2 cups (480 ml) RICE VINEGAR

1 cup (200 g) SUGAR

¼ cup (33 g) SALT

⅓ cup (75 ml) SESAME OIL

1 tablespoon RED PEPPER FLAKES

¾ cup (75 g) MINCED FRESH GINGER

2 teaspoons SHIO KOMBU

1 teaspoon LEMON ZEST

¼ cup (40 g) SESAME SEEDS

1 tablespoon FRESH DILL

recipe continues on page 154

Pickled Herring Battera with Acme Smoked Fish

Wash the cucumbers. Slice them on the bias very thinly without cutting all the way through the cucumber. Sprinkle the cucumbers with the salt and gently massage it. Let them sit in a bowl for about 30 minutes, then rinse off the salt.

In a bowl, combine the remaining ingredients except the dill and whisk until the salt and sugar are dissolved. Pour over the salted cucumbers and leave for at least 1 hour, though they taste better after 12 hours and can last for 3 days. Just before serving, sprinkle with the dill.

Reserve the pickling liquid and use it again (and again).

In search of more Japanese-inflected food in the United States, I headed to San Francisco's Japantown to see my friend Baz (David Bazirgan, see more on page 157) at Dirty Habit. His rendition of sunomono is so streamlined you'll taste the virtue of each and every element—just as it should be.

UNI AND CUCUMBER SUNOMONO, FROM DAVID BAZIRGAN (BAZ), BAMBARA, CAMBRIDGE, MASSACHUSETTS
SERVES 2

For the sunomono dressing:

1⅓ cups (315 ml) DASHI

½ cup (120 ml) RICE WINE VINEGAR

¼ cup (60 ml) SHOYU

¼ cup (60 ml) MIRIN

Put all the ingredients in a bowl and mix well.

To assemble:

2 cups (250 g) ENGLISH CUCUMBER, *chopped*

1 cup (115 g) RADISHES, *shaved*

12 FRESH TONGUES OF UNI (SEA URCHIN), *to garnish*)

⅓ cup (30 grams) FURIKAKE, *to garnish*

Toss the cucumber and radishes in the sunomono dressing. Garnish with the uni and furikake. Serve chilled.

NORTH AMERICA

Barbara Lynch, No. 9 Park

BOSTON

Unlikely as it sounds, my first encounter with vinegar was as a photography student at the Massachusetts College of Art in Boston. Poorly stored film—you know, that stuff used to capture photographs before there were camera phones—would occasionally befall the fate of cellulose triacetate degradation, or "vinegar syndrome." In extreme heat film would become dry and brittle, cracking to the point of almost shattering; the emulsion and the acetate film base would separate, become exposed to oxygen and moisture, and convert into acetic acid.

Acetic acid is common in darkroom photography, often found in stop bath, a chemical solution used to halt the processing of black-and-white film; the chemicals that cause film to develop work only in alkaline environments. I used to leave the darkroom emitting the stench of vinegar, but to me it smelled like a sense of accomplishment—that is, until an assignment was ruined. I had bought rolls of gray-market Kodak Tri-X 400 film to shoot in a low-light situation. When I attempted to push the film to 3200 ISO (three times the intended speed of the film), the negatives came out gritty rather than grainy, which was unexpected. I thought I had done something wrong, but it happened to the next roll, and the one after that. I brought strips of negatives to my teacher, who instantly knew that I had been had, a case of poorly kept film sold to a naive photo student. From then on, I was wary of the ill effects of acetic acid. Fast forward to a semester later: I was photographing the dinner rush at an acclaimed Boston restaurant when the chef gave me a quarter-bottle of Gegenbauer Noble Sour P.X. One sip of this peerless solution would introduce a different sort of vinegar syndrome, one that would alter my appreciation for acidity for the rest of my life.

Long before I decided to tour the world in search of the best and most unusual vinegars, my formative years were filled with college IDs, a handful of majors, half a dozen universities, and, in the end, a sole degree, a BFA in photography. My real education came from cooking double shifts in greasy spoons, in hopes of one day working at illustrious fine dining establishments. One night, after manning flattops and fryolators, I walked through Boston's Kenmore Square, and from across the Mass Pike I heard "Dirty Water" by the Standells echoing through a jubilant Fenway Park after a Red Sox game. The chorus sums up so much about this phase of my life: "Well, I love that dirty water. Oh, Boston, you're my home." I'll admit it: I'm an avid Red Sox fan, which I know is sacrilege for a New Yorker, but it's in this refrain, with its double reference to the River Charles and the endless washing of dishes that I witnessed in my first restaurant kitchens, that I found my true sense of home in Boston.

Barbara Lynch is a modern-day Julia Child; she cooks haute cuisine on Beacon Hill that you don't need to be a Boston Brahmin to enjoy. No. 9 Park may be steps away from Boston's gold-domed State House, but Lynch's food is as approachable as it is intricate. I had heard stories of a notoriously blunt Irish girl from blue-collar South Boston, but I've come to know Lynch as one of the kindest, most nurturing people I've ever met. When I was first escorted into her pristine professional kitchen, as a dopey student there to get a glimpse of "the dinner rush," I sensed something bigger than a semester-long assignment.

The pass was lined with paper chits, furiously marked up by black Xs and Os. Orders were announced, and within minutes plates of exquisite food were expedited out of the kitchen quicker than seemed possible. Two and half turns, and a hundred covers later, Lynch would slip out into the alleyway for a smoke and a sip of wine, regaling me with stories of the industry. At some point during these chats, we must have come to an understanding; I'd show up at least once a week to photograph a "day in the life" of her restaurant and, in exchange, I would be fed leftovers from service. For a thrifty college kid, this was gourmet gold, and I felt that I was getting the better end of the bargain by far.

No. 9 Park turned into my second home, a three-year relationship that nourished my burgeoning art. Hundreds of rolls of film later—and after countless bites of prune-stuffed gnocchi with foie gras and vin santo glaze—I had gained the equivalent of a lifelong culinary education—not to mention an inside look at what it takes to operate a top-tier restaurant.

Surrounded by white tablecloths at No. 9 Park, you wouldn't guess that Lynch was raised by a woman who worked three jobs, brought up nine kids, and had no time to cook. Lynch now appraises every ingredient that is brought into her restaurant. And where her mother used white distilled vinegar with newspapers to wash their windows, Lynch considers vinegar an essential part of cooking. Every day, Lynch makes her daughter, Marchese, a salad of minced cucumbers, tomatoes, and fennel with a half-tablespoon of Carr's Ciderhouse apple cider vinegar (from Hadley, Massachusetts); it's not overpowering, it doesn't make you pucker, it's brilliantly bright.

Lynch, who has long subscribed to the French philosophy of using vinegar with just about everything, especially butter and cream sauces to cut the fat, is keenly aware of when powerful can become piercing. Whether making a mayonnaise or even wine, you aim for the right amount of acidity. And nothing infuriates Lynch more than an overdressed salad. Vinaigrette should be as crisp as fresh-picked lettuces. Gualtiero Marchesi, unofficial godfather of modern Italian cuisine and among Lynch's favorite chefs, taught her this culinary lesson, with particular resonance for the use of vinegar: Less is more. Marchesi's restaurant is an hour northeast of Milan in the Franciacorta sparkling wine region, and like that libation, his Sauce Caramello is straightforward and also complex. With only three ingredients—sugar, water, and vinegar—Sauce Caramello is the perfect partner to a big bowl of fritto misto (mixed fry). This lesson became the basis for how I gauge most any sauce, no matter how involved the recipe; is the food a medium for the sauce, or its muse?

*Sauce Caramello
with Fritto Misto*

SAUCE CARAMELLO WITH FRITTO MISTO, FROM BARBARA LYNCH, NO. 9 PARK, BOSTON, MASSACHUSETTS, BY WAY OF GUALTIERO MARCHESI SERVES 4

For the sauce caramello:

2 cups (400 g) SUGAR

1/2 cup (120 ml) ROOM-TEMPERATURE WATER

6 tablespoons (90 ml) WHITE WINE VINEGAR

1 pinch SALT

RED PEPPER FLAKES, *optional*

In a medium saucepan over medium-low heat, combine the sugar and water. Cook, stirring occasionally with a wooden spoon, until the sugar has dissolved. Turn the heat up to medium-high and continue to cook until the sugar begins to caramelize, about 10 minutes. Working off the heat, add the vinegar; use caution, as the sauce will foam up. Stir and season with the salt. If you'd like a little heat, add a pinch of red pepper flakes. Return to heat for another 2 minutes for it all to come together. Remove fron the heat and allow the sauce to cool to room temperature. Sauce Caramello can be stored at room temperature for up to a day and up to a week in the refrigerator. Warm the sauce over low heat to bring it back to room temperature.

For the fritto misto:

1/2 cup (65 g) ALL-PURPOSE FLOUR

1/2 cup (65 g) CORNSTARCH

1/4 teaspoon KOSHER SALT

1/4 teaspoon FRESHLY GROUND BLACK PEPPER

2 cups (480 ml) ICE-COLD WATER OR SPARKLING WATER

1 quart (1 L) CANOLA OIL

1 VIDALIA ONION, *sliced 1/4-inch (6-mm) thick*

2 MEDIUM ZUCCHINI, *cut into batons*

1 bunch BROCCOLI, *cut into florets*

1 pound (455 g) SQUID, *cleaned and cut crosswise into 1/2-inch (12-mm) rings, tentacles left whole*

recipe continues on page 162

Mix the flour, cornstarch, salt, and black pepper in a glass bowl. Slowly whisk in the water or sparkling water. Some lumps may remain. Set the bowl in a larger bowl with enough ice water to keep the batter chilled.

Fill a medium, heavy stainless-steel saucepan halfway up with the oil. Heat over medium heat until the temperature registers 375°F (190°C) on a deep-fry thermometer. Test the oil with a drop of batter. It should form a small ball and begin to sizzle.

Working with 2 or 3 pieces of one kind of vegetable at a time, coat them in the batter, giving each one a quick shake to remove excess batter. Carefully drop them one by one into the oil. Using tongs or a slotted spoon, turn the pieces as they cook so all the sides are lightly golden. Drain fried vegetables on a paper towel–lined surface, lightly seasoning each piece as it is pulled. Working in batches, finish frying all the vegetables, followed by the squid. Serve immediately alongside Sauce Caramello.

A condiment can be a star, the reason you keep eating whatever it is you're eating it with. It should augment the experience, not take away from it. In the following instance, Lynch makes a versatile pepper jelly, with notes of heat bolstered by its brightness. Try it on a cheese plate alongside sharp cheddars and springy goat cheese, or even use it as a sandwich spread. I like it on a BLT. The point here is that seasoning can come on the side in enjoyably unexpected ways.

PEPPER JELLY, FROM BARBARA LYNCH, NO. 9 PARK, BOSTON, MASSACHUSETTS MAKES ABOUT 1³/₄ QUARTS (1.7 L), OR 7 (8-OUNCE / 240-ML) JARS

1 tablespoon OLIVE OIL

2 RED PEPPERS, about 1 ½ cups (220 g), *diced*

2 YELLOW PEPPERS, *diced,* about 1½ cups (220 g)

1 JALAPEÑO CHILE, *diced,* about 2 tablespoons

3 cups (720 ml) APPLE CIDER VINEGAR

3½ teaspoons POMONA PECTIN, *activate as per the brand's directions*

4 cups (800 g) SUGAR

SALT

In a medium saucepan, over medium heat, sauté the peppers in the olive oil for 5 minutes, until slightly cooked but still firm. Add the vinegar, bring to a boil, and cook for a few minutes. Whisk in the pectin and sugar gradually to prevent clumping, return to a boil, and boil for another few minutes, stirring occasionally, then remove from heat.

Place a small amount of jelly in a bowl and allow to cool in the refrigerator. This will allow you to see the jelly's consistency. If you prefer a thicker jelly, return to the stovetop and simmer briefly to further reduce. Season with salt.

To store, either follow canning instructions from a reliable source or let cool in a heatproof container and then refrigerate. It will keep for months.

David Bazirgan, known as Baz, is something of a pasta maestro. He was the chef de cuisine at No. 9 Park, where I first started taking food seriously. I used to sidle up beside him with my camera during service. Though he was austere, his food was anything but; his pared-down plates let the ingredients speak for themselves. The key to the following dish is getting the butter to the right point of browning, so that when you deglaze, it retains all the roasted notes you worked so hard for.

*Tagliatelle with Brown
Butter, Lemon Vinegar, and
Pine Nut Gremolata*

TAGLIATELLE WITH BROWN BUTTER, LEMON VINEGAR, AND PINENUT GREMOLATA,

FROM DAVID BAZIRGAN (BAZ), BAMBARA, CAMBRIDGE, MASSACHUSETTS SERVES 4

For the gremolata:

¾ cup (100 g) PINE NUTS, *toasted and crushed*

¾ cup (35 g) TOASTED BREAD CRUMBS

½ cup (25 g) CHOPPED FLAT-LEAF PARSLEY

2 tablespoons LEMON ZEST, *from about 2 lemons*

SALT

Mix all ingredients together in a bowl and set aside.

For the sauce:

1 cup (2 sticks / 225 g) BUTTER

½ cup (120 ml) LEMON VINEGAR

SALT

In a medium saucepan over medium-low heat, melt the butter and let brown for a few minutes, swirling the pan every so often. You will see the butter turn brown and milk solids separate and fall to the bottom. Keep an eye on it. You don't want it to burn. Add vinegar to the brown butter, heat gently for another 30 seconds or so, then season with salt and set aside.

To serve:

4 (4-ounce / 115-g) bundles TAGLIATELLE, *homemade or store-bought*

PARMIGIANO-REGGIANO, *for grating*

Boil a large amount of salted water, cook the pasta until al dente, then drain, reserving some of the pasta water.

Toss the pasta in the butter sauce until well coated. Add a couple of tablespoons of pasta water to help emulsify, then place in a warm pasta bowl.

Garnish with a generous amount of gremolata, then grate an ample quantity of cheese over the top. Serve immediately.

My first foray into the "back of the house" (restaurant term for a professional kitchen) was at Clio, the marquee dining experience at the Eliot Hotel in Back Bay. I'd stroll by Mass Ave, between Commonwealth and Newbury Street, and peer through the small picture window that looked into Ken Oringer's kitchen, and his mind. Clio was among the city's best restaurants, and Oringer's genius greatly admired. He was so ahead of the curve in approach and technique that there are many concepts and ingredients he used that I've yet to come across in any another restaurant.

Oringer began cooking at a family friend's Italian restaurant in New Jersey at age fifteen. Even at this young age he found baseline balsamic more intriguing than the generic gallon jugs of red and wine vinegars his family kept under their kitchen sink. There weren't any Whole Foods at this time, so Oringer would go to specialty markets in Manhattan's Little Italy or Chinatown to get something unique to expand his pantry. In 1989, he was working for David Burke at the celebrated River Café in Brooklyn when a bottle of umeboshi vinegar was brought back from Japan for the cooks. It was sour as hell, but still had the perfume of ripe plum, unlike anything Oringer had tasted before. This experience set Oringer off in search of more vinegars at stores like Dean & Deluca and Zabar's.

Oringer eventually moved to San Francisco for work, and there he made trips to nearby wine country, discovering a preponderance of vinegars made from grape must. Offered a job to work with acclaimed chef Jean-Georges Vongerichten, Oringer made his way to Boston in 1990, and JG, being a Frenchman from Alsace, loved his acid. In his kitchen there were fifteen different types of vinegar, from sweet potato to elderflower, with infusions of herb stems and onion berries. This idea of a diversified and multicultural pantry would carry through to Clio's opening years later, in 1997.

Oringer knew there was an abundance of local New England ingredients with a comparable amount of acidity to that of vinegar, but cranberries, rhubarb, and Cape gooseberries were seasonal. Vinegar was available year-round and could come from outside of Boston yet still be part of the city's diverse culinary scene.

In 2002 Oringer opened Uni, a sashimi bar right in Clio's lounge. The challenge was understanding the nuances of each fish and its oiliness; Japanese snapper asks for a lighter acid, and tuna needs something more assertive, as do many silver-skin fish that have a stronger finish, like mackerel. Adding acidity was a balancing act. Oringer, who hadn't even eaten sushi until college, was now flying in fish from Tokyo's famed Tsukiji fish market. (He continued to utilize his favorite New England fishermen as well.) To get customers to eat raw fish made by a guy from New Jersey, he had to parlay his years of experience as a chef and the confidence that customers had in his preparations. In this recipe, Oringer uses the often-discarded white rind of watermelon as an accompaniment to fatty tuna. It's opulent and familiar at the same time, and remarkably easy.

PICKLED WATERMELON RIND FOR TUNA SASHIMI,
FROM KEN ORINGER, UNI, BOSTON, MASSACHUSETTS
MAKES 3 CUPS (720 ML)—2 CUPS (480 ML) BRINE, WHICH YOU CAN REUSE, AND 1 CUP (240 ML) PICKLE

WHITE WATERMELON RIND from 1 (3-pound / 1.4-kg) piece watermelon

1 cup (240 ml) RICE WINE VINEGAR

1 cup (200 g) SUGAR

¼ cup (33 g) SALT

¼ teaspoon WASABI, *freshly grated preferred, or powdered*

2 tablespoons WHOLE SZECHUAN PEPPERCORN

1 tablespoon WHOLE CLOVES

1 tablespoon FENNEL SEEDS, *whole*

1 pound (455 g) SUSHI GRADE TUNA, *sliced ¼-inch (6-mm) thick for sashimi*

recipe continues on page 169

Pickled Watermelon Rind
for Tuna Sashimi

Trim the white watermelon rind clear of all red and green parts. Cut into small dice and place in a heatproof bowl or jar.

Combine the rice wine vinegar, sugar, salt, wasabi, Szechuan peppercorns, cloves, and fennel seeds in a small saucepan and bring to a boil over high heat. Pour the hot liquid on top of the watermelon rinds, and let cool. Cover, then place in the refrigerator overnight; they'll keep for up to a month.

To serve, slice sashimi and place on a plate, overlapping each piece with the next. Brush a little of the pickling liquid on top of each piece of tuna and garnish with a few watermelon rind pickles per slice.

Jamie Bissonnette is a punk. Yeah, he's tatted from finger tips to nape, and the emphatic way he talks about food is like the spoken-word part of a hard-core song before the screaming starts, but at Coppa, his Italian enoteca, he serves self-effacing small plates. Bissonnette is Ken Oringer's business partner at Toro, a Spanish tapas restaurant in Boston's South End; just down the street on Shawmut Avenue, you can sit on the patio at Coppa and pick at *stuzzichini* (bar snacks) like *boquerones* (white anchovies in vinegar) and *funghi in salamoia* (marinated mushrooms).

These dishes are telling of Bissonnette's remarkable recall for taste memories, which he uses to expound impassioned flavor arrangements. He remembers sitting in a shopping cart as a child, yelling, "I'm hungry, I'm hungry," to his mother, who sated him with a slice of liverwurst and a dill pickle from the deli. Bissonnette imbues his food with the acidity he recalls dripping off the pickle. He grew up in Connecticut with German-Swedish heritage, lots of sour cabbage and red wine vinegar; his grandmother made a big deal of never using low-end store-bought vinegars, and always had a crock on the counter, to which she regularly added unfinished glasses of wine.

Beaming with New England pride, Bissonnette recites a rich history of preserving fish by the Narragansett Indians in Rhode Island,

and in the same breath acknowledges his love a good Maine lobster roll with mayo on a buttered bun. Adding that he prefers his fried fish with a rémoulade, a sweet pickle-studded condiment based off Scandinavian tartar sauce, he notes New England's call for acidity. Ask him about the humble dish of Boston Baked Beans stewed in molasses. The ordinary variety can be cloyingly sweet, he notes, but add a couple of drops of vinegar, and you will want to eat a whole bean pot! Baked scallops, cod, or haddock with these beans may change your tune.

You can't do Boston without downing some oysters, but rather than a traditional mignonette, Bissonnette uses the bivalves' propensity as filter feeders to his advantage. Leave an oyster in pickling liquid, or prepare it in the style of escabeche (a Spanish dish, typically composed of fried fish that is marinated and served tepid or cold), and it'll soak in all the flavors, while still retaining the texture of a raw oyster.

OYSTERS ESCABECHE, FROM JAMIE BISSONNETTE, COPPA, BOSTON, MASSACHUSETTS SERVES 2 TO 4

1 dozen ISLAND CREEK OYSTERS, *or any medium-size East Coast oysters*

½ cup (120 ml) WHITE WINE VINEGAR, *such as Cava or Champagne*

½ cup (120 ml) BRUT CAVA, *or any dry sparkling wine*

¼ cup (60 ml) GRAPESEED OIL, *or any lightly flavored neutral oil*

1 tablespoon ROOIBOS TEA WITH BERGAMOT LEAVES, *or 2 tea bags*

1 LARGE SHALLOT, *minced,* about ½ cup (70 g)

Shuck the oysters into a bowl over ice, keeping them in their own liquor. Save the bottom shells for presentation and set aside. Allow the oysters to sit for 20 minutes, then use their liquid to clean off any pieces of shell or sand. Strain the liquid and pour it back over the oysters, repeating a few more times. Place the oysters in another bowl resting over ice.

In a small saucepan, combine the vinegar, Cava, and grape-seed oil. Bring to a simmer over medium heat, then add the tea and remove from the heat. Allow the liquid to steep with the tea for 10 minutes. Strain the liquid through a cheesecloth or fine-mesh strainer over the oysters and add the shallot. Let the oysters cool on the ice and store them in their liquid.

While oysters are cooling, clean the bottom shells. Scrape the abductor muscle off and scrub the shells thoroughly. If you're not using them immediately, you can clean them in the dishwasher; just remember to chill them down before using.

To serve, make sure the oysters are cold, or let them sit in the fridge for up to 6 days; the best flavor is usually after a day or two. You can garnish them with whatever you'd like; Bissonnette suggests sliced chives, cracked grains of paradise or black peppercorns, urfa pepper flakes, fleur de sel, chiffonade lovage or celery leaves, or simply as is. To plate, put one oyster in each shell with a small amount of the escabeche liquid and whatever garnishes you choose.

Oysters Escabeche   171

Bissonnette's newest venture (again collaborating with Ken Oringer) is Little Donkey in Cambridge's Central Square; the emphasis is small plates with global flavors, from tapas to antipasti. When Bissonnette travels for inspiration, he not only gathers ingredients and ideas; he also collects honey. At one point he had hundreds of small jars as mementos. In this multifaceted vinaigrette, Bissonnette reminds us that cuisine is in fact an amalgam of who we are, not just where we've been.

HONEY ZA'ATAR VINAIGRETTE, FROM JAMIE BISSONNETTE, LITTLE DONKEY, BOSTON, MASSACHUSETTS
MAKES ABOUT 3 CUPS (720 ML)

1½ cups (360 ml) GOOD HONEY, *fresh from the farmers' market or your local apiary*

¼ cup (60 ml) MILD WHITE VINEGAR, *such as Chardonnay*

2 tablespoons ZA'ATAR, *the freshest spice blend you can find, or make your own*

2 tablespoons ROASTED SESAME SEEDS, *such as Korean cham-kkae, but don't try to roast your own, as they'll burn and taste acrid*

2 teaspoons ESPELETTE CHILE FLAKES

½ cup (120 ml) OLIVE OIL

FLEUR DE SEL, *to season*

In a medium bowl, combine all the ingredients except the oil and salt, then slowly whisk in the oil until fully combined. Season with salt. Try it on fatty pork, grilled meats, or roasted poultry.

Matthew Jennings shares Bissonnette's interest in global flavors, running Townsman as a brasserie with international allure on the edge of Boston's Chinatown. Raised in Massachusetts, Jennings remembers those romaine days, before mesclun was a thing and green leaf dominated. With such a limited range of roughage, you had to get creative with your dressing, so Jennings's mom used to add Parmesan and black pepper to Ken's Steakhouse red wine vinegar and olive oil dressing. He upgraded during culinary school. On a trip to Florence, Jennings brought back half a dozen very special vinegars, but upon return, he stepped out into the unforgiving New England winter and slipped on the ice, breaking every bottle.

Jennings took this as a sign that he needed to learn to fill his own pantry with more accessible products. He had always adored apple cider vinegars, which you can sometimes source from apple orchards that make cider, but once he came across Société-Orignal's Balconville apple vinegar, especially the late harvest bottling, he bought up a large supply from the Canadian producer. Today, Jennings uses a range of his own homemade creations, including an unfiltered pear cider with added barley aged in old whiskey casks and a charred rice vinegar maturing in an Evan Williams barrel.

Jennings believes vinegar is at its best when uncooked, so he uses Misto sprayers to spritz a dish before it leaves the pass; meats off the grill get a quick glaze, and fried Brussels sprouts are finished with a house-made smoked red pepper vinegar and a dollop of malt vinegar aioli. He won't deny the importance of vinegar in sauce making—even Espagnole, one of Escoffier's five mother sauces, involves deglazing a pan with it—but Jennings would rather keep his vinegars in the raw bar. A set of relishes dress up a *plateau de fruits de mer*, accentuating the seafood by adding a hint of acid, which brings out their natural salinity.

BLUEBERRY AND JALAPEÑO RELISH, FROM MATTHEW JENNINGS, TOWNSMAN, BOSTON, MASSACHUSETTS MAKES 3 CUPS (720 ML)

1 quart (580 g) BLUEBERRIES

1 cup (150 g) JALAPEÑO, *cut into brunoise*

¼ cup (13 g) MINCED FENNEL FRONDS

¼ cup (35 g) MINCED SHALLOTS

¼ cup (60 ml) FRESH LEMON JUICE

¾ cup (180 ml) CIDER VINEGAR

2 tablespoons HONEY

½ cup (100 g) SUGAR

2 tablespoons URFA PEPPER FLAKES

SALT

recipe continues on page 174

Combine all ingredients and pulse gently in a food processor until a chunky, juicy relish has formed. Store in an airtight container for up to 2 weeks.

CELERY AND SUMAC RELISH, FROM MATTHEW JENNINGS, TOWNSMAN, BOSTON, MASSACHUSETTS

MAKES 3 CUPS (720 ML)

1 pound (455 g) CELERY STALKS

⅓ cup (65 g) SUGAR

⅛ teaspoon SALT

¼ cup (60 ml) FRESH LEMON JUICE

½ cup (120 ml) RICE WINE VINEGAR

1 tablespoon SUMAC, *freshly ground if possible*

Peel the celery and remove any strings from the stalks. Cut them into small dice.

Put the sugar, salt, lemon juice, vinegar, and celery in a saucepan and cook over medium-high heat, stirring until the sugar and salt dissolve and the celery has released some of its liquid, a few minutes. Continuing to stir frequently, bring the syrup to a gentle simmer, then cover and cook for about 8 minutes, stirring occasionally. Uncover the pan and continue to cook, stirring frequently, until all of the liquid is absorbed. Cool completely, then fold in the sumac. You can store the relish in the refrigerator in a tightly sealed jar for a couple of months.

There's a difference between a sauce and a side, and then there are sauces that *are* sides, and this is one. It's good with fried foods, but also great with cured and cold poached seafood (e.g., crab, shrimp, lobster). Make room on your *plateau* for another ramekin.

MALT AIOLI, FROM MATTHEW JENNINGS, TOWNSMAN, BOSTON, MASSACHUSETTS MAKES 2 CUPS (480 ML)

1 teaspoon DIJON MUSTARD

1 tablespoon FRESH LEMON JUICE

1 teaspoon MINCED GARLIC

1 teaspoon SALT, *or to taste*

FRESHLY GROUND BLACK PEPPER

3 EGG YOLKS

1 cup (240 ml) CANOLA OIL

1 cup (240 ml) FRUITY OLIVE OIL

2 tablespoons MALT VINEGAR

Make sure all ingredients are room temperature before beginning.

Place the mustard, lemon juice, garlic, salt, pepper to taste, and the egg yolks in a bowl. Place the bowl on top of a towel to stabilize it and slowly whisk in the canola oil and then the olive oil in a thin, steady stream. Once the mixture reaches a thick, mayonnaise consistency, add the malt vinegar and adjust the seasoning if needed. The aioli can be made a day ahead—it gains a bit more depth that way—and it keeps in the refrigerator for a week or longer.

I can't recall how I met Jitti Chaithiraphant. I knew he made a Moxie vinegar from the quintessential New England soft drink, which ended up in Matthew Jennings's foie gras torchon dish as a jelly. He does that for the chef, says, "What kind of vinegar do you want?" and it happens. Jitti is just one of those guys who shows up serendipitously, as he did in Boston over two decades ago.

Bangkok-born, he's lived a vagabond life in the few years since we've become acidity allies. Jitti started cooking in the early 1990s, but after a few salaried years of mainly cooking Thai food, he left the industry, only to return a decade later. It wasn't until he took a job with chef Michael Leviton at Lumiere, a bistro in West Newton, Massachusetts, that Jitti gained his first experience with Western cuisine: seasonal, farm-to-table, locavore. Jitti began traveling the country on what seemed like an eternal apprenticeship, studying under such luminaries as Sean Brock, John Shields, Michael Anthony, and Frank Stitt. In trade for his free labor, Jitti gained a deep appreciation for naturally preserved foods.

He began studying ancient agricultural practices and the role of fermentation on farms, but in municipal Boston, his dream of homesteading lay dormant while he watched an overripe pineapple rot in his apartment. This piece of fruit symbolized the origins of Jitti's journey toward becoming a vinegar maker. He looked outside his window and saw an apple tree, and quickly proceeded to pick said apples. With cores and skins bobbing about in a solution of water and sugar, hoping to attract acetobacters, Jitti was in pursuit of the time-honored dream of wild fermentation: no added yeasts, no aeration, just a SCOBY (symbiotic colony of bacteria and yeast) and serenity.

Rummaging through farmers' markets, ethnic markets, and supermarkets, fermenting whatever he could get his hands on, Jitti now forages for wild ingredients like pinecones and black walnuts, a practice he picked up while living on an organic farm in Virginia. I visited Jitti just after New Year's, his house strewn with boxes, as if he had just moved in or was packing to leave. We ate lunch together, a green curry with rice and peas, ready when I arrived, and wonderfully warming on a cold day. He turned on the GPS feature on his phone, and in a map application showed me all the nice hikes within a reasonable distance; in spring, summer, and fall Jitti gathers, and in winter, he hoards. Surrounded by scattered buckets filled with annotated and time-stamped contents unrecognizable to my eye, Jitti lives among these living cultures.

There's a back sunroom converted into a fermentation lab with columns of metro shelves, recorked wine bottles, and plastic soda jugs. There we sipped sweet potato vinegar, butternut squash vinegar, and parsnip vinegar. Noticing a theme, I counted back a few months and

realized what we were tasting were the fall foods that only recently converted to acetic acid. They were young and lacked the depth of a more developed batch, but they had potential to evolve, as Jitti believes we all do when we adapt to our environment. The most noteworthy vinegar was a banana preparation, heady and with tropical notes like a Hefeweizen (beer). It was made only with skins, something most of us just throw away. Jitti says he's found evidence in the Incan diet that proved they knew of banana skin health benefits way back in the fifteenth century. That's Jitti's quiet optimism for you, willing to wait for nature's course.

Jitti Chaithiraphant, Heritage Vinegar

BANANA VINEGAR, FROM JITTI CHAITHIRAPHANT, HERITAGE VINEGAR MAKES ABOUT 2 QUARTS (2 L)

10 ORGANIC BANANA SKINS

3 quarts (2.8 L) WATER

1¾ cups (385 g or 420 ml) ORGANIC BROWN SUGAR, PALM SUGAR, or MAPLE SYRUP

1 WHOLE ORGANIC APPLE, *sliced, or* 2 tablespoons MOV (mother of vinegar; see page 308)

First, allow the bananas to fully ripen and then wait a bit longer; the darker the skin turns, the better the flavor. Pour the water and sugar into a bucket or separate into large mason jars,

recipe continues on page 178

adding equal amounts to each vessel. Add the banana skins, using a weight or small plate to keep them submerged, preventing them from molding. Add a few slices of apple or MOV and cover with cheesecloth.

After a few days you'll see white kahm yeast floating on the surface; feel free to stir it once a day, and eventually the kahm will sink to the bottom.

After 5 to 6 weeks, you will see a thin, clear film forming on the surface; this is the beginning of the SCOBY. The healthier your banana (this is why we use organic), the more likely you'll get a thicker SCOBY.

Your banana vinegar should be ready in 10 to 12 weeks. Strain and bottle. Discard the skin, but save your fresh banana skins from now on!

Jeremy Sewall's wildly popular restaurants Island Creek Oyster Bar and Row 34 are built on his legacy; Jeremy is a relative of Samuel Sewall, known for his involvement in the Salem witch trials and for serving as chief justice of the Massachusetts Superior Court. Jeremy's cooking is a manifestation of his forefathers; he's proud of his Boston heritage, and adept at crafting an everlasting impression with his regional cuisine. We first met when I was a lowly cook. I found him solemn at first, but as I got to know him, he became like a drinking buddy or big brother.

Years later I photographed his cookbook, *The New England Kitchen*. After each of the hundred-plus dishes we documented, I was tempted to take another bite; it's rustic New England cooking, adapted for contemporary tastes. What follows is a trio of delicate mignonettes, an all-purpose ginger syrup to drizzle over crudo (raw fish), and textbook sweet-and-sour peppers, each intended to elevate plain-sailing seafood to extraordinary levels.

MIGNONETTE, FROM JEREMY SEWALL, ISLAND CREEK OYSTER BAR, ROW 34, BOSTON, MASSACHUSETTS

MAKES ³/₄ CUPS (180 ML)

¼ cup (35 g) MINCED SHALLOTS

¼ cup (60 ml) DRY WHITE WINE, *something you'd enjoy drinking with oysters*

¼ cup (60 ml) WHITE WINE VINEGAR

1 teaspoon FRESHLY GROUND BLACK PEPPER

Combine all ingredients in a small bowl and serve.

SPICY MIGNONETTE, FROM JEREMY SEWALL, ISLAND CREEK OYSTER BAR, ROW 34, BOSTON, MASSACHUSETTS

MAKES ABOUT 1 CUP (240 ML)

¼ cup (35 g) MINCED SHALLOTS

¼ cup (60 ml) DRY WHITE WINE

¼ cup (60 ml) WHITE WINE VINEGAR

1 teaspoon FRESHLY GROUND BLACK PEPPER

1 FRESNO CHILE, *seeds and ribs removed, minced*

2 tablespoons CHOPPED CILANTRO

1 tablespoon FRESH LIME JUICE

Combine all ingredients in a small bowl and serve.

BASIL MIGNONETTE, FROM JEREMY SEWALL, ISLAND CREEK OYSTER BAR, ROW 34, BOSTON, MASSACHUSETTS
MAKES ³/₄ CUPS (180 ML)

½ cup (120 ml) CHAMPAGNE VINEGAR

2 tablespoons THAI BASIL LEAVES

2 tablespoons CHOPPED LEMONGRASS

2 tablespoons CHOPPED GINGER

½ cup (120 ml) DRY WHITE WINE

¼ cup (35 g) MINCED SHALLOTS

1 teaspoon FRESHLY GROUND BLACK PEPPER

In a small saucepan, bring the vinegar to a boil with the basil, lemongrass, and ginger. Remove from heat and let cool to room temperature. Strain into a bowl, mix in the remaining ingredients, and serve.

GINGER SYRUP, FROM JEREMY SEWALL, ISLAND CREEK OYSTER BAR, ROW 34, BOSTON, MASSACHUSETTS
MAKES ABOUT 1 CUP (240 ML)

¼ cup (25 g) GINGER, *peeled and very thinly sliced*

½ cup (120 ml) CHAMPAGNE VINEGAR

½ cup (100 g) SUGAR

In a medium saucepan, combine the ginger, vinegar, and sugar, bring to a boil over medium heat, then reduce the heat and simmer for about 10 minutes. The syrup becomes thicker and sweeter as it cooks. Let cool to room temperature, strain, and serve. It will keep covered in the refrigerator for up to a month.

SWEET-AND-SOUR PEPPERS WITH RARE SEARED TUNA STEAK, FROM JEREMY SEWALL, ISLAND CREEK OYSTER BAR, ROW 34, BOSTON, MASSACHUSETTS SERVES 4

For the peppers:

3 tablespoons OLIVE OIL

1 tablespoon CHOPPED GARLIC

¼ cup (50 g) SUGAR

¼ cup (60 ml) SHERRY VINEGAR

1 LARGE RED ONION, *cut into ¼-inch (6-mm) slices*

1 LARGE RED PEPPER, *peeled,* * *cut in half, seeds removed, then cut into ¼- to ½-inch (6- to 12-mm) strips*

1 LARGE YELLOW PEPPER, *peeled,* * *cut in half, seeds removed, then cut into ¼- to ½-inch (6- to 12-mm) strips*

¼ cup (60 ml) VEGETABLE STOCK

**Use a sharp Y-shaped peeler for best results*

Heat the olive oil in a large sauté pan over medium heat, add the garlic, and lightly toast it, about 1 minute. Add the sugar and vinegar and mix until dissolved, about another minute. Toss in the onions and peppers, bring to a simmer, then add the vegetable stock, bring to a simmer again, and simmer for 5 minutes. Take off the heat and let cool. At this point, you can store the peppers in their liquid until ready to use, or cover in an airtight container and place it in the refrigerator; they will last for up to 1 week.

For the tuna:

2 pounds (910 g) FRESH TUNA

SALT and BLACK PEPPER

½ cup (120 ml) OLIVE OIL

PARSLEY, *to garnish, optional*

recipe continues on page 183

*Sweet-and-Sour Peppers with
Rare Seared Tuna Steak*

Season the tuna with salt and black pepper. In a sauté pan over medium-high heat, add ¼ cup (60 ml) of the olive oil and let it heat for 30 seconds. Sear two pieces of tuna at a time, cooking each side for about 1½ minutes for rare. Discard the oil and repeat with the remaining oil and pieces of tuna. Let the fish sit for a few minutes and then, if you wish, slice into ½-inch (12-mm) pieces across the grain.

To serve, portion the sweet-and-sour peppers into four shallow bowls, with a couple of spoonfuls of the cooking liquid included. Place the tuna on top and garnish with parsley, if desired.

It's no exaggeration to say Gabriel Bremer is soft spoken. We met in 2004, moments after he took over Salts, a longstanding establishment steps away from the MIT campus. The dining room was sophisticated and quaint, and was led by Bremer's wife, Analia Verolo, whose Uruguayan background explained a tannat-filled wine list. Though the majority of Bremer's dishes came from a fine dining perspective, he regularly hinted toward home cooking. At his new restaurant, La Bodega by Salts, aside from a stuffed whole-roasted duck, which had been a menu highlight and the bane of Bremer's existence since day one at Salts, he's joked of having a more casual spot, cooking conventional recipes recalibrated (don't worry, the duck's still on the menu at La Bodega).

For example, a white gazpacho, garnished with a bouquet of edible flowers from his farm, sherry gelée, orange powder, and soft yogurt and macadamia nut truffles. An ornate single serving of *postre chaja*, a layered sponge cake with peaches and meringue from Uruguay named after an indigenous bird called the crested screamer, this is as loud as Bremer food gets. A soup, salad, and dessert.

WHITE GAZPACHO, FROM GABRIEL BREMER, LA BODEGA
BY SALTS, CAMBRIDGE, MASSACHUSETTS
MAKES ABOUT 1 QUART (960 ML)

¼ day-old BAGUETTE

7 cups (1.6 L) WATER

1½ cups (210 g) WHOLE
  BLANCHED ALMONDS

2 cups (300 g) GREEN
  GRAPES

3 cloves GARLIC

¼ cup (60 ml) OLIVE OIL,
  SPANISH PREFERRED

3 tablespoons SHERRY
  VINEGAR

SALT

WHITE PEPPER

For the garnish:

½ cup (60 g) RADISH,
  sliced thinly lengthwise

¼ cup (40 g) GRAPES,
  cut in half lengthwise

¼ cup (25 g) ALMONDS,
  sliced thinly lengthwise

Cut the baguette into 1-inch (2.5-cm) slices, then place them into a large bowl with 4 cups (960 ml) tap water. Let soak until soft, 5 to 10 minutes. Remove the bread and discard the water.

In a blender, combine the almonds, grapes, garlic, and 3 cups (720 ml) water and blend until smooth. Add the softened bread, the olive oil, and vinegar and blend once again until smooth. Pass the soup through a fine-mesh strainer and season with salt and pepper. Chill for 1 hour before serving.

Spoon the soup into very shallow bowls and garnish with radishes, grapes, and toasted almonds.

POSTRE CHAJA, FROM GABRIEL BREMER, LA BODEGA
BY SALTS, CAMBRIDGE, MASSACHUSETTS
MAKES 4 3 X 4 INCH CAKES

For the peach sorbet:

500 grams (2¼ cups / 540 ml)
  PEACH PUREE

65 grams (¼ cup plus 1 tbsp)
  SUGAR

44 grams (3 tbsp) WATER

40 grams (8 tsp) LIQUID
  GLUCOSE

Combine all the ingredients in a saucepan and bring to a boil over medium-high heat. Remove from the heat and let cool. Pour into a container, cover, and chill in the refrigerator overnight. Place into an ice cream machine and freeze according to the manufacturer's instructions.

For the meringue:

250 grams (8 oz) LARGE
    EGG WHITES
    (8 large egg whites)

375 grams (1¾ cups plus
    2 tbsp) SUGAR

25 grams (1 tbsp plus 2 tsp)
    PEACH VINEGAR

In a double boiler, whisk together the egg whites, sugar, and vinegar, then cook to 140°F (60°C). Transfer the mixture to a mixer and whip until stiff peaks form. Place half of the meringue into a pastry bag and keep in the refrigerator until you're ready to use it. Spread the remaining meringue onto a baking sheet lined with a nonstick pad (like a Silpat) and place in the oven on low heat, at 200°F (95°C) to dehydrate and crisp, an hour or two, checking every so often. You want it firm but not taking on any color. If it turns ecru, you've gone too far.

For the cake:

125 grams (1 cup) ALMOND
    FLOUR

120 grams (9½ tbsp) SUGAR,
    *separated into 100-gram
    (8-tbsp) and 20-gram
    (1½-tbsp) portions*

38 grams (2½ tbsp) CAKE
    FLOUR

150 grams (5¼ oz) WHOLE
    EGGS (3 large eggs)

20 grams (11¾ oz) EGG
    YOLKS (1 large egg yolk)

100 grams (3½ oz) EGG
    WHITES (3 large egg
    whites)

Preheat the oven to 400°F (205°C).

In a mixer, combine the almond flour, 100 grams of the sugar, the cake flour, whole eggs, and egg yolks and mix on medium-high speed for 10 minutes. In another mixer bowl, combine the egg whites and the remaining 20 grams of sugar and whip until stiff peaks form. Fold the egg whites into the almond flour

*recipe continues
on page 186*

mixture until fully incorporated. Spread the mixture out onto a parchment-lined baking sheet and bake for 12 to 14 minutes, until golden brown. Remove from oven, let cool to room temperature.

To assemble: Cut out a small round of the sponge cake, 3 to 4 inches (7.5 to 12 cm) in diameter. Place a small scoop of the peach sorbet on top of the cake. Cover the sorbet with the soft meringue and finish with pieces of the crispy meringue. Garnish with a little diced fresh peach if you like.

Postre Chaja

NEW YORK CITY

Brunch is a uniquely American meal (though it originated in England, it was first popularized in the United States in the 1930s). The portmanteau of breakfast and lunch, it combines the notion that breakfast can be eaten well into the afternoon with the optimistic view that alarm clocks and snooze buttons don't exist on weekends. On the Lower East Side of New York City, hipsters and locals slink out of bed with mussed hair and yesterday's clothes. Clinton Street Baking Company is their mecca, and many wait in line for hours for Clinton Street's world-famous blueberry pancakes. Busloads of Japanese tourists are dropped off around the corner, waiting to douse the fluffy stacks in warm maple butter.

Chef Neil Kleinberg and his wife, DeDe Lahman, are the gatekeepers, but they're also amazingly hospitable souls, happy to take care of the disheveled crowd of hungry young folks. Brunch food is notoriously fatty, perfect to soak up last night's libations, but acid plays an integral role in hollandaise sauce, and there's none better than Clinton Street's to start the day, so get in line!

HOLLANDAISE SAUCE, FROM NEIL KLEINBERG, CLINTON STREET BAKING COMPANY, NEW YORK CITY SERVES 2 TO 4

Diner-goers should know that eggs Benedict is fundamentally reliant on the quality of the hollandaise. It's the first thing you need to perfect in making eggs Benedict, before you poach your eggs, toast your English muffin, or griddle your ham/slice your smoked salmon/sauté your spinach. It's got to be the right warmth to run over your eggs with the fluidity of hot fudge. Though the steps are not complex, making hollandaise is a scrupulous study in time and temperature.

recipe continues on page 188

16 tablespoons (2 sticks / 225 g) UNSALTED BUTTER

3 LARGE EGG YOLKS

2 teaspoons FRESH LEMON JUICE

½ teaspoon SALT

¼ teaspoon GROUND WHITE PEPPER, *if you use black, you'll see the specks in the sauce*

¼ teaspoon CAYENNE

Fill a saucepan about three-quarters full with water, but make sure that a stainless steel bowl set atop the pan would not touch the water. You're going to use the bowl as a double boiler. Bring water to a simmer over medium heat.

In another small saucepan, melt the butter over medium-low heat. Set aside in a warm place.

In the stainless steel bowl, whisk together the egg yolks, lemon juice, salt, pepper, and cayenne. Whisk in 2 tablespoons room-temperature water.

Place the bowl on top of the simmering water and continue to whisk the yolks until combined. Use a potholder; that bowl is going to get hot. Though you don't want it to get too hot, which can cause the eggs to curdle. After 1 minute, the yolks will become foamy and loose. After 2 minutes, the foamy texture will begin to subside and the yolks will thicken slightly. Make sure to whisk around the sides of the bowl so that the yolks do not congeal. If they appear to be thickening too quickly or clumping, remove the bowl from the pan and let the eggs cool down.

After 3 minutes of continuous whisking, the eggs will be even thicker and creamy. (Take a break here if you need it. Remove the bowl from the heat, then resume.) The yolks are close to being cooked; after 4 minutes, they'll thicken into ribbons and you will be able to see the bottom of the bowl; keep whisking! After 5 minutes, the yolks will be thick and golden and should have the texture of a thin mayonnaise. Remove the bowl from the pan.

Add the warm melted butter in a steady stream into the yolks, whisking the entire time. The sauce will begin to emulsify after about 1 minute. The hollandaise is now ready. It's best to keep hollandaise in a container in a warm water bath, similar to a bain-marie. Make sure the sauce is covered so a skin doesn't form on the surface. If the hollandaise thickens up, whisk in a tablespoon of room-temperature water. Do the same thing if your hollandaise ever "breaks" or separates. It will keep for a few hours, so get poaching some eggs!

In the mid-aughts, Brooklyn became home to a new generation of DIY food makers, a throwback to bygone days brought on by borough hipsters and homemakers alike. Among their primary obsessions: preservation. Pickling was so in vogue that if you didn't make your own in-house it was like a foodie demerit, but before pickling was cool, Jon Orren's pickled pears once won first prize at a pickle festival. It was the moment he saw that his avocation could become his career, and ultimately he launched Wheelhouse Pickles in 2005.

Orren has been a pickle fanatic for ages; at age six or seven he ate so many pickles that his mom refused to buy him more, and she suggested he just take some cucumbers from the garden, chop them up, and put them in the excess brine; he's been pickling ever since. What Orren tries to stress with Wheelhouse is that all vegetables, from beets to turnips, and even fruit, can be pickled. Orren's riff on the classic Branston Pickle, a British condiment of pickled diced vegetables cooked down with vinegar, tomato, apple, and spices, typically found as part of a ploughman's lunch (a cold meal of bread, meat, and cheese), adds the sweet, spicy, and tangy bite it needs.

PLOUGHMAN'S PICKLE, FROM JON ORREN, WHEELHOUSE PICKLES, BROOKLYN, NEW YORK MAKES ABOUT 1 QUART (1 L)

½ teaspoon BROWN MUSTARD SEEDS

½ teaspoon WHOLE CORIANDER SEEDS

¼ teaspoon FENNEL SEEDS

6 whole ALLSPICE BERRIES

2 WHOLE CLOVES

½ teaspoon whole BLACK PEPPERCORNS

1 pinch DRIED CHILE FLAKES

⅛ teaspoon GROUND CINNAMON

5 ounces (140 g) PARSNIPS, *peeled and grated*, about 1⅓ cups

10 ounces (280 g) TURNIPS, *peeled and grated*, about 2½ cups

4 ounces (115 g) CARROTS, *peeled and grated*, about 1 cup

2½ ounces (70 g) LEEKS, *rinsed, dried, and finely diced*, about ⅓ cup

2 ounces (55 g) SHALLOTS, *finely diced*, about ⅓ cup

3 ounces (85 g) GRATED CAULIFLOWER, about ½ cup

5 tablespoons (75 ml) OLIVE OIL

2 teaspoons KOSHER SALT

2½ ounces (70 g) TART APPLE, *such as Granny Smith, peeled and finely chopped*, about ½ cup

2½ ounces (70 g) FINELY CHOPPED PITTED DATES, about ½ cup

1 tablespoon FINELY MINCED GARLIC

1 tablespoon TOMATO PASTE

2 ounces (55 g) BREAD-AND-BUTTER PICKLES, *finely chopped,* or SWEET RELISH, about ½ cup

1¾ cups (420 ml) MALTY BEER, *such as brown ale, stout, porter, or amber*

1 tablespoon WORCESTERSHIRE SAUCE

¼ cup (60 ml) APPLE CIDER VINEGAR

Preheat the oven to 450°F (230°C) and put an empty baking sheet in the oven.

In a medium sauté pan, toast the mustard, coriander, fennel, allspice, cloves, and peppercorns until they become fragrant and you hear the first audible cracking/popping noise, a minute or two. Remove the spices from the heat and transfer to a spice grinder. Add the chile flakes and cinnamon and grind until the mixture becomes a fine powder. Set aside.

Combine the parsnips, turnips, carrots, leeks, shallots, cauliflower, 3 tablespoons of the olive oil, and 1½ teaspoons of the salt in a large bowl and mix well. Remove the hot baking sheet from the oven and carefully spread the vegetable mixture in an even layer across the baking sheet. Return to the oven and roast for 25 to 30 minutes, turning occasionally, until the vegetables have given up most of their moisture and are beginning to brown.

Heat the remaining 2 tablespoons olive oil in a large sauté pan over medium heat. Add the roasted vegetables, spice mixture, apples, and dates, and cook until the apples and dates begin to soften, about 3 minutes.

Add the garlic and tomato paste and cook until the tomato paste just begins to form a film on the bottom of the pan, 2 to 3 minutes. Add the pickles or relish, the beer, Worcestershire, vinegar, and the remaining ½ teaspoon salt. Simmer for 10 minutes, stirring occasionally, to cook off the alcohol and reduce mixture slightly—it should still be somewhat liquid.

Blend the mixture in batches in a blender or food processor, either pulsing for a chunky and rustic consistency or running continuously for a smooth puree that can be used as a savory spread.

Cool the mixture, then transfer it to storage containers and refrigerate. The spread will keep up to 4 weeks. Alternatively, keep the mixture hot and can it according to the manufacturer of your canning kit's instructions.

For an order of cloud-like gnocchi nestled in warm tomato sauce and topped with a generous spoonful of cold ricotta, well, there's no better place to go than Frankies Spuntino at 457 Court Street. The Franks (their surnames Castronovo and Falcinelli) are the new icons of "old school" Brooklyn, our generation's arbiters of good taste. Their home-made pastas are exceptional, but invariably it's their well-dressed salads I crave. Every bite has the precise amount of acidity, thanks to their cipollini onion cider vinaigrette, which makes a simple green salad seem anything but simple.

The complexity a little vinegar can give is only compounded by the depth a lot of vinegar can inspire; case in point: sauerbraten. When the Franks opened up their Bavarian-inspired Prime Meats, focusing on fresh-baked pretzels and house-made sausages (weisswurst, bratwurst), classics like crispy pork schnitzel and spaetzle also graced the menu. I crossed my fingers that sauerbraten would find its way to our cozy little corner of the borough and rejoiced when it did. Regarded as one of Germany's national dishes, this "sour (pot) roast" is awash in a vinegar-forward marinade, which begins by tenderizing a typically tough cut of meat, then long braising until it is meltingly tender and tremendously flavorful. Note that the Franks suggest marinating the meat for three days, so you'll need to plan ahead. It can be eaten hot with red cabbage and potato dumplings, carved cold as lunchmeat, seared on a flattop like hash, or, as I did in college, served as "sauerbraten au gratin."

SAUERBRATEN, FROM FRANK CASTRONOVO AND FRANK FALCINELLI, FRANKIES SPUNTINO AND PRIME MEATS, BROOKLYN, NEW YORK SERVES 6 TO 8

1 piece of BEEF BRISKET, TRIMMED, about 2 pounds (910 g)

For the marinade:

2 CARROTS, *roughly chopped, about 1 cup* (140 g)

2 LEEKS, *white and light green parts, roughly chopped,* about 1 cup (90 g)

2 CELERY STALKS, *roughly chopped,* about 1 cup (100 g)

1 HEAD GARLIC, *split lengthwise*

1 BAY LEAF

2½ cups (600 ml) DRY RED WINE, *such as Syrah or Blaufränkisch*

2½ cups (600 ml) RED WINE VINEGAR

5 cups (1.2 L) WATER

½ teaspoon JUNIPER BERRIES

½ teaspoon ALLSPICE

½ tablespoon WHOLE BLACK PEPPERCORNS

Place the meat in a large Dutch oven with the carrots, leeks, celery, garlic, and bay leaf.

Combine the wine, vinegar, water, juniper berries, allspice, and peppercorns in a large braising pot and bring to a boil over high heat. Pour the mixture over the meat, cool to room temperature, and let marinate in the refrigerator for 3 days.

After 3 days, remove the meat from the pot and pat dry. Strain and reserve the marinade.

For the sauerbraten:

¼ cup (60 ml) CANOLA OIL

1 MEDIUM WHITE ONION, *thinly sliced,* about ¾ cup (95 g)

2 GRANNY SMITH APPLES, *cored and roughly chopped,* about 1 cup (180 g)

⅔ cup RAISINS, about 3 ounces (85 g)

1 FRESH BAY LEAF

recipe continues on page 194

Preheat the oven to 275°F (135°C).

In a Dutch oven, heat the canola oil over medium-high heat and sear the brisket until browned all over, about 5 minutes per side. Remove the brisket, reserving the fat. Add the onion and cook for about 10 minutes, stirring occasionally, until well caramelized. Drop the heat to medium, deglaze the pan with half of the reserved marinade, and scrape the bottom of the pan to release any browned bits. Add the apples, raisins, and bay leaf, place the brisket on top, and cover with the remaining marinade. Bring to a simmer over medium heat, then cover and transfer to the oven. Braise for 2 to 2 ½ hours, until fork tender.

I firmly believe that all significant meat dishes need an equally delicious vegetable side, like a superhero and a sidekick. This one has become a Thanksgiving staple in my family. Its original iteration was as a texture-adding topping for a butter lettuce salad but after a while it became more of the centerpiece, so one day I decided to isolate it as its own recipe. The balsamic brown butter is a rich and tart vinaigrette that you'll undoubtedly use for other salads as well. Both the mushrooms and hazelnuts crunch with a deep, dark roastiness, complemented by crispy fried sage leaves.

BROWN BUTTER BALSAMIC MUSHROOMS WITH HAZELNUTS AND SAGE, MY RECIPE SERVES 2 TO 4

1 pound (455 g) MIXED MUSHROOMS, *such as maitake, oyster, and trumpet*

2 tablespoons OLIVE OIL

SALT and BLACK PEPPER

¼ cup (35 g) WHOLE HAZELNUTS

4 tablespoons (½ stick / 55 g) BUTTER

10 FRESH SAGE LEAVES

2 tablespoons BALSAMIC VINEGAR, IGP, *the cheaper stuff*

1 tablespoon FRESH LEMON JUICE

FLAKY SALT, *optional*

recipe continues on page 196

*Brown Butter Balsamic
Mushrooms with
Hazelnuts and Sage*

Preheat the oven to 300°F (150°C).

Trim the mushrooms of any woody ends. Toss them in the olive oil and add a little bit of salt and black pepper to season. Place on a baking sheet and roast for 45 minutes, until they're roasted coffee-bean brown.

Meanwhile, place the hazelnuts on a baking sheet in the oven and roast for about 20 minutes, until lightly browned and fragrant. Once warm to the touch, remove hazelnut skins with a kitchen towel. Remove and set aside to cool. You'll crunch or chop these up once they're cool enough to touch.

Combine the butter and sage in a small saucepan and melt over medium heat. Reduce the temperature to medium-low and let the butter brown. You'll see little brown bits forming at the bottom; they're the tasty milk solids, and you don't want those to burn, so keep an eye on them. Once the butter has browned, remove the sage leaves and drain on a paper towel–lined plate. Add the vinegar to the melted butter. Do not lean over the pan, as the vapors will be pretty strong. Whisk to combine. Add a little salt and black pepper, then turn the heat to medium-low and let reduce for about 30 seconds. Finish with the lemon juice and set aside. If the vinaigrette separates, you can mount it with a tablespoon of cold butter to emulsify.

To assemble, place the mushrooms on a plate and spoon the balsamic brown butter over them until they're well coated. Sprinkle with hazelnuts and top with the sage leaves. Finish with a bit of flaky salt if you like.

April Bloomfield's rise to fame in the United States actually began in the United Kingdom at The River Café. The story goes that Mario Batali scouted her at the suggestion of Jamie Oliver and introduced her to her business partner Ken Friedman, with whom she opened The Spotted Pig in lower Manhattan in 2004. She's been revered in the New York City dining scene ever since.

April's fish and chips may be the only recipe in this book that doesn't use vinegar in the process, but malt vinegar with fish and chips is such a standard that I felt compelled to include it here. What's more, any cook who substitutes vinegar for lemon in a classic Caesar dressing (in April's view, if a lemon is too old and has lost its essential oils, it's not substantial enough to stand up against the eggs, oil, and anchovies), deserves a say about acidity. Bloomfield's mom's pantry was stocked with her grandmother's pickled red cabbage and onions, so pickled that they'd make your belly ache. In her restaurants, it's a bit more controlled. She serves beets roasted with a touch of water, balsamic, thyme, and garlic, the balsamic amplifying the root's sweetness, as it does on sautéed chicken livers.

Bloomfield roasts kidneys in a hot pan with butter, bolstered by the umami-rich and vinegar-based Worcestershire sauce. (For another English classic, try Worcestershire in Welsh rarebit, the best cheesy toast you'll ever have.) The warming spices of Branston Pickle (see page 190) are central to a ploughman's lunch, because Bloomfield says, "the most boring food in the world is that without acidity."

FISH AND THRICE-COOKED CHIPS, FROM APRIL BLOOMFIELD, THE SPOTTED PIG, NEW YORK CITY SERVES 6

For thrice-cooked chips:

8 RUSSET POTATOES, UNPEELED, about 3 pounds (1.4 kg)

12 cups (2.8 L) CANOLA OIL

FLAKY SEA SALT

Cut the potatoes into ¾-inch (2-cm) spears. Place in a large pot of cold water and bring to a boil with the lid on. Allow to boil until the potatoes begin to break down and look slightly fluffy at the edges, 5 to 10 minutes. Strain and spread out to air-dry.

Heat the oil in a deep-fryer to 325°F (165°C). Drop a handful of potatoes in without overcrowding the fryer and fry for 8 to 10 minutes, until the potatoes have absorbed some fat.

recipe continues on page 198

Remove with a slotted spoon to a wire rack, drain, and cool.

Heat the oil to 350°F (175°C). Drop the potatoes back in and fry until they reach a deep golden brown and the edges are extra crispy. Remove from oil with a slotted spoon and season with flaky salt. Reserve oil for deep-frying the fish.

For the batter:

1 cup (125 g) ALL-PURPOSE FLOUR

1 cup (130 g) CORNSTARCH

¼ teaspoon BAKING POWDER

2 teaspoons DRY ACTIVE YEAST

2 EGG YOLKS, *mainly for color*

12 ounces (360 ml) BEER, *preferably pale ale*

Sift the dry ingredients into a large bowl. In a separate bowl, whisk together the egg yolks and beer. Incorporate the dry ingredients into the wet ingredients and allow to proof for about 30 minutes.

For the fish:

CANOLA OIL, *for frying, reuse from the Thrice-Cooked Chips*

6 (4- to 5-ounce / 115- to 140-g) PORTIONS FLAT, FLAKY WHITE FISH, *such as haddock or cod*

ALL-PURPOSE FLOUR, *for dredging*

FLAKY SEA SALT

Heat the oil in the fryer to 350°F (175°C).

Dredge the fish in the flour, then in the batter mixture. Drop the fish gently into the hot oil, being careful to avoid letting the fish stick to the bottom of the fryer. While the fish is frying, drizzle a little extra batter into the oil on top of the fish for extra texture and crispy bits. Fry until the batter turns a rich golden brown, 6 to 7 minutes. Remove from the oil and strain. Season with salt.

This dish is best served with a bottle of malt vinegar and a cold beer.

Fish and Thrice-Cooked Chips

Alex Raij is an Argentine Jew from Minnesota who fell in love with Basque food through a Basque man in New York, the epitome of a melting pot story. With her husband, Eder Montero, she operates Txikito and El Quinto Pino in Manhattan's Chelsea area, and both restaurants serve a variety of Northern Spain's shareable plates. Another restaurant they run, La Vara, is a few blocks from my house in Brooklyn; it explores the Moorish side of Spanish food, a bit more spiced than straight-up Basque cuisine.

At Txikito's bar you can have a Gilda, a favorite *pintxo*, or small snack, of Manzanilla olive, guindilla pepper, and an anchovy on a toothpick. Gildas, like *boquerones* (fresh white anchovies, salt cured, vinegar brined, and olive-oil packed), are ideal tapas that don't disguise their natural flavors. Too much acid can take away from their authenticity, and you have to be careful with vinegar in the Spanish paradigm. It's a cuisine that hinges on being *equilibrado*, or balanced.

Oil and vinegar taste great together, but they're not so friendly on a chemical level. They don't naturally want to emulsify, so when you add vinegar to oil, the latter surrounds the former instead of combining. Big shots of vinegar to a dish can create dissonance, which Raij is aware of when she cooks her mother's rabbit leg escabeche (which she does with loin at La Vara); vinegar is added toward the end so it doesn't permeate the meat but, rather, perfumes it. We joke about how vinaigrette in America is so assertive, but Raij admits to loving Catalina dressing, the nicer name for that manufactured "French dressing" from the 1950s, with its soft tangerine color and eternal shelf stability. One of its key ingredients is xanthan gum, which Raij now uses for her own vinaigrettes to help evenly distribute the vinegar over any salad.

SALAD OF GREEN APPLE, SHAVED FENNEL, CRUMBLED MORCILLA, AND APPLE CIDER VINAIGRETTE, FROM ALEX RAIJ, TXIKITO, EL QUINTO PINO, LA VARA, NEW YORK CITY SERVES 4

For the vinaigrette:

1 GRANNY SMITH APPLE

1 cup (240 ml) CIDER VINEGAR, use HIGH-QUALITY CIDER VINEGAR, *such as O-Med from Spain*

1 pinch SALT

1 cup (240 ml) OLIVE OIL

2 tablespoons XANTHAN GUM

Peel and grate the apple. In a small saucepan, combine the apples and half of the vinegar with just enough water to cover. Add the salt and bring to a simmer over medium heat. Cook until softened, about 2 minutes. Transfer to a blender, add the remaining vinegar, and blend on high speed. Slowly add the olive oil in a thin stream until fully incorporated. Season with salt. With the motor running, add half of the xanthan gum, then add the rest, if needed, until it barely gels. The vinaigrette can be kept, covered, in the refrigerator for a few days.

For the salad:

2 SMALL LINKS SPANISH OR ARGENTINE-STYLE MORCILLA (*blood sausage, no rice*), *casing removed, then crumbled* (about 5 ounces / 140 g)

1 to 2 tablespoons OLIVE OIL

¼ teaspoon CUMIN

GROUND WHITE PEPPER

SALT

2 LARGE BULBS FENNEL

2 GRANNY SMITH or FUJI APPLES, *unpeeled*

CILANTRO, *to garnish*

In a small frying pan, fry the morcilla in the olive oil over medium-low heat until the fat starts to render out, a couple of minutes. Then add the cumin and white pepper and salt to taste. Stir and continue to cook, breaking the sausage into a crumble with a wooden spoon, a few more minutes.

recipe continues on page 203

Salad of Green Apple,
Shaved Fennel, Crumbled Morcilla,
and Apple Cider Vinaigrette

Drain on a paper towel–lined plate and set aside, uncovered, so it stays dry and crispy. This will act as your crouton.

Trim the tops and bottoms of the fennel bulbs, then cut them in half.

Prepare a lightly salted ice bath.

Using a mandoline, shave the fennel from the cut sides into almost paper-thin ribbons. Hold the fennel in the ice bath until serving, up to 3 hours. When you're ready to use it, drain the fennel on paper towels.

Cut the apple, skin on, into thin matchsticks.

In a serving bowl, combine the apple, cilantro, and fennel and dress with vinaigrette to coat. Top with crumbled morcilla.

Eleven Madison Park, affectionately known by its acronym, EMP, sits at the base of a thirty-story Art Deco skyscraper whose imposing entrance is only surpassed by its grand dining room. I think of Daniel Humm, the towering Swiss-born chef who would easily be seven feet tall with a toque on, as being similar to his restaurant's architecture—unapproachable from afar but charming and contemplative once you meet him up close. Humm tells me that his kitchens use a lot of lime because it's very acidic but imparts very little taste; it achieves the sensation of acidity without overpowering the dish. EMP also uses a bit of white balsamic in their kitchen, which in Humm's mind is super clean with a touch of sweetness, and abides by his kitchen philosophy that "whatever ingredient goes on the plate should taste like the best version of itself."

Often, Humm uses vinegar as a texture modifier. During a talk at Harvard University, he stated three main purposes for vinegar: "It adds flavor, changes the structure of ingredients, and plays a role in preservation." He conducted an experiment with egg yolks, in which they were marinated in various vinegars for different amounts of time, many of which yielded creamy yolks, lightly pickled, and bursting like a sunny-side-up egg without ever having been cooked over heat. This method is used in EMP's Eggs Benedict dish, served in a caviar tin with a pickled quail egg, alongside mini English muffins designed to be eaten like blinis.

This high-concept brunch item reflects how Humm thinks about all of his menus, as heightened dining experiences framed with the comforts of relatable food memories. Consider an oyster: You can straightforwardly shuck one and eat it. Well, at EMP, theirs is dressed up a bit, with some crispy buckwheat and the chef d'oeuvre: mignonette snow. It's prepared by whisking the mignonette into liquid nitrogen until it hardens, then pulsing the flash-frozen liquid into a fine powder, creating a silken mouthful when dusted on top of the oyster.

OYSTERS WITH MIGNONETTE SNOW, FROM DANIEL HUMM, ELEVEN MADISON PARK, NEW YORK CITY SERVES 8

For the mignonette snow (due to this recipe's exactness, it's best to measure in grams):

200 grams CHAMPAGNE

300 grams CHAMPAGNE VINEGAR

100 grams WATER

10 grams SALT

10 grams SUGAR

20 grams BLACK PEPPERCORNS

200 grams SHALLOTS, *peeled and sliced*

LIQUID NITROGEN, *as necessary (Follow the recommended safety guidelines; this stuff is not for amateurs. Detailed handling instructions can be found in* Eleven Madison Park: The Cookbook.)

Combine the champagne, vinegar, water, salt, sugar, peppercorns, and shallots in a saucepan over medium heat, bring to a simmer, and cook for 1 minute. Strain the vinegar mixture into a bowl and let cool, then chill in the refrigerator until cold.

Fill a large bowl halfway full with liquid nitrogen. Slowly pour the vinegar mixture into the nitrogen, whisking to break up any large chunks. When the mixture is completely frozen, transfer to a food processor and grind to a fine powder. Keep frozen. Before you use the snow, it's best to put it in a cooler or plastic quart container for an hour, for the nitrogen to dissipate. The snow will keep in a cooler at room temperature for 3 to 4 hours and in a quart container in the freezer for 8 to 12 hours. Or, if you'd like to serve immediately, you can stir the snow in the bowl until it stops smoking, which means the nitrogen has boiled away. After that, it will still be quite cold for about 5 minutes, and after that you'll be good to go.

For the oysters:

8 OYSTERS, *preferably Widow's Hole from Long Island*

LUCKY SORREL LEAVES, *to garnish*

Shuck the oysters. Top with a bit of crispy buckwheat and spoon the mignonette snow over each oyster. Garnish with sorrel leaves. Serve on crushed ice.

Note: If you're wary of using liquid nitrogen, or just don't have a source for it, EMP offers another accoutrement that is equally good on top of an oyster: pickled mustard seeds. At the restaurant, they also serve it with crispy buckwheat, but you can use any puffed grain for texture.

Eleven Madison Park, Oysters with Mignonette Snow

PICKLED MUSTARD SEEDS, FROM DANIEL HUMM, ELEVEN MADISON PARK, NEW YORK CITY MAKES ABOUT 1 CUP (240 ML)

1 cup (240 ml) WHITE BALSAMIC VINEGAR

⅓ cup (65 g) SUGAR

2⅔ tablespoons WATER

2 teaspoons SALT

⅔ cup (192 g) YELLOW, BROWN, or MIXED MUSTARD SEEDS

Combine the vinegar, sugar, water, and salt in a medium bowl and whisk to fully dissolve the salt and sugar. Place the mustard seeds in a heat-resistant container. Bring the pickling liquid to a simmer in a saucepan over high heat. Pour the pickling liquid over the seeds to cover. Let cool to room temperature. Refrigerate overnight before using. Keep in the pickling liquid, refrigerated, for up to 2 weeks.

*You can blend this up to make a mustard that can be used for the Mustard Pretzel recipe on page 296.

In the big city, I knew there had to be chefs who made their own vinegar, but it took me a while to find one. When you walk into Betony in Midtown Manhattan, you're greeted by a marbled floor, a high ceiling, and a brushed black metal bar. On the day I visited while researching this book, Eamon Rockey, the restaurant's general manager, made his way down from the mezzanine, finely jacketed, and ushered me back upstairs. An Eleven Madison Park alum, Rockey was joined by chef Bryce Shuman, who also worked at EMP for six years, rising to the role of executive sous chef before leaving to open up Betony in 2013. Shuman was sitting upstairs at a square four-top, on the table a half-sheet tray and a number of plastic quart containers filled with vinegars: fig and currant, fennel, plum, cucumber . . . I had found what I was looking for: a restaurant that produces their own vinegar.

Their vinegar quest came about because Betony once had too many sixtels of beer for their draft lines. They took this as a sign, and fermented the spare sixtel to make a house malt vinegar that's been in rotation ever since. They worked with Garrett Oliver, brewmaster at Brooklyn Brewery, to pick which beer to try acidifying next. The malt vinegar has not moved too far away from the bar, as it's used in a cocktail, the Old Dog Shandy (see page 287), mixed with smoked honey and a dark porter over pebble ice, then lightly spritzed with a tobacco tincture that makes it feel (and smell) like you're having a drink with your pipe-smoking grandfather.

The fresh-vegetable or fruit-juice vinegars are done one of two ways: either a bit of sugar is added so there's enough sugar for a cider or champagne yeast to eat, or a neutral spirit, like vodka, is added until the liquid attains the right gravity (percentage of alcohol) to be efficiently converted. The cucumber's 9 to 9.5 percent ABV (alcohol by volume) is strong enough that you could catch a buzz by sniffing it. Once the acetobacter is introduced, Shuman lets it go for about a month or so in their boiler room, where temperatures are 85 to 90°F (30 to 32°C), which really pushes fermentation. Some are then aged in small wine fridges at about 62°F (17°C), together with a bunch of lactic ferments, like pickles, a bog butter buried in moss, and a Moroccan *smen*, another type of fermented butter.

An ultra-composed dish of chicken, cherry, and chanterelle (think elements like cherries glazed with cherry juice, vinegar, or glucose then stuffed with foie gras) uses an infused cherry vinegar to finish, made by macerating a ton of fresh cherries by weight in a champagne vinegar. But it is this playful take on what I like to think of as state-fair-food-meets-camping-snack that combines two of my favorite techniques, pickling and frying.

FRIED PICKLED BRUSSELS SPROUTS WITH TRAIL MIX YOGURT, FROM BRYCE SHUMAN, FORMERLY OF BETONY, NEW YORK CITY SERVES 2 TO 4

For the pickling liquid:

MAKES ABOUT 2 QUARTS (2 L)

4 cups (960 ml)
  CHAMPAGNE VINEGAR

2¼ cups (450 g) SUGAR

2¼ cups (540 ml) WATER

¼ cup (33 g) SALT

Combine all the ingredients in a large saucepan and whisk well to dissolve.

For the pickled Brussels sprouts:

2 pounds (910 g) MEDIUM
  BRUSSELS SPROUTS,
  *2 to 3 dozen depending on
  size, trimmed*

2 quarts (2 L) PICKLING
  LIQUID, *see above*

Put the Brussels sprouts in a heatproof container. Bring the pickling liquid up to a boil over high heat and pour over the Brussels sprouts. Allow the mixture to come down to room temperature, then cover and refrigerate.

For the tempura batter:

MAKES ABOUT 6 CUPS (1.4 L)

5 cups (1.2 L) WATER

1 cup (130 g) CORNSTARCH

2 cups (320 g) RICE FLOUR

1½ tablespoons SALT

1 teaspoon XANTHAN GUM

In a medium bowl, whisk the water, cornstarch, rice flour, and salt until fully incorporated. Whisk in the xanthan gum until completely hydrated and the mixture starts to thicken. Pour the batter into a whipped-cream dispenser and charge with two N_2O chargers.

*recipe continues
on page 210*

Fried Pickled Brussels Sprouts
with Trail Mix Yogurt

For the trail-mix yogurt:

MAKES ABOUT 3 CUPS (720 ML)

2 cups (480 ml) GREEK
  YOGURT

½ cup (75 g) DRIED
  CHERRIES, *roughly
  chopped*

¼ cup (30 g) PISTACHIOS,
  roughly chopped

1 tablespoon FRESH
  LEMON JUICE

1 teaspoon SALT, *or to taste*

In a large bowl, combine all the ingredients.

For the fried Brussels sprouts:

6 cups (1.4 L) RICE BRAN
  OIL, *vegetable or canola oil
  will also work*

PICKLED BRUSSELS
  SPROUTS, *see above*

1 cup (130 g) CORNSTARCH

TEMPURA BATTER,
  see page 208

SALT

Heat the oil in a deep fryer to 365°F (185°C).

In a large bowl, toss the pickled Brussels sprouts in the cornstarch. In another bowl, toss the Brussels sprouts with the tempura batter until they're fully coated.

To fry, remove a small batch of Brussels sprouts from the batter, shaking off any excess, and fry for about 2 minutes, until the batter is crispy. Remove from oil, drain on a paper towel, and salt immediately.

To assemble: When you're done frying, transfer the Brussels sprouts to a serving bowl, and serve with a bowl of trail mix yogurt for dipping.

To get to the Kuma Inn, you ascend the stairs to the second floor of a tenement building on New York City's Lower East Side, and there you'll find King Phojanakong in the corner, cooking up his mix of

Thai-Filipino food. His dad (King Sr.) is Thai, his mom Filipino. King grew up in Stuyvesant Town, a cluster of high-rise buildings east of Gramercy Park. It's a short subway ride away from Chinatown, where King was surrounded by Asian food as a kid. Those flavors stayed with him through his Michelin-starred kitchen training, and they inform the way he's refined the national dish of the Philippines: adobo.

Although the adobo method is indigenous to the Philippines, the adobo we know today is a fusion of Filipino, Spanish, and Chinese flavors. It's a popular dish among traveling seamen because of its long shelf life, the result of its high concentration of acidity and salt. Stewed meat, most often chicken or pork, is first marinated overnight, then cooked and (here's the game changer) pan-fried to finish. This adds another level of flavor and aromatizes the air while you impatiently wait for that first bite. The meat is so tender and sweet it sticks to your teeth; each bite will send your palate to paradise. King's mom still thinks she makes it better than he does.

CHICKEN ADOBO, FROM KING PHOJANAKONG, KUMA INN, NEW YORK CITY SERVES 4

1 WHOLE CHICKEN, about 3 pounds (1.4 kg), *cut into 8 pieces (2 wings, 2 drumsticks cutting off the thighs at the joint, and split breast, all of which a butcher can do)*

5 cloves GARLIC, *crushed*

1 teaspoon WHOLE BLACK PEPPERCORNS

3 BAY LEAVES

1 cup (240 ml) CANE VINEGAR or RICE WINE VINEGAR

¾ cup (180 ml) SOY SAUCE

1 cup (240 ml) WATER

STICKY RICE, *steamed, for serving*

In a medium saucepan, combine all the ingredients. If necessary, add more liquid (equal parts vinegar, soy, and water) to cover. Bring to a boil, reduce to a simmer, and cover. Braise 30 to 40 minutes or until tender.

recipe continues on page 212

Optional, but highly recommended: pan-fry the chicken in a sauté pan over medium-high heat, adding a tablespoon or two of oil for fat, until browned, a few minutes. Serve over steamed rice.

Chicken Adobo

If you're Pinoy (from the Philippines), it's practically obligatory for there to be a bottle of Suka Pinakurat on your table. A spicy vinegar and elemental ingredient for many *sawsawan* (dipping sauces), it's known as *sinamak*, and consists of garlic, chiles, and ginger steeped in coconut vinegar. When used sparingly it adds fiery brightness to a dish, and can turn a bland bowl of sticky rice into magic. Used liberally, it will clear your sinuses in that "hurts so good" kind of way.

SINAMAK (CHILE-INFUSED VINEGAR),
FROM KING PHOJANAKONG, KUMA INN, NEW YORK CITY
MAKES ONE 750-ML BOTTLE

1 HEAD GARLIC, WHOLE CLOVES, *peeled*

1 cup (150 g) WHOLE THAI CHILES, RED and GREEN

3 tablespoons SLICED GINGER, *1-inch (2.5-cm) pieces*

2 tablespoons WHOLE BLACK PEPPERCORNS

3 cups (720 ml) CANE, COCONUT, or RICE VINEGAR

Fill an empty 750-ml wine bottle with all the ingredients except the vinegar and shake to evenly distribute. Top off bottle with vinegar and close. Let the mixture infuse for a minimum of 3 days. The garlic may turn green, depending on the vinegar—it's just the garlic's sulfur compounds reacting to trace amounts of copper sulfate, and it's safe to eat.

This stuff is great as a dipping sauce with grilled and fried foods. You can combine it with a splash of soy or fish sauce for even more flavor. It will keep for 3 to 6 months in the refrigerator, or 1 to 2 months at room-temperature.

Would I tell you how great chile vinegar is with grilled foods and not offer a recipe? Here, Chicken Inasal, a popular dish from Bacolod City, known as the "City of Smiles," is considered Pinoy barbecue.

CHICKEN INASAL, FROM KING PHOJANAKONG, KUMA INN, NEW YORK CITY SERVES 4

2 pounds (910 g) CHICKEN THIGHS, 6 to 8 pieces

¼ cup (60 ml) CANOLA OIL

¼ cup (60 ml) FISH SAUCE

6 tablespoons (90 ml) COCONUT VINEGAR

¼ cup (60 ml) KALAMANSI JUICE, or LIME JUICE

1 tablespoon BROWN SUGAR

1 stalk LEMONGRASS, *crushed, cut into 2-inch (5-cm) pieces*

2 tablespoons SLICED GINGER

5 cloves GARLIC, *crushed*

Combine all the ingredients in a large bowl, toss to coat the chicken, and marinate for 2 to 4 hours in the refrigerator.

Set up a grill with a hot side and a cool side. Grill the chicken on indirect heat for about 40 minutes, flipping after 20 minutes. Take off the grill when the thighs reach an internal temperature of 160 to 165°F (71 to 74°C). In the Philippines, they use annatto oil to baste, which gives the chicken a sunny orange hue. You can try a 2:1 ratio of butter to chili oil for an extra kick.

As a child, whenever I played Risk, that strategic board game in which you conquer continents, my strategy was to control Oceania en route to taking over the world. I've always had an affinity for those countries on the Risk board (Australia, New Zealand, New Guinea and outlying islands) because of this. And, on a more elemental level, because purple is my favorite color, and Oceania is purple in the game of Risk. When I first stepped foot into Public, an AvroKO-designed restaurant in Manhattan's SoHo district, chef Brad Farmerie presented me with an assortment of ingredients I had never seen before, like bush tomatoes, a small shrub usually dried and ground for seasoning, and wattleseed, which tastes like a mix of a nutty coffee and dark chocolate, and I immediately felt the desire to explore further (if not to conquer the world).

Farmerie's interest in Australian and New Zealand cuisines (which includes kangaroo carpaccio, on his menu) caught my attention immediately. Public embraces dishes like Curry Coconut Laksa, a popular peppery noodle dish from Southeast Asia, widespread in Malaysia, and sundry spices from the Middle East to Japan, all of which reflect the international influences at play in the Oceanic region. Farmerie's formal training was in the United Kingdom, spending years under renowned New Zealand–born chef Peter Gordon of The Sugar Club in London. This may help explain Farmerie serving Tasmanian Sea Trout with Piccalilli (an English relish similar to that of the Branston Pickle, except seasoned with mustard and turmeric). Here the recipe calls for salmon.

SALMON CRUDO WITH PICCALILLI, FROM
BRAD FARMERIE, PUBLIC, NEW YORK CITY SERVES 4

For the piccalilli:

MAKES 1 QUART (960 ML)

- ½ head CAULIFLOWER, *cut into very small florets*, about 3 cups (55 g)
- 2 SPANISH ONIONS, *diced*, about 1½ cups (190 g)
- 3 SHALLOTS, *diced*, about 1 cup (140 g)
- ½ CUCUMBER, *peeled, seeds removed, diced*, about ¾ cup (100 g)
- SALT
- 1⅓ cups (315 ml) CHAMPAGNE VINEGAR
- 1⅓ (315 ml) cups CIDER VINEGAR
- ½ teaspoon ALEPPO PEPPER FLAKES
- ⅔ cup (130 g) SUPERFINE SUGAR
- ¼ cup (24 g) YELLOW MUSTARD POWDER
- 2 tablespoons GROUND TURMERIC
- 1½ tablespoons CORNSTARCH
- BLACK PEPPER

In a large bowl, combine the cauliflower, onions, and shallots with 1 tablespoon salt and refrigerate overnight.

recipe continues on page 216

The following day, rinse the cauliflower and onions in a colander under cold water, then toss with the cucumber and set aside.

Combine all the remaining ingredients except the cornstarch, salt, and pepper in a large saucepan and bring to a simmer over medium heat.

Combine the cornstarch with 2 tablespoons water, whisk to dissolve it, then whisk into the vinegar mixture.

Pour the vegetables into the vinegar mixture and take off the heat. Salt and black pepper to taste. Allow to cool. Cover and refrigerate for a few days before using.

For the salmon:

1 pound (455 g) FRESH KING SALMON FILLET, *skin off, pin bones removed, bloodline trimmed*

OLIVE OIL

FLAKY SEA SALT

SHICHIMI TOGARASHI, *optional*

Slice a few pieces of fish and lay them on a plate. Brush each piece with olive oil, sprinkle with flaky sea salt, and, if you like, add a sprinkle of shichimi togarashi. Add a small spoonful of piccalilli to each piece, anywhere from 1 teaspoon to 1 tablespoon—it's really up to your liking, as you'll have plenty of piccalilli to go around.

Salmon Crudo with Piccalilli

Farmerie has a considerable repertoire of savory to sweet chutneys, from mango-pineapple to apple-black pepper. Chutneys are essentially pickled produce chopped up and cooked down into a jam, however one that retains a sweet-and-sour aspect from their initial vinegar brine. During the British colonization of India in the early seventeenth century, travelers relied on eating preserved foods, a custom that had its beginnings as far back as 500 BC. The British empires exported this idea to their colonies, the reason we see chutney in Australia and even the United States. It's great on any grilled meat or even a cheese plate.

EGGPLANT CHUTNEY, FROM BRAD FARMERIE, PUBLIC, NEW YORK CITY MAKES ABOUT 16 OUNCES (480 ML)

1⅓ tablespoons CUMIN SEEDS

1⅓ teaspoons FENUGREEK SEEDS

1⅓ tablespoons YELLOW MUSTARD SEEDS

¼ cup GINGER, *sliced*

½ cup (70 g) GARLIC CLOVES

1⅓ tablespoons TURMERIC, *ground*

1 cup plus 2 tablespoons (300 ml) OLIVE OIL

⅔ cup plus 1 tablespoon (148 g) SUGAR

⅓ cup (75 ml) RED WINE VINEGAR, *preferably Cabernet Sauvignon*

⅓ cup (75 ml) WHITE WINE VINEGAR, *preferably Chardonnay*

2¼ teaspoons SALT, *plus more to taste*

2 teaspoons ALEPPO CHILI POWDER

½ MEDIUM YELLOW ONION, *diced*, about ⅔ cup (85 g)

¼ cup (25 g) MINCED GINGER

¼ cup (35 g) MINCED GARLIC

1 EGGPLANT, about 1½ pounds (680 g), *peeled and cut into ¾-inch (2-cm) cubes*

¼ to ½ cup CILANTRO CHIFFONADE, *depends on how much you want*

In a cast-iron skillet, dry-toast the cumin, fenugreek, and mustard seeds over medium heat until fragrant. Transfer to a spice mill or clean coffee grinder, and grind into a fine powder. Set aside.

In a food processor, combine the ginger, garlic, and turmeric and ¼ cup (60 ml) of the olive oil and process to a paste. Set aside.

In a small bowl, combine the sugar, vinegars, salt, and chile powder, and set aside.

Combine the onion, ginger, garlic, and and ⅓ cup (75 ml) of the remaining olive oil in a pan, heat to medium-low heat, and sweat until softened and golden, 8 to 10 minutes. Add the reserved spice mixture and spice paste and cook for 5 minutes. Add vinegar mixture and bring to a boil, then turn off the heat and let cool. This makes the chutney base.

Heat ¼ cup (60 ml) of the remaining olive oil in a large skillet, add half of the eggplant, and cook until golden and al dente, 5 to 7 minutes. Remove from the skillet and repeat with the remaining olive oil and eggplant. Season with a little salt, then add the cooked eggplant to the chutney base and bring to boil over high heat. Cook until the eggplant is soft but still holds its shape, 2 to 3 minutes. Cool, then put into a container and refrigerate at least overnight before using. Fold in chiffonade cilantro just before serving.

Before Andy Ricker's name became synonymous with northern Thai cuisine in the United States, he learned to cook in order to avoid doing dishes (he still hates washing dishes). Pok Pok, his restaurant with locations now in Portland, Oregon; Brooklyn, New York; and Los Angeles, offers a habit-forming selection of sour citrus and fresh herb flavors. Ricker's first revelation when he traveled to Thailand was that limes there actually impart a flavor, smell, and sweetness, and are used less for their acid than for their aromatic qualities. There's not a great deal of vinegar in Thai cooking, typically white distilled with different colored chiles for dipping sauces (*naam jim*) and the pervasive dish *prik nam som* (Thai chiles pickled in vinegar), but vinegar isn't really something you splash in the pan when cooking Thai food. Pickled fruit (green mangoes, *mayom* gooseberries) are eaten as snacks, like crunching a bag of chips, especially tasty with booze.

At Pok Pok there's a salted lime and a salted plum vodka Collins at the bar, both the beneficiaries of pickled products. Also on the counter, Ricker serves his Som drinking vinegars, in flavors ranging from tamarind to turmeric, but these don't have anything to do with Thailand. Som does mean "sour" in an old Thai dialect, but these vinegars are based on products from China, Taiwan, and Korea that Ricker found in Asian markets. They are essentially shrubs, the flavor of the fruit conveyed through a vinegar base. He uses them to complement spicy, bitter, and savory notes in his cooking, while also offering them as a mixer or nonalcoholic drink option.

THE MID-ATLANTIC

On a 200-plus-acre nature preserve in Delaplane, Virginia, a creek of contaminated water almost made it to the Potomac. Daniel Liberson's family bought the estate in 2006, and in a joint effort with the Nature Conservancy and the Army Corps of Engineers, set forth on the largest private undertaking of a stream restoration in Virginia's history. It had been ruined by herd mentality, of cattle that is, trampling the riverbanks and defecating into the water supply. The initiative to save Bolling Branch Stream involved the creation of a buffer comprised of thousands of native plants. Thanks to this, the stream now runs clear again, and the local flora—which includes paw-paw, spicebush, and mulberry—is thriving.

Liberson, with the humor of a Jewish comedian from the Catskills Borscht Belt and the cynicism of a seasoned cook, picked weeds off his family's estate, in time calling this practice "foraging," stockpiling ingredients to build his accidental vinegar company, Lindera Farms. Liberson collected ramps in the early spring, applied malolactic fermentation to the leaves, and began creating vinegar with a layered effect that tastes like "drunk nachos" in his own words. "There are notes of sour cream and chives!" His harvest year usually ends with ripe persimmons in the late fall, but unlike the wine calendar, in which a bottling is often released a full year or more later, Liberson is able to harness the true potential of his vinegars within a few months. He doesn't force the product, though, because as a vinegar maker, often you have to be a noninterventionist, equipped with patience and the knowledge that vinegar will be ready when it's ready.

Liberson every so often packs his car for a business road trip, stopping by some of the top fine dining restaurants in the country; Sean Brock of McCrady's bought his whole supply of last year's ramp vinegar. This is because Liberson sources well—like the glowing Golden Angels Apiary honey, and hickory syrup from Falling Bark Farm, where

Joyce and Travis Miller take only fallen bark from the shagbark hickory trees, a sustainable resource, and then roast it to create coffee and cigar-like smokiness, making for one of the more idiosyncratic vinegars I've ever had.

The Dabney in Washington, DC, aims to be the restaurant embodiment of the Mid-Atlantic. Jeremiah Langhorne is behind the undertaking. He too worked with Brock at McCrady's in Charleston, an obvious feeding ground for adventurous fermentation; when Langhorne relocated he had to reorient himself and discover what items could represent the region.

The Langhornes have been in Virginia since the seventeenth century, and Jeremiah's family were very good documentarians. His brother wrote a book on their genealogy, his grandfather made country hams, but as a kid he didn't see any relevance in these traditions. Langhorne has vowed to never let the past get away from him again, which may explain his fixation on Bay Sauce, a 160-year-old recipe found in a 1980s issue of *Good Housekeeping* magazine, to which his family had contributed recipes. Made from young black walnut leaves and used in many Virginia households as early as the 1820s, Bay Sauce has nothing to do with the Chesapeake region's Old Bay seasoning. A mix of fermented walnut leaves, wild ginger, horseradish, onions, garlic, cloves or allspice, cider vinegar, and salt, it's like mushroom-y ketchup, made sustainable with an overlooked but plentiful product source.

You'll have to go to The Dabney to try this Bay Sauce. I would offer the recipe, but it takes at least a year to make, and its umami-laced acidity needs to be continually tended to. Most of the vinegars made and used at the restaurant are for finishing dishes, more *à la minute* than annual.

VINEGAR BUTTER SAUCE, FROM JEREMIAH LANGHORNE, THE DABNEY, WASHINGTON, DC MAKES ABOUT ½ CUP (120 ML)

1 tablespoon GARLIC-INFUSED OLIVE OIL, *store-bought, or make your own by steeping peeled garlic in warm olive oil until fragrant*

1 tablespoon MINCED SHALLOT

1 splash VEGETABLE STOCK

2 tablespoons BUTTER

JUICE from a slice of LEMON

1 pinch SALT

1 pinch ESPELETTE PEPPER

2 tablespoons VINEGAR OF YOUR CHOICE, *try something clean, then work up to something complex*

Heat a sauté pan over medium heat, then add the garlic oil and minced shallots. Once the shallots begin to turn golden brown, add the vegetable stock. Remove from the heat and quickly whisk in butter, then add the lemon juice, salt, and pepper. Remove from the heat and add the vinegar. Season to taste. Serve over fish or vegetables.

It's called passive guidance, or that's what Isaiah Billington and Sarah Conezio of Keepwell Vinegar call their vinegar-making process. When I arrived to meet them in Washington, DC, where they had lined up a dozen or so vinegars in oblong bottles, hues of a muted rainbow. Ex–pastry chefs from Woodberry Kitchen in Baltimore, Maryland, they follow the ethos of chef-owner Spike Gjerde, a leader in localizing a sustainable pantry. After years spent working with sweets, it's ironic that Billington and Conezio use a minuscule amount of added sugar in their vinegars; rather, they look for raw materials to provide natural sucrose or glucose.

They've tried maple syrup, as well as sorghum, which, only if needed, is added to Concord grape, GoldRush apple, or beet vinegars. In one bottle we sampled, celery leaves imparted a slightly copper-like and oxidized flavor (think sucking on a penny), similar to that of sherry vinegar. It's interesting to visit a vinegar maker in the making; they officially launched just a few months prior to our meeting. It takes time to build an inventory, but this is also the time to dream up the product you're going to make next.

The historic Bloomindale neighborhood, part of DC's Northwest quadrant, is home to the much-beloved restaurant The Red Hen. The chef, Michael Friedman, grew up in a Jewish household in an Italian community, which explains the dynamism of his place. Reproducing the classics takes a courteous cook, and Friedman embraces the idea of period pieces like antipasti salad, redolent with dried oregano coating cubes of provolone and salami. The Red Hen's house caper vinaigrette is a nod to those salads of his youth.

Friedman uses these classic flavors in recipes like red-wine-vinegar-braised octopus, in which the vinegar breaks down the proteins, or by whipping red wine vinegar into homemade sausage, which produces a ragu with that same old-fashioned acidity. In his best Alsatian accent, Friedman quotes a mentor of his, Gabriel Kreuther, for whom he worked at The Modern in New York City: "Salt elevates flavor and acid pushes it through."

SQUID INK LINGUINI WITH CLAMS, PICKLED FRESNO CHILES, CHICKPEAS, PEA SHOOTS, AND BREAD CRUMBS, FROM MICHAEL FRIEDMAN, THE RED HEN, WASHINGTON, DC SERVES 2

For the pickled chiles:

MAKES ABOUT 2¹/₂ CUPS (600 ML)

2 cups (480 ml) CIDER VINEGAR

¹/₂ cup (100 g) SUGAR

¹/₄ cup (33 g) KOSHER SALT

3 cups (450 g) THINLY SLICED FRESNO CHILES

In a large bowl, combine the vinegar, sugar, and salt. Mix well. Add the chiles to the pickling liquid and refrigerate overnight. The chiles can ferment for a day at room temperature and will keep, refrigerated, for 2 weeks in the pickling liquid.

For the pasta:

2 tablespoon OLIVE OIL

4 tablespoons (15 g) THINLY SLICED SCALLIONS

8 ounces (225 g) CALAMARI, *cleaned and cut into strips*

1 cup (160 g) CHICKPEAS, *cooked and drained*

4 tablespoons (40 g) PICKLED FRESNO CHILES, *see recipe above*

¹/₂ cup (120 ml) WHITE WINE

4 tablespoons (55 g) UNSALTED BUTTER

8 ounces (225 g) FRESH SQUID INK LINGUINI

A healthy bunch of PEA TENDRILS

6 LARGE BASIL LEAVES, *roughly chopped*

SALT

¹/₄ cup (25 g) TOASTED BREAD CRUMBS

Bring a pot of water to a boil.

While the water is coming to a boil, heat a medium sauté pan over medium heat until hot. Add the olive oil, then add the scallions and sauté for 30 seconds. Add the calamari to the pan and increase the heat to high.

Squid Ink Linguini with Clams,
Pickled Fresno Chiles, Chickpeas,
Pea Shoots, and Bread Crumbs

226

Sauté the calamari for 1 minute, then add the chickpeas, chiles, white wine, and butter. Move the pan around to reduce the wine while emulsifying the butter, which will create a rich pan sauce. (This might take a couple of attempts to nail perfectly. The important thing is that you get a light, creamy sauce, and that it doesn't break.)

Drop the pasta into the water and cook until just al dente, about 1 minute. Drain the pasta and add to the pan. Add the pea tendrils and basil and remove the pan from the heat. Toss the pea tendrils in the pasta to just wilt, then add salt to taste.

Place the pasta in a bowl and top with the bread crumbs.

Friedman is also one of the sweetest chefs I've ever met, so to match his darling demeanor, I present to you an adaptation of his classic Italian dessert: a light, whipped, balsamic-inflected custard, served with ripe seasonal fruit that's been enhanced by a quick maceration in vinegar.

BALSAMIC ZABAGLIONE WITH PEACHES IN CHAMPAGNE VINEGAR, FROM MICHAEL FRIEDMAN, THE RED HEN, WASHINGTON, DC SERVES 4

4 PEACHES, *cut in half, pits removed*

¼ cup (60 ml) CHAMPAGNE VINEGAR

1 cup (240 ml) HEAVY CREAM

⅓ cup (75 ml) BALSAMIC VINEGAR

⅓ cup (75 ml) HONEY

5 LARGE EGG YOLKS

ZEST OF 1 LEMON, about 1 tablespoon

In a medium bowl, toss the peaches in the champagne vinegar and marinate for an hour in the fridge.

In a stand mixer, whip the heavy cream until soft peaks form, about 5 minutes. Transfer the whipped cream to a bowl and reserve in the refrigerator.

recipe continues on page 228

Fill a medium saucepan halfway with water. Heat the water until it comes to just under a boil—you want a good amount of steam. Maintain medium heat on the pot for the steam.

In a medium bowl, combine the balsamic vinegar, honey, egg yolks, and lemon zest. Place the bowl over the saucepan (it shouldn't be touching the water) and begin whisking. Rotate the bowl while whisking to ensure all the sauce is being moved.

After 5 to 7 minutes, the zabaglione should have almost doubled in size—if you run your whisk through it and the trail holds in the zabaglione, you're done. Remove the custard from the heat and whisk vigorously until it is cool to the touch.

Fold the whipped cream into the zabaglione. This will help keep its structure and add great texture and body. Reserve in the refrigerator or immediately spoon over peaches.

THE SOUTH

In Wise County, rural Virginia, the Appalachian Mountains play backdrop to the movie (named for the Loretta Lynn song) *Coal Miner's Daughter*. The film shows a community of laborers working menial jobs that were endemic to the area. Although he now runs the acclaimed restaurant McCrady's in Charleston, South Carolina, Sean Brock's heart is still in Appalachia where he was raised.

Brock is at the culinary forefront of preservation techniques and heirloom-seed saving, constantly questioning where our food traditions come from before they're gone. When he was growing up, his grandmother kept a vinegar mother under the sink, and it's still active to this day. Ask him and he'll recite you the story of Hoppin' John, a dish of black-eyed peas and rice, and those of other Lowcountry delicacies like cornbread, shrimp and grits, and fried chicken. But he'll soon turn the conversation to modern producers, like gristmill owner Glenn Roberts at Anson Mills and his Carolina Gold Rice, and Julian Van Winkle, master (whiskey) distiller at Pappy Van Winkle—all while downplaying his own accolades (of which there are many).

Brock may have ushered in a newfound respect for the grains and soil of his native lands, but he's more interested in paying it forward, in preserving these makers' craftsmanship, than he is in taking any credit. He, too, is an artisan, and his vinegar-making skills are part of fermenting folklore. He's developed dishes like Pig Tail Braised Collards in Milk Stout Vinegar and Charleston Ice Cream with Rice Wine Vinegar, but Brock's lightheartedness is revealed in his creation of Mountain Dew vinegar.

For his more common base ingredients, Brock uses a steam juice extractor, a pot within a pot that has a hose protruding out of the bottom. You can put whatever you hope to distill in the steaming basket on top, which then makes a consommé-like liquor that drips to the bottom. Brock uses neutral spirits to catch the flavorful liquid, and then ferments the mixture into vinegar. You can also use this method to infuse vinegar in thirty minutes or less. One of Brock's most spectacular dishes is Seasonal Tomatoes with Raspberry Vinegar. What makes it so special is that it's not fancy or highfalutin. It's for anyone to enjoy.

*Seasonal Tomatoes with
Raspberry Vinegar*

SEASONAL TOMATOES WITH RASPBERRY VINEGAR,
FROM SEAN BROCK, MCCRADY'S, CHARLESTON, SOUTH
CAROLINA SERVES 2

1 tablespoon or more
RASPBERRY VINEGAR,
preferably homemade

A few RIPE HEIRLOOM
TOMATOES, MIXED
VARIETIES, *cut into thick
slices or wedges*

FLAKY SEA SALT

Drizzle vinegar over fresh tomatoes, finish with salt, and enjoy!

Travis Milton comes from a similar background to that of Brock, even working at McCrady's, but Milton returned to the Appalachia of his youth, hoping to dig deeper into its regional cuisine, part of one of the most diverse foodsheds in North America. There are ingredients that aren't available outside of the area, like hickory cane corn and greasy beans.

In West Virginia, a strong community of coal diggers from Italy brought Old World meals with them into the mines, like pepperoni rolls, small breads stuffed with spicy sausage that would last a day and a half in their back pockets, the spicy oil acting as a preservative. Milton knew that vinegar must have also been part of the local diet, especially since no citrus grows in those mountains, so he went in search of signs of fermentation.

Milton grows seeds that have been in his family for ten generations, turning a simple kilt (wilted) lettuce salad into a meal with historical resonance. His grandfather had an apple orchard; from this his grandmother would make apple butter, and the peels and cores were mainly used for (pig) slop, but they'd save some scraps to ferment into vinegar to dress their greens.

As a cook, Milton went into the woods to spend time consulting for Sandor Ellix Katz, a food writer and author of *Wild Fermentation* who lives in Eastern Tennessee, the heart of Appalachia. Whenever they came across molds they didn't recognize, they'd call Milton's father, a microbiologist, to ask, "What microbes are working here, and what will kill us?" Milton will admit that fermentation takes some trial and error. Sorghum was a tough one, and after a two-stage ferment, it got really, really funky, so much so that he couldn't bring himself to taste it.

Yes, vinegar can sometimes seem to have a life of its own, but most of Milton's recipes are straightforward and they're all totally trustworthy. He loves turnip green vinegar, used to deglaze poaching turnips. The result is turnip flavor times a thousand, and the unassertive root vegetable all of a sudden delivers an absolute pop. Speaking of soda (pop), Milton's personal stash of Cheerwine vinegar is no fable, and if you're lucky, you may someday try his Cheerwine Pie.

Chris Shepherd loves preserving; the man makes his own miso, gochujang, shrubs, and vinegar. While cooking at Underbelly in Houston, Texas, his interest in fermentation became curriculum at nearby Rice University. In exchange for teaching students how to cook, Shepherd's staff can use the university's science labs for certain kitchen preparations. The deal has enabled Shepherd to say yes to farmers who come in with forty extra cases of Korean plums, or bumper crops of satsuma citrus: no produce left behind. A ten-thousand-square-foot building at Rice houses eighty gallons of vinegar. Shepherd and the university are together exploring the possibilities of creating a fermentable foodshed.

Vinegar is the key to offsetting Underbelly's highly spiced Creole food, a convergence of cuisines that highlights the best of Houston's diverse food culture, which ranges from Southern barbecue to Vietnamese cooking. It was in a 1960s pamphlet called "Hillbilly Cooking, Mountaineer Style" that Shepherd first came across vinegar pie. This Depression-era recipe used vinegar instead of citrus to create a custard base (similar to that of chess pie, a Southern specialty).

Intrigued, Shepherd asked his pastry chef to give it a shot. When a customer called serendipitously to inquire if they made vinegar pie, a favorite from her childhood, Shepherd asked her to bring in her family's recipe for reference, and the rest is history.

VINEGAR PIE, FROM CHRIS SHEPHERD, UNDERBELLY, HOUSTON, TEXAS SERVES 8

For the crust:

11 tablespoons (155 g) BUTTER

⅓ cup (75 ml) SUGAR

1 LARGE EGG

1 teaspoon (260 g) VANILLA EXTRACT

2 cups ALL-PURPOSE FLOUR

½ teaspoon SALT

In a stand mixer, mix the butter and sugar until creamy. Add the egg and vanilla and mix until combined. Add the flour and salt and briefly mix just to combine; do not overmix. Wrap the dough in plastic wrap and place in the refrigerator for 30 minutes.

Preheat the oven to 350°F (175°C). Spray a 13-inch (33-cm) tart pan with cooking spray. Remove the dough and roll it ½ inch (12 mm) thick on a floured surface. Press the dough into the prepared tart pan, add weights of your choosing (e.g., pie weights or beans in aluminum foil), and bake for 15 minutes, or until the edges start to brown. Remove the weights and finish baking until the bottom of the crust is completely cooked, about 10 minutes more.

Vinegar Pie

For the filling:

4 LARGE EGGS

2 cups (400 g) SUGAR

5 tablespoons (38 g)
    CORNSTARCH

¼ teaspoon SALT

JUICE of ½ LEMON

4 tablespoons (60 ml)
VINEGAR OF YOUR
CHOICE, *use a neutral-
toned one, so it doesn't color
the custard*

2 cups (480 ml) WATER

2 tablespoons BUTTER

1 teaspoon VANILLA BEAN
PASTE, *or use extract if
needed*

**Put the eggs and sugar in a large saucepan and whisk together.
Add the cornstarch and salt and whisk until smooth. Mix in
the lemon juice, vinegar, and water, and place over medium
heat, whisking constantly so it does not burn, and bring to a
boil. Boil for 1 full minute, then remove from the heat and add
the butter and vanilla. Pour into the baked tart shell and place
plastic wrap directly onto the surface of the pie. Chill overnight
before serving.**

When Poole's Diner opened in Raleigh, North Carolina, in 1945, the
only thing you could order there was pie. By the early 1950s, Poole's
had expanded their menu to become a luncheonette, with red leather
banquettes, a horseshoe bar, all the features that we associate with a
retro diner. For decades it was stuck in time, until Ashley Christensen
came along. Christensen restored an institution, but she also revived
a city's passion for what a slice of pie represents, which was part of her
larger agenda: to preserve Poole's for years to come. She also updated
the chalkboard menus and added a section dedicated to one of her
favorite food groups: salad. Now she offers farm-fresh greens dressed
in lively vinaigrettes, a recipe for one of which follows.

BLACKBERRY BANYULS VINAIGRETTE, FROM ASHLEY CHRISTENSEN, POOLE'S DINER, RALEIGH, NORTH CAROLINA
MAKES ABOUT 1¹/₂ CUPS (360 ML)

1 tablespoon MINCED SHALLOT

¹/₃ cup (75 ml) BANYULS VINEGAR

1 tablespoon HONEY

8 FRESH BLACKBERRIES, *gently crushed with a fork,* about ¹/₄ cup (60 ml)

SALT

¾ cup (180 ml) NEUTRAL VEGETABLE OIL

FRESHLY GROUND BLACK PEPPER

In a small bowl, cover the shallots with the vinegar and marinate for 15 minutes. This allows the shallots to bleed flavor directly into the vinegar and to soak up some of the vinegar so they will pack a sharp pickle-like punch, even after the oil is added.

Whisk in the honey, blackberries, and a pinch of salt. Be sure the honey is totally incorporated into the vinegar, because if it isn't it won't fully do its job as a binding agent. Pour the oil into a measuring cup with a pouring spout. Begin whisking the vinegar mixture in a circular motion. Either use a bowl with a rubberized bottom or place a damp towel underneath the bowl to keep it from spinning as you whisk. Slowly drizzle the oil into the vinegar mixture in a thin, steady stream, aiming it at the side of the bowl so that it is taken up into the current of the vinegar whirlpool; avoid pouring directly into the center of the bowl, as there is not as much vinegar there and the oil will be less likely to emulsify. Whisk continuously until all of the oil is added to the bowl.

Taste the vinaigrette and season with salt. If you underseason at this point, it will make a more versatile base for pairing with other ingredients of varying salt levels.

Try serving this vinaigrette with a plate of country ham, paper-thin Sprite melon, and burrata, or simply on peppery salad greens like arugula or red mustard leaves.

When fig season is over, Hugh Acheson makes fig vinegar. Centrally located in and around Athens and Atlanta, Georgia, Acheson has put up a mini-empire built on a wholesome philosophy rooted in age-old Southern cooking practices. A Canadian from Ottawa, he found a second home, or homecoming of sorts, in his adopted cities, married a Georgia native, and made it his mission to feed his children in a way that also nourishes their minds. Food doesn't always have to adhere to strict rules and systems, but it can be a source of valuable life lessons. Even a big old piece of braised pork shoulder can lend credence to the axiom—"It takes a village"—a butcher, a farmer, and a vinegar maker all played a part in helping to satisfying your soul.

Blackberry Banyuls
Vinaigrette

CIDER-VINEGAR BRAISED PORK SHOULDER WITH LEEKS, APPLE, AND SWEET POTATO GREENS, FROM HUGH ACHESON, FIVE & TEN, ATHENS, GEORGIA; EMPIRE STATE SOUTH, ATLANTA, GEORGIA SERVES 8

5 pounds (2.3 kg) WHOLE BONE-IN PORK SHOULDER

4 teaspoons KOSHER SALT, *plus more to taste*

1 teaspoon FRESHLY GROUND BLACK PEPPER

1 tablespoon CANOLA OIL

1 ONION, *peeled and thinly sliced*

2 CELERY STALKS, *thinly sliced*

4 cloves GARLIC, *thinly sliced*

1¾ cups (420 ml) APPLE CIDER VINEGAR

4 BAY LEAVES

3 sprigs FRESH THYME

3 cups (720 ml) CHICKEN STOCK

8 MEDIUM LEEKS, *dark green parts removed and sliced into ½-inch (12-mm) rings*

1 teaspoon BUTTER

½ cup (120 ml) OLIVE OIL

1 teaspoon DIJON MUSTARD

2 CRISP RED APPLES, *such as Fuji, cores removed and thinly sliced with the skin on*

1 pound (455 g) SWEET POTATO GREENS, *or any hearty greens, washed and dried*

Preheat the oven to 325°F (165°C).

Pat the pork shoulder well with paper towels. Season the pork shoulder with 2 teaspoons of the salt and the black pepper and let sit at room temperature for 15 minutes.

Heat the canola oil in a large braising pan or Dutch oven over medium-high heat until barely smoking. Sear the seasoned pork shoulder in the hot oil for 5 minutes on each side, or until the pork has a nice, caramel-brown crust. Remove the pork shoulder from the pan and rest it at room temperature.

Lower the heat to medium, add the onion and celery, and cook, stirring occasionally, until the onion and celery are softened and slightly browned, 8 minutes. Add the garlic and 1½

recipe continues on page 240

Cider-Vinegar Braised Pork Shoulder with Leeks, Apple, and Sweet Potato Greens

239

cups (360 ml) of the apple cider vinegar, raise the heat to high, and cook for another 8 minutes, or until the liquid has reduced by half. Add the bay leaves, thyme, chicken stock, 1 teaspoon of the remaining salt, and the pork.

Cover the pan with a lid, or use aluminum foil if you don't have a lid, and place the pan in the oven for 1½ hours. Carefully turn over the pork shoulder, cover again, and cook for another 1½ hours. Add the leeks to the pan and evenly distribute them, making sure they are immersed in the liquid, then cover again and cook for 45 minutes, or until the leeks are tender. Remove the pan from the oven and carefully take out the pork shoulder and leeks, and let them rest at room temperature. Leave the oven on.

Place the pan on medium-high heat, remove the bay leaves and thyme sprigs, and cook for 20 to 25 minutes, or until the braising liquid has reduced to a light gravy consistency. Remove the pan from the heat and add the cooked leeks and butter to the pan, stirring to melt the butter.

Place the pork shoulder on a baking sheet and put back in the oven for 10 minutes, or until it warms through.

In a large bowl, combine the remaining ¼ cup (60 ml) vinegar, the remaining 1 teaspoon salt, the olive oil, and the mustard and whisk well to form a vinaigrette. Add the apples and sweet potato greens to the bowl and mix well. Add another pinch of salt if needed.

Use two forks to tear the pork into chunks. To serve, spoon some of the leek mixture onto a plate, place torn chunks of the pork shoulder on top of the leeks, and spoon a little sauce from the pan over the pork. Serve with the salad.

Growing up, Edward Lee's family cupboard was full of kimchi made by his grandmother. Except for some rice vinegar in *naengmyeon* buckwheat noodles, a dish with a gochujang (spicy fermented chili paste) base, sesame oil, and a ton of acidity via vinegar, his upbringing was all but lacto-fermented. Born in Brooklyn, Lee traveled to Louisville with his Korean pantry, literally and figuratively, amalgamating his instinctive cuisine into his restaurant, 610 Magnolia. There he has his own greenhouse and growing program, and anything that comes out of the ground may very well be made into a pickle, even kimchi.

Lee has added homemade persimmon vinegar to his supply, a technique taught to him by Japanese food writer Nancy Singleton Hachisu. He leaves the persimmons to mature in his backyard, then smashes up the fruit, adds them to a big crockpot, covers it with cheesecloth, and leaves it to ferment for a minimum of three months. This process starts every fall, and once a week Lee checks in on its progress: he makes sure there's not too much mold, and during rainy days, he'll bring it inside. The vinegar is ready by spring, but it only nets about five gallons and is used sparingly at his restaurants. Considered an annual tradition, it's signal to the splendors of delayed seasonality, a time to reflect, and to look forward to starting over.

GOCHUJANG WINGS WITH ALABAMA WHITE SAUCE, FROM EDWARD LEE, 610 MAGNOLIA, LOUISVILLE, KENTUCKY SERVES 2 TO 4

Lee lacquers his chicken wings with funky fermented gochujang glaze and, in keeping with most Korean food, offsets its sweetness by adding acid, this time in the form of Alabama White Sauce.

12 WHOLE CHICKEN WINGS, *tips on*

SALT

BLACK PEPPER

For the marinade:

½ cup (120 ml) GOCHUJANG

6 tablespoons (90 ml) SWEETENED CONDENSED MILK

2 tablespoons FISH SAUCE

1½ tablespoons WORCESTERSHIRE SAUCE

1 tablespoon APPLE CIDER VINEGAR

1 tablespoon SESAME OIL

recipe continues on page 242

Preheat the oven to 300°F (150°C).

Clean the wings and pat them dry. Season generously with salt and black pepper. Let the salt absorb for 20 minutes at room temperature.

Meanwhile, make the marinade by whisking together all the ingredients in a small bowl. Brush half of the marinade onto the wings, set on a rack on a baking sheet, and bake for 30 minutes.

Turn heat up to 425°F (220°C), take the wings out of the oven, and brush with another smooth layer of marinade, leaving some for a final brushing. Return to the oven, roast for another 10 minutes, and add yet another layer of marinade. Roast for 5 to 10 minutes more, until the wings are nicely browned and cooked in the middle.

Alternatively, if you have a smoker, smoke the wings at 225°F (110°C) for 1 hour. Remove from the smoker and brush additional marinade onto the wings. Roast in a 425°F (220°C) oven for 8 to 10 minutes, until browned and crispy on the outside.

For the sauce:

1 CUP (240 ML) MAYONNAISE, *Duke's preferred*

¼ cup (60 ml) APPLE CIDER VINEGAR

1 tablespoon YELLOW MUSTARD

1 tablespoon PREPARED HORSERADISH

2 cloves GARLIC, *minced*

2 teaspoons WORCESTERSHIRE SAUCE

½ teaspoon CELERY SEEDS

¼ teaspoon SMOKED PAPRIKA

SALT and BLACK PEPPER

In a medium bowl, whisk everything together and chill for at least 30 minutes. Salt and black pepper to taste. Best if made a day ahead. Use as a dipping sauce for the wings.

Gochujang Wings with
Alabama White Sauce

THE MIDWEST

There once was a basement in Cleveland, Ohio, overflowing with carboys of fermenting beer and wine. Tired of paying Williams-Sonoma prices for specialty vinegars, chef Jonathon Sawyer saw an opportunity to stock his own pantry without breaking the bank, and Tavern Vinegar Company was born. Sawyer's house was built during the mid-1800s, and its original cold cellar fluctuated between 50°F (10°C) and 70°F (21°C), a perfect place and range for fermenting. Sawyer got his hands on exclusive wines, like Jean-Louis Chave, Côte Rôtie from Gaillard 1994, and bottles of 1980s Bollinger, all of which either couldn't be sold on the market or were supposedly corked. He turned these rough gems into precious barrel-aged vinegars and supplied his restaurants (Greenhouse Tavern, Noodle Cat) with the majority of their bases for vinaigrettes, pickles, marinades, poaching liquids, braising, and the occasional bordelaise sauce. Production having outgrown his basement (even after moving houses), Sawyer continues to expand his vinegar business, partnering with Middle West Spirits in Columbus, in hopes of further fermenting craft beer, wine, and sake vinegars for use in all his restaurants.

The Corn Belt is generally defined as Illinois, Iowa, Minnesota, and Nebraska, the top four corn-producing states in the nation, though it is sometimes said to include parts of Indiana, Kentucky, Michigan, Ohio, North and South Dakota, and Wisconsin relies heavily on agricultural businesses to boost its economy, so I assumed there must be somebody growing something there that sooner or later ferments—with any luck, by design.

My research took me up to Cody, Nebraska, where George Paul Johnson first planted grapes in 1999. The Sandhills region, half prairie and half dunes, is unforgiving, especially during the harsh, snowy winters, so it took a while, but eventually George Paul landed on a few varietals that could withstand the climate and short growing seasons: Brianna, Prairie Red, and Temparia.

The first wines were remarkably fruity and balanced with a nice touch of acidity, reminding George Paul of balsamic. This inspired him and his family to give vinegar making a go, and they applied for, and were given, a Nebraska Agricultural Innovation and Value-Added Agriculture grant. A decade after those first vines, they opened a facility to process hundreds of gallons a year of red, white, raspberry, and apple wines into vinegar. Chefs in Lincoln and Omaha, in Chicago and St. Louis, now have their own local vinegar maker who uses the same original cultures as he did a decade ago. George Paul even produces balsamic-style vinegar, named "Emilia" after his daughter (and with an echo of Reggio Emilia, where some balsamic is from), which takes about five years to make. Because of its popularity, there's now a waiting list, proof that good things come to those who wait.

In my wife's hometown of Clarkston, Michigan, there's an old church that twenty years ago was converted into Clarkston Union ("The Union"), home of the best mac and cheese in the country, if not the world. I swear, go and try to find a better one. It's made with cream sauce layered with slices of yellow Pinconning, an aged Colby-style, semi-soft, cow's-milk cheese made in Michigan, then topped by a crave-worthy crunchy crust of sharp cheddar and panko. Proprietors Ann Stevenson and Curt Catallo recently sold their millionth mac. Their comfort dish has been christened by musician and local resident Kid Rock as "the most macked" and endorsed by Guy Fieri on his Food Network show *Diners, Drive-Ins and Dives.*

A couple of blocks away in this small town, Ann and Curt also operate Union Woodshop, a barbecue joint with a back-lot smoker that has been burning at a constant low temperature since the day they opened in 2009. Chef Aaron Cozadd didn't want to restrict himself to a single style of BBQ. He knew that a good rub and some time with smoldering hickory wood was enough to make very tasty meat, from beef brisket (try the burnt ends!) to half chickens. However, Cozadd focused on a set of regional sauces that could transport a diner to places like Memphis, Tennessee, or Lockhart, Texas.

I usually reach for their Raleigh, North Carolina, vinegar-based sauce, as well as their Holly Hill, South Carolina, mustardy variety, both of which beg to be poured over pulled pork. But here's the pro tip: order the Porker, a house-ground pork patty with Michigan maple bacon, house-made hot links (sausages), pickled chiles, and cold-smoked cheddar, a mighty burger/sandwich with a daub of South Carolina mayo on top (made by spiking mayonnaise with the aforementioned BBQ sauce at a 1:1 ratio) that takes this impressive stack of a meal into the stratosphere.

NORTH CAROLINA BBQ SAUCE, FROM AARON COZADD, UNION WOODSHOP, CLARKSTON, MICHIGAN

MAKES ABOUT 1 QUART (1 L)

2 tablespoons KOSHER SALT	¼ cup (55 g) BROWN SUGAR
2 teaspoons CAYENNE	¼ cup (60 ml) KETCHUP
1 to 2 tablespoons RED PEPPER FLAKES, *or up to 3, depending on your heat level preference*	3½ cups (840 ml) CIDER VINEGAR

In a medium bowl, mix all the ingredients together, adding the vinegar last. Transfer to a jar, cover, and let it sit overnight in the fridge for the flavors to bloom. It will keep covered in the refrigerator for up to 1 month.

SOUTH CAROLINA BBQ SAUCE, FROM AARON COZADD, UNION WOODSHOP, CLARKSTON, MICHIGAN

MAKES ABOUT 1 QUART (1 L)

2½ cups (600 ml) YELLOW MUSTARD

1 cup (240 ml) CIDER VINEGAR

¾ cup (165 g) BROWN SUGAR

½ to 1 tablespoon PAPRIKA, *depending on your heat level preference, I like to use smoked*

⅔ tablespoon WORCESTERSHIRE SAUCE

½ to 1 tablespoon CRACKED BLACK PEPPER, *to taste*

⅔ tablespoon CAYENNE

In a medium bowl, mix all the ingredients together. It can be served immediately, though the flavors will come together more if left to sit overnight. It will keep covered in the refrigerator for up to 1 month.

Some barbecue purists think adding a sauce is sacrilege, way too sweet for the meat; it's the vinegar that can save a sauce from becoming too saccharine. Cozadd sought to show vinegar's utility in confectionary too, and turned to a childhood favorite of his called "sea foam." Also known as honeycomb candy, it is often sold in its chocolate-dipped form, so most people are unaware of what's underneath: a light and airy honeyed bite. Its characteristic crunch comes from a reaction between baking soda and vinegar; like a middle school science fair experiment, it bubbles up and creates air pockets that form a unique structure. Again, Cozadd likes delivering diverse flavors around a central dish or ingredient; here, the sea foam candy can be topped with chile flakes, fennel seeds, or lavender.

SEA FOAM CANDY, FROM AARON COZADD, UNION WOODSHOP, CLARKSTON, MICHIGAN
MAKES ABOUT 1 POUND (455 G) CANDY

2¼ cups (450 g) SUGAR

3 tablespoons HONEY or CORN SYRUP

¼ cup (60 ml) CIDER VINEGAR, *though you can experiment with different types*

1 cup (240 ml) WATER

1 tablespoon plus 1 teaspoon BAKING SODA

Toppings, enough to liberally sprinkle on top:

ALEPPO CHILE FLAKES

LAVENDER FLOWERS

TOASTED FENNEL SEEDS

Optional (but highly recommended): Dip to coat in MELTED TEMPERED MILK or DARK CHOCOLATE

Before you begin, have a whisk, heatproof spatula, and baking sheet with a silicone mat.

Combine everything but the baking soda in a deep pot; the mixture will foam up to at least twice its size, if not more. Place over high heat, cover, and bring the mixture to a boil. The lid will prevent sugar from crystallizing on the sides of the pan.

As water begins to cook off, the boiling will become louder. Affix a candy thermometer and bring the boiling mixture to 290°F (145°C).

Carefully whisk in the baking soda, stirring rapidly to incorporate it and then stopping quickly to allow the air bubbles to form. Immediately pour it out onto the lined baking sheet and sprinkle your toppings on one side. Let cool for 45 minutes to 1 hour, then break into bite-size pieces and enjoy. Store in an airtight container in a dry, cool place. It will keep for weeks.

Sea Foam Candy

When I visit my in-laws during Christmas, or anytime I'm an hour's drive from Ann Arbor, Michigan, I make my pilgrimage to the Midwest food mecca that is Zingerman's.

Co-owner Ari Weinzweig attended the University of Michigan and graduated with a degree in Russian history, but while washing dishes at a local restaurant he learned that he loved the food business. In 1982, he and partner Paul Saginaw started a delicatessen, which drew hungry campus dwellers for sandwiches. The shelves were stocked with local and international specialty food items, some exclusive to Zingerman's.

I've always been impressed with their vinegar wall, which features dozens of producers, and the best part is that you're allowed to taste a sample of any product available! While I've done a lot of tastings there, I was most excited to talk to Weinzweig and managing partner Grace Singleton about their selection process, and what they look for in a quality vinegar. Singleton, an avid biker, spoke of vinegar's healthful and helpful properties in relieving leg cramps by combating the buildup of lactic acid. Ari focused on taste and started opening bottles of Martin Pouret's Orléans vinegars from France and La Vecchia Dispensa's balsamic from Italy, both producers that I had recently visited.

Having tasted these products in their natural environments, I was curious to see how they seemed to a retail consumer. Ari believes "anyone can learn to tell the difference," that if you spend time tasting any single ingredient you learn to detect what you like and what you don't. Zingerman's looks for flavor carried by tradition: A story sells, but it still has to taste good.

Paul Virant thinks of his Chicago restaurant Vie as a "preservation kitchen," also the title of his cookbook, which guides the reader on how to cook with pickles, preserves, and *aigre-doux*—a sweet-sour concoction that can be used to season foods throughout the year. Before opening Vie in 2004, Virant's then-girlfriend (to whom he's now married) had given him a vinegar culture, and both relationships have been growing ever since. Virant grew obsessed with preserving, found an Alsatian jam maker, Christine Ferber, who had already published an aigre-doux book, and went to France to take a class with her.

Ferber built balanced flavor from mountain berries and their complementary spices to enrich reduction sauces in a way that Virant had never experienced. He left envisioning an elderberry aigre-doux, maybe glazing a duck breast with a syrupy condiment, and a shrub (the drink) using the fruit of shrubs (berries). Pairing the natural tannins in berries with that of vinegar accentuates the innate sweetness of the protein, just as with a fine wine. Virant also had the thought of using a more vegetal profile, preserving the beginning of spring with green garlic, carrots, and radish, which one can imagine served with an autumnal lamb roast.

ELDERBERRY AIGRE-DOUX, FROM PAUL VIRANT, VIE, CHICAGO, ILLINOIS MAKES 1 QUART (1 L)

1 cup (240 ml) RED WINE

⅓ cup (75 ml) RED WINE VINEGAR

½ cup (100 g) SUGAR

¼ teaspoon SALT

¼ teaspoon ANISE SEED

¼ teaspoon WHOLE CLOVES

¼ teaspoon BLACK PEPPER

¼ teaspoon GROUND NUTMEG

¼ teaspoon WHOLE ALLSPICE

5 cups (500 g) ELDERBERRIES

Combine the wine, vinegar, sugar, salt, and spices in a large saucepan and bring to a boil. Pack the elderberries into 3 clean, warm canning jars. Strain the preserving liquid and fill the jars with the hot liquid, heated to 180°F (80°C). Seal with 2-piece canning lids. Process the filled and covered jars in a boiling water canner for 30 minutes (begin counting the processing time when the water returns to a boil). At the end of the processing time, remove the jars and cool. Store sealed jars in a cool, dry location. Once open, it will keep for 1 month in the refrigerator.

SPRING GARLIC, CARROT, AND RADISH
AIGRE-DOUX, FROM PAUL VIRANT, VIE, CHICAGO, ILLINOIS
MAKES 2 QUARTS (2 L)

1 cup (135 g) GREEN
GARLIC, *sliced*

¼ cup (60 ml) OLIVE OIL

⅓ cup (40 g) CARROTS,
cut into coins

⅓ cup (40 g) RADISHES,
cut into quarters

¼ cup (60 ml) HONEY

¼ cup (60 ml) CHAMPAGNE
VINEGAR

SALT and BLACK PEPPER

¾ cup (40 g) FLAT-LEAF
PARSLEY LEAVES,
chopped

In a saucepan over medium heat, cook garlic in olive oil until translucent, a few minutes. Add the carrots and cook for another minute, then add the radishes and cook for another minute. Add the honey and vinegar and cook for 1 to 2 minutes, until everything holds together a bit. Season with salt and black pepper, then add the parsley.

Follow the canning instructions for the Elderberry Aigre-Doux.

THE WEST COAST

For a city that's only seven miles square, San Francisco has a disproportionate influence at the vanguard of the greater food movement in this country. Visit the Ferry Plaza Farmers Market—one of the foremost forums for culinary interchange in the United States—early on a Saturday morning, and you'll see the city's top chefs with their wheelie carts collecting inspiration at every stall. The quality of the produce is so high that you can put an unadorned piece of fruit on a plate and call it an appetizer. What's fascinating to see, of course, is how the chefs interpret and prepare such pristine goods.

Nick Balla and Cortney Burns are masterful when it comes to manipulation. At Bar Tartine, their walls were a library of foodstuffs in a state of transformation, which they've now carried on to their new project, Motze, a temporary, Japanese-influenced restaurant. They make their own cheeses, cure their own fish roe, sprout grains for bread and porridge, and culture butter to spread on top. I have had some of the most stimulating meals of my life there. Their way of preserving food is about safekeeping, capturing ingredients precisely at their most flavorful moment and transforming them into something new and somehow inevitable.

WINTER VEGETABLE ESCABECHE, FROM NICK BALLA AND CORTNEY BURNS, FORMERLY OF BAR TARTINE, SAN FRANCISCO, CALIFORNIA MAKES ABOUT 2 QUARTS (2 L)

This winter dish of pickled vegetables uses a fresh pear cider vinegar that Balla and Burns start in the early fall, when pears are at the peak of their season. They tend to buy lots and juice the ugly ones. These blemished fruits are cheaper than their prettier counterparts, which makes them ideal for making vinegar.

recipe continues on page 255

Winter Vegetable
Escabeche

Vegetables:

4 cups, about 2 pounds,
  *roughly chopped, any
  assortment of the following*:
  TURNIPS, KOHLRABI,
  CARROTS, FENNEL,
  ONION, WINTER
  SQUASH or PUMPKIN,
  RUTABAGA

For the pear syrup:

1 quart (960 ml) PEAR
  CIDER OR JUICE,
  store-bought or homemade

In a medium saucepan over low heat, reduce the pear cider or juice by 6 to 8 times its original volume. It should be sweet and as thick as honey is at room temperature. Stir frequently. Or, as an alternative method, reduce the juice in a stainless steel pan in a food dehydrator—no stirring required.

*For the brine (make enough to
  cover the vegetables):*

3 to 4 parts PEAR VINEGAR
  to 1 part PEAR SYRUP

A few CLOVES of CHOPPED
  GARLIC

1 SMALL KNOB of GINGER

1 small bunch STRONG
  AROMATIC HERBS,
  fresh or dried: SAGE,
  FIR TIPS, THYME,
  MARJORAM, and/or DILL

1 tablespoon BLENDED
  SPICES: BLACK
  PEPPER, FENNEL
  SEED, ANISE SEED,
  and/or CARAWAY

1 DRIED GREEN or RED
  CHILE

SALT

In a pot, combine all the brine ingredients together and bring to a simmer.

To assemble: Cut the vegetables into chunks, removing the skin where necessary. Dry char in a cast-iron pan or grill over a fire until the outside of the vegetable chunks begins to blister. They should still be slightly raw in the middle.

Allow the vegetables to cool slightly and pour the brine over the top. They can be eaten immediately while still slightly warm or refrigerated indefinitely for future use.

"Offal good" is his catch phrase, making organ meat great is his game. Chris Cosentino and I have known each other for over a decade. I first met him as a cook, then became his photographer. I recently became his coauthor (for his cookbook, *Offal Good*), and hope to continue as his collaborator. With Chris I've eaten balls, brains, sperm sacs (cod milt), and udder, but it's never due to a dare; I trust him thoroughly, and each new piece of offal is a chance to face down your apprehensions.

Cosentino brings the comfortable and the uncomfortable into conversation with each other, allowing people to let their guards down and just enjoy the goodness that is a well-cooked piece of meat. Brains are like the crème brûlée of organs. When hard-seared they gain a crispy exterior, while the insides stay luscious and fatty. Most of these variety meats benefit from a bit of acid, and this dish is no exception. You can try the Black Butter alone if you're scared of brains, but trust Chris; I do.

BRAINS IN BLACK BUTTER, FROM CHRIS COSENTINO, COCKSCOMB, SAN FRANCISCO, CALIFORNIA SERVES 2

For the brains:

1 FRESH CALF'S BRAIN, about 1 pound (455 g), *soaked in water overnight to remove blood, and rinsed*

COURT BOUILLON, *see recipe below*

2 tablespoons BUTTER

¼ pound (115 g) CHANTERELLE MUSHROOMS, *cleaned*

A few branches THYME

2 tablespoons CAPERS

1 tablespoon CHAMPAGNE VINEGAR

½ cup (120 ml) CHICKEN STOCK

2 slices PULLMAN LOAF or BRIOCHE, *cut ½-inch (12-mm) thick*

1 cup (20 g) ARUGULA LEAVES

FLAKY SALT

Poach the brain for a few minutes in the court bouillon, remove from the heat, and let cool in the refrigerator. Once cooled, split the lobes.

Melt the butter in a large sauté pan over high heat. Sear the brains on the presentation (top) side first, until they're crispy and begin to firm up, a few minutes. Add the mushrooms and thyme, then flip over the brain and baste with butter until the butter is black and the brain is warm throughout (you can check this with a cake tester), another minute or two. Remove the brain and set aside.

Turn the heat down to medium and add the capers and champagne vinegar to deglaze, promptly adding the chicken stock right after, and reduce by half, about 5 minutes, then remove from the heat.

Grill the bread and set it on a plate, laying down a bed of the arugula on each piece. Add a nice amount of the chanterelle-caper mixture on top, then the brains, finishing with the rest of the sauce. Finish with salt.

For the Court Bouillon:

MAKES 1 GALLON (3.8 L)

1 gallon (3.8 L) WATER

1 CARROT, *roughly chopped,* about 1 cup (140 g)

1 CELERY STALK, *roughly chopped*, about 1 cup (100 g)

1 ONION, *roughly chopped,* about 1 cup (110 g)

1 HEAD GARLIC, *split lengthwise*

½ bunch THYME

1 BAY LEAF

1 tablespoon FENNEL SEEDS

1 tablespoon BLACK PEPPERCORNS

1 tablespoon SALT

1 LEMON, *juiced and peeled*

½ cup (120 ml) WHITE WINE

Combine all the ingredients in a large nonreactive stockpot and bring to a boil. Let simmer for 10 minutes, then strain before using.

With a youthful face but a pastry chef's wisdom beyond his years, Francis Ang is able to seduce flavors as if they were the amped-up exemplar of whatever it is they should taste like. Ang's virtuosity is hard to match, so rather than ask for a skillfully constructed dessert, we went the savory route, at which he is also quite adept, and braised lamb belly with the same sense of brilliance. The lamb was served in *bao*, steamed Chinese buns, also called *mantou*, which are a fitting blank canvas for big flavors and fatty meats. Of Filipino origin, the combination of braise and black vinegar glaze is reminiscent of a darker, more cooked down version of adobo (see page 211).

LAMB BELLY STEAMED BUNS WITH BLACK VINEGAR GLAZE, FROM FRANCIS ANG, FORMERLY OF DIRTY HABIT, SAN FRANCISCO, CALIFORNIA; CURRENTLY OF PINOY HERITAGE
SERVES 6

For the twice-cooked lamb belly:

1½ pounds (680 g) LAMB BELLY or LAMB BREAST

1½ tablespoons KOSHER SALT

2 SHALLOTS, *sliced,* about ¾ cup (105 g)

2 HEADS GARLIC, *cut in half lengthwise*

6 cups (1.2 kg) PORK FAT (LARD)

Salt the lamb belly and cure it overnight in the refrigerator.

Preheat the oven to 300°F (150°C). Place the lamb, shallots, and garlic in an ovenproof pan. Add the pork fat and cover with aluminum foil. Roast for about 2 hours, until the lamb belly can be pierced with a fork. This technique is called confit (cooked in fat); it will slowly and evenly cook the meat as well as impart all the aromatics it's cooked with. Remove from the oven and let the meat cool in the fat until you're ready to use it. It will keep, kept in its fat, for at least a week in the fridge.

recipe continues on page 260

*Lamb Belly Steamed Buns
with Black Vinegar Glaze*

For the black vinegar glaze:

2½ tablespoons SHAOXING WINE (CHINESE RICE WINE) or DRY SHERRY

¼ cup (60 ml) SOY SAUCE

⅓ cup (75 ml) BLACK VINEGAR

3 tablespoons PALM SUGAR or BROWN SUGAR

⅓ cup (75 ml) WATER

1 strip ORANGE PEEL

2 STAR ANISE

1 CINNAMON STICKS

½ teaspoon AGAR AGAR, *a gelling agent derived from algae, available at specialty markets*

Combine all the ingredients in a medium saucepan, bring to a boil, and simmer for 3 minutes. Strain into a bowl and chill; the black vinegar glaze should solidify. Cut the mixture into small chunks and liquefy in a blender.

To serve:

A dozen bao buns, steamed as per manufacturer's instructions:

Optional:

PICKLED MUSTARD GREENS

CRUSHED TOASTED PEANUTS seasoned with SZECHUAN PEPPERCORNS

Heat a pan with oil to 350°F (175°C). Take the lamb belly out of the fat and cut it into 1-inch (2.5-cm) slices. Fry on both sides; you won't need any extra fat or oil to do so; it has plenty.

Meanwhile, steam the buns.

Apply a healthy amount of black vinegar glaze onto the bun, then place the belly inside and glaze the top of the meat as well.

You can garnish with mustard greens and peanuts, or even fresh herbs like cilantro.

Albert Katz is the Oakland-based chef and entrepreneur behind Katz Pantry (established in 1993), an organic family-owned farm and store that draws its inspiration from the Alice Waters school of thought, which holds that the best food is comprised of organic, locally grown ingredients. Although Katz Pantry is known today for their artisanal preserves, olive oils, honeys, and vinegars, Katz struck out with vinegar when he first began experimenting with it in the nineties. It wasn't until after 2000 that Katz met Jim Paar, a grape grower who understood some of the science behind vinegar making. After a long period of trial and error, Katz discovered that sweet-and-sour vinegars could be made better through natural winemaking processes, rather than cooking down the must as is done to make balsamic. Thus, Katz uses the Orléans method to make his vinegars—and he very well may have been the first in this country to do so for commercial purposes.

There wasn't much competition when Katz launched his line of vinegars in 2004. California vineyards primarily produced wine, the attitude being that vinegar was a far inferior venture, and, of course, the booming prices of California wine at the turn of the twenty-first century meant a far greater return for growers who invested in winemaking. But Katz stuck with it and strove to meet his community's demand for high-quality, homegrown foodstuffs. His Late Harvest Viognier Honey Vinegar, in particular, is a must-try.

PORTLAND, OREGON

Chimichurri is a finely chopped mixture of herbs, aromatics, oil, and vinegar, like a vinaigrette crossed with an herb salad, a relative to the French *persillade*. It is often served alongside Argentinean grilled meats or fish, acting as a palate cleanser and refresher all in one. I've had no better than that of Gabrielle Quiñónez Denton and Greg Denton from Ox in Portland, Oregon. It greatly enhances skirt steaks and bone-in halibut chops. I start with their base recipe to build my grilled chicken wing adaptation, using the chimichurri as foundation for a green hot sauce, then garnishing the dish with more fresh herbs. But really, this sauce can be used for anything, from adorning fried eggs to a grilled cheese accompaniment; it's really that versatile.

CHIMICHURRI, FROM GABRIELLE QUIÑÓNEZ DENTON AND GREG DENTON, OX, PORTLAND, OREGON
MAKES ABOUT 2 CUPS (480 ML)

½ cup (65 g) FINELY MINCED YELLOW ONION

½ cup (25 g) CHOPPED FLAT-LEAF PARSLEY

1 tablespoon CHOPPED FRESH OREGANO

1 teaspoon GRATED or FINELY MINCED GARLIC

1½ teaspoons KOSHER SALT

1 teaspoon FRESHLY GROUND BLACK PEPPER

½ teaspoon CHILE FLAKES

1 cup (240 ml) OLIVE OIL

½ cup (120 ml) RED WINE VINEGAR

In a medium bowl, combine the onion, parsley, oregano, garlic, salt, pepper, and chile flakes. Pour in the olive oil and vinegar and mix well. Use immediately, or store, covered, in the refrigerator, for up to a couple of days. Use before the herbs start to brown. To keep for longer, combine all of the ingredients except the vinegar, then add the vinegar before serving.

CHIMICHURRI CHICKEN WINGS, MY RECIPE
SERVES 2 TO 4

2 cups (480 ml) CHIMICHURRI, *see recipe above*

4 JALAPEÑO PEPPERS, *2 roasted, 2 raw (remove seeds), plus more to garnish, optional*

¼ cup (60 ml) RED WINE VINEGAR

OLIVE OIL

2 pounds (910 g) CHICKEN WINGS, *drummettes preferred*

SALT

PARSLEY and OREGANO, *leaves picked, to garnish*

1 YELLOW ONION, *thinly sliced, to garnish*

recipe continues on page 264

Chimichurri Chicken Wings

In a blender, combine the chimichurri with the jalapeños, vinegar, and 1 tablespoon of olive oil. Set aside.

Season the chicken wings with a liberal amount of salt and let sit for 10 minutes.

Fire up a grill, or heat a grill pan over medium-high heat. Toss the wings in enough oil to coat, and then start cooking them, turning every so often, until you get a nice char on the exterior and they're fully cooked through, about 20 minutes. When the wings are done, toss them in a bowl with the modified chimichurri sauce.

Garnish with parsley and oregano leaves and thin slices of onion and, if you like, additional fresh, or even pickled, jalapeños.

Scott Dolich, chef-owner of Park Kitchen in Portland, Oregon, saw his culinary career begin in a butcher shop. It wasn't his job to cut up the animals, but he did get to take home all the bits that didn't sell: the neck, the shanks, the head, the ears. His mom gave him Julia Child's *The Way to Cook*, and from there, he was hooked, simmering hearty stews and serving leeks vinaigrette alongside roasted potatoes and grilled chicken. It was magic. Dolich quickly realized that not everything had to be complex; as long as there were bites of brightness throughout, the meal would connect as a whole.

Malt, bourbon, and wine vinegars are made in-house. Dolich's bourbon vinegar is especially good. It's sweet and charcoal-y, and he uses it to acidulate the "beans" in his signature Franks & Beans dish, made with pressure-cooked hazelnuts in place of legumes, served with house-made hot dogs. This recipe was part of a push to eliminate all citrus from his restaurants, and even olive oil, because he thought those ingredients made his food de facto Mediterranean. Dolich's goal was to get to the essence of Pacific Northwest cuisine.

Running a bar without limes and lemons is nearly impossible, though you wouldn't know it if you sipped their hop shrub, a cocktail that crosses a shandy with a boilermaker.

Here is his modernized approach to Leeks Vinaigrette, with the addition of smoked fish. Dolich and David Sapp, a chef at Park Kitchen, created this interplay of classic French with nods to Jewish and Japanese cuisines. The resulting dish reflects the glory of Pacific Northwest cuisine.

SMOKED BLACK COD, BRAISED LEEKS, CHARRED LEEKS, LEEK ASH, BLACK LEEK CREAM, POACHED BLACK RADISH, AND DIJON VINAIGRETTE,
FROM SCOTT DOLICH AND DAVID SAPP, PARK KITCHEN, PORTLAND, OREGON SERVES 4

For the cod:

1½ pounds (680 g) BLACK COD, *portioned into 6-ounce (170-g) pieces*

BUTTER, *enough to submerge the fish*

Either purchase smoked, or cold-smoke the fish (a way of smoking without exposing to heat; you can use a prebuilt kit, or make your own smoker) at 85°F (30°C) for 20 minutes before poaching it in warm butter until cooked *mi-cuit* (about halfway). Reserve in the refrigerator.

For the radishes:

2 ROUND BLACK RADISHES, about ¼ pound (115 g)

2 cups (480 ml) VEGETABLE STOCK

Clean the radishes well by washing under cold water. In a saucepan, combine the radishes and vegetable stock, and bring to a simmer. Simmer for about 20 minutes, until softened. Remove the radishes from the vegetable stock, reserving the stock for the Braised Leeks, and let the radishes cool. Cut the poached radishes into ¼-inch (6-mm) coins and reserve for plating.

For the braised leeks:

1 MEDIUM LEEK, WHITE
PART ONLY, about ¼
pound (115 g); *reserve the
green tops for the Leek Ash*

2 cups (480 ml) VEGETABLE
STOCK, SAVED FROM
POACHED BLACK RADISH

Cut the leek white into 2-inch (5-cm) sections. To do so, stand the leeks on end and cut them in half lengthwise. Cut these leek halves in half lengthwise again. You should now have four 2-inch (5-cm) leek quarters. Separate out each layer of the leek so that you have multiple "leek flags." Bring the vegetable stock to a boil and add the leeks. Cover and let sit to cook until slightly softened and warm throuhgout, a few minutes. Reserve the leeks for plating.

For the charred leeks:

1 MEDIUM LEEK, WHITE
PART ONLY, *cut into
½-inch (12-mm) coins,* about
¼ cup (20 g); *reserve the
green tops for the Leek Ash*

SALT and BLACK PEPPER

4 tablespoons (½ stick / 55 g)
BUTTER

Season the leek coins with salt and pepper. Melt the butter in a large sauté pan over medium-high heat and sear the leeks on one side until that side is golden brown, 2 to 3 minutes. Remove from the heat and reserve for plating.

For the leek ash: Preheat the oven to 175°F (80°C) and prepare a hot grill.

Separate out the layers of the reserved leek greens and lay them out on the hot grill without oil. Let the leeks char until they are very well browned but not burnt. Lay them on a baking sheet and put them in the oven for about 1 hour, until completely desiccated and crispy. Pulverize the charred leeks in a blender or coffee grinder or in a mortar with pestle.

For the black leek cream:

2 MEDIUM ONIONS, about 1 pound (455 g), *peeled and sliced*

2 tablespoons BUTTER

1 teaspoon SALT

1 cup (240 ml) MILK

½ cup (120 ml) HEAVY CREAM

1 BAY LEAF

⅛ teaspoon XANTHAN GUM

½ teaspoon LEEK ASH, *see above*

1 teaspoon SQUID INK

In a medium saucepan, over medium-low heat, sweat the sliced onions in the butter with the salt until translucent, a few minutes. Add the milk, cream, and bay leaf and stew until very soft and reduced, another few minutes. Take the bay leaf out and transfer the mixture to a blender; while the blender is running, dust in the xanthan gum and then add the Leek Ash and squid ink. Chill on ice and reserve for plating.

For the vinaigrette:

1¾ tablespoons WHITE WINE VINEGAR

2½ tablespoons DIJON MUSTARD

¼ cup (60 ml) OLIVE OIL

2 tablespoons WATER

2 pieces SMALL GREEN ENDIVE, *cut obliquely into fork-friendly U shapes, for garnish*

In a blender or a bowl, blend or whisk all the ingredients together until emulsified.

Spread a thin layer of the black leek cream and sprinkle leek ash over the plate. Artfully place warm pieces of charred leeks and poached black radish on the leek cream and ash without obscuring each other on the plate. Toss the pieces of endive in the Dijon vinaigrette and place a few leaves on the plate with the radishes and leeks. Then put the smoked black cod in the middle of the plate, propped on top of the vegetables.

SEATTLE, WASHINGTON

Renee Erickson's Seattle-based oyster bar, The Walrus and the Carpenter, can be found on Ballard Avenue, along the banks of Salmon Bay. Patrons come from far and wide to slurp down a dozen or so oysters and drink copious amounts of Champagne. Ah, the good life, of which Erickson is a great advocate, an allusion perhaps to Paris's Belle Époque? Erickson has certainly provided a "golden age" for seafood in Seattle, but it's this beef tartare dish that has a *joie de vivre* worth living for.

BEEF TARTARE, DATE VINEGAR, EGG YOLK, WALNUTS, AND MINT, FROM RENEE ERICKSON OF THE WALRUS AND THE CARPENTER, SEATTLE, WASHINGTON

SERVES 4

½ cup (60 ml) OLIVE OIL

¼ cup (35 g) FINELY CHOPPED SHALLOTS

1 teaspoon SALT, *plus more to taste*

2 tablespoons DATE VINEGAR

12 ounces (340 g) LEAN BEEF, IDEALLY STRIP LOIN, *fat removed, finely chopped, grass fed and dry aged if you can find it*

½ cup (25 g) MINT LEAVES, *roughly chopped*

½ cup (60 g) WALNUTS, *toasted and chopped*

YOLKS FROM 4 EGGS, *preferably organic*

FLAKY SEA SALT, *to finish*

GRILLED BREAD or POTATO CHIPS

In a medium bowl, stir together the olive oil, shallots, salt, and vinegar. Add the steak and mix so it's seasoned evenly. Stir in the mint and walnuts. Taste and add more salt to season if needed.

To serve, form the meat into four mounds on four plates. Make a well in the top of the tartare and place an egg yolk in each well. Sprinkle more sea salt on the yolk and serve with grilled bread, or pile it on crispy salted potato chips.

Beef Tartare, Date Vinegar, Egg Yolk, Walnuts, and Mint

269

MONTREAL

A shining light in Montreal's culinary scene, Derek Dammann is a big, broad-shouldered man and a gentle soul of a chef. His cooking, honed in London under the tutelage of Jamie Oliver at his restaurant Fifteen, is flawless and homey. It's food that seduces you with its congeniality, so that at first you might not recognize just how sophisticated it is. During Montréal en Lumière, an annual outdoor winter festival with a twenty-four-hour roster of activities, from art exhibitions to gastronomy, I first sampled his *tire d'érable*, a taffy made by boiling down maple sap far past the point of syrup. You cook it till it approaches the hard-ball stage, then swiftly pour it on fresh snow and roll it on a tongue depressor (a wider version of a popsicle stick) to form an irresistible treat.

TIRE D'ERABLE OVER SNOW, FROM DEREK DAMMANN, MAISON PUBLIQUE, MONTREAL, CANADA SERVES 4 TO 6

This is best made in winter, when you can collect freshly fallen snow on a baking sheet, but in a pinch you can always buzz up some ice in a blender; you'll want a nice fine powder, one you'd ski on.

1½ cups (360 ml) APPLE VINEGAR, *see opposite*

TONGUE DEPRESSOR STICKS

In a saucepan over medium-high heat, cook the Apple Vinegar until it barely reaches hard-ball sugar stage, 242 to 244°F (117 to 118°C). Let it cool very slightly, then spoon over snow in a straight line. Take a tongue depressor stick and start at one end of the vinegar streak, twirling the stick to catch what is now a caramel. Don't worry about getting some ice crystals in there—they're added pleasure.

APPLE VINEGAR, FROM DEREK DAMMANN,
MAISON PUBLIQUE, MONTREAL, CANADA
MAKES ABOUT 3 CUPS (720 ML)

3 GRAVENSTEIN APPLES

2½ cups (600 ml) RICE
WINE VINEGAR

½ cup (120 ml) MAPLE
SYRUP

1½ teaspoons KOSHER
SALT

Cut the apples into quarters and place them in a nonreactive container. In a saucepan over medium-high heat, combine the remaining ingredients and bring to a boil. Pour the hot liquid over the apples and place a plate on top of the apples to keep them completely submerged. Cool to room temperature and store covered in the refrigerator for at least 6 weeks before using.

DRUNKEN VINEGARS

I enjoy a mixed drink as much as the next guy, and I love my booze with a kick of acidity, so naturally I had to question why mixologists rely almost entirely on citrus and never use vinegar. I've observed how shrubs have recently become all the rage in cocktail programs around the country, but straight vinegar can also add a boost and a layer of flavor that you can't get with lemon and lime. Plus, vinegar is a more homogeneous product than citrus juice, so batching out works well for consistency's sake. Unless otherwise indicated, the cocktail recipes here list ingredients to make one drink.

When you first find yourself seated in front of Damon Boelte, you can't help but stare. He's a tall, lanky Oklahoman with the long locks and beard of a rock star. And in a sense that's what he is, as he plays with his twin brother in a band called, appropriately enough, Brothers. When we first met a decade ago, he was clean-shaven, hair coiffed in the style of those old-time speakeasy mixologists, but Boelte is a straight-up bartender, affable in a way that typifies a Sooner. Go see him behind the bar at Grand Army, on a quiet little corner of Downtown Brooklyn. He's likely to be there, with a Western-style hat and turquoise jewelry, ready to pour you a drink that will turn into three.

BALSAMIC NEGRONI, FROM DAMON BOELTE, GRAND ARMY, BROOKLYN, NEW YORK MAKES A 48-OUNCE (1.4-L) PITCHER, SERVES 4 TO 8

16 ounces (180 ml) CAMPARI

16 ounces (180 ml) COCCHI VERMOUTH DI TORINO

16 ounces (180 ml) GIN, BEEFEATER preferred

½ pint (165 g) STRAWBERRIES, *sliced*

½ ENGLISH CUCUMBER, *sliced*

ICE

½ cup (120 ml) BALSAMIC VINEGAR, DOP

In the pitcher, mix together Campari, vermouth, and gin. Add the sliced strawberries and cucumber, let sit for 30 minutes for all the flavors to mingle, then top with ice.

To serve, put a few ice cubes in a rocks glass, pour in 6 ounces (120 to 180 ml) of the Negroni, and float 1 tablespoon of the balsamic vinegar on top.

Balsamic Negroni

VINEGAR AND TONIC, FROM DAMON BOELTE, GRAND ARMY, BROOKLYN, NEW YORK MAKES 1 DRINK

HALF A LIME

ICE CUBES

1 ounce GIN, *preferably Mahón*

1 ounce WHITE TXAKOLI WINE

½ to 1 ounce CHAMPAGNE VINEGAR or CAVA VINEGAR, *to your liking*

TONIC, *to top, Schweppes or Fever-Tree*

SLICE OF LIME, *to garnish*

In a Collins glass, muddle the lime, then fill the glass with ice cubes. Pour in gin, wine, and ½ ounce of vinegar and taste to see if you want more acidity; if so, add another ½ ounce. With a bar spoon in the glass, pour the tonic down the handle while stirring to best integrate all the ingredients. Garnish with a slice of lime.

If you're looking to set up a bar with interesting tinctures, Brian Means is your man. He approaches shrubs from a culinary perspective, and with his formulas the whole is more than the sum of its parts. The following shrubs have their own distinct flavor profiles; the Tomato Tarragon would make a great Bloody Mary or a finishing ingredient for a tomato soup. Play around with these shrubs in your cooking, but make sure you have one of his cocktails at hand while doing so.

TOMATO TARRAGON SHRUB, FROM BRIAN MEANS, FORMERLY OF DIRTY HABIT, SAN FRANCISCO, CALIFORNIA MAKES ABOUT 1 QUART (1 L)

4 MEDIUM RED RIPE TOMATOES

1 cup (240 ml) TARRAGON VINEGAR

1 cup (200 g) CANE SUGAR

1 bunch FRESH TARRAGON

Puree the tomatoes in a blender or Vitamix and then strain through a chinois or fine-mesh strainer to separate out the seeds.

recipe continues on page 278

Combine the remaining ingredients in a large saucepan and add the tomato puree. Bring to a simmer over medium-high heat, then reduce the heat and simmer for 10 to 15 minutes, stirring occasionally so the sugar doesn't burn. Remove from the heat and then place in an ice bath to cool down immediately. Remove the tarragon.

Place in a storage container and place in the refrigerator, where it will keep for 1 to 2 months.

CELERY APPLE SHRUB, FROM BRIAN MEANS, FORMERLY OF DIRTY HABIT, SAN FRANCISCO, CALIFORNIA MAKES ABOUT 1 QUART (1 L)

Enough celery to make 1 cup (240 ml) CELERY JUICE, about 1 bunch

1 cup (240 ml) APPLE CIDER VINEGAR

1 cup (200 g) CANE SUGAR

½ cup (120 ml) APPLE JUICE, *preferably fresh, not store-bought*

Juice the celery in a juicer and strain through a chinois or fine-mesh strainer

Combine the vinegar and sugar in a medium saucepan and heat over medium heat to dissolve the sugar. Remove from the heat and add in the celery and apple juice. Let cool in an ice bath, then place in storage container, then place in the refrigerator until ready to use. It will keep for 1 to 2 months.

In the following recipe, Means uses a somewhat bitter molasses in a boozy and bright cocktail, inspired by the sailing straits of the Caribbean and Brazil. The herbaceous Green Chartreuse is counterbalanced by the bracing Blackstrap Gastrique, and the heady effect keeps your mind adrift.

THE COMMODORE, FROM BRIAN MEANS, FORMERLY OF DIRTY HABIT, SAN FRANCISCO, CALIFORNIA MAKES 1 DRINK

1 ounce HAMILTON BLACK RUM

½ ounce AVUÁ AMBURANA CACHAÇA

½ ounce GREEN CHARTREUSE

¾ ounce FRESH LIME JUICE

¼ ounce BLACKSTRAP GASTRIQUE, *see below*

LIME WHEEL, *for garnish*

Combine all the ingredients in a mixing tin and add ice. Shake for about 10 seconds, then double strain into a cocktail coupe. Garnish with a lime wheel.

BLACKSTRAP GASTRIQUE MAKES ABOUT 1½ CUPS (360 ML)

½ cup (120 ml) BLACKSTRAP MOLASSES

¼ cup (60 ml) MAPLE SYRUP

1 cup (240 ml) RED WINE VINEGAR

Combine all the ingredients in a small saucepan and bring to a simmer over medium heat. It will produce a rather strong aroma while cooking, so you might want to leave a window open. Stir constantly for 10 to 15 minutes to fully incorporate the molasses and reduce the liquid down. Remove from the heat and place in an ice bath to cool. Place in a storage container, keep in the refrigerator until ready to use. It will keep for up to 3 months.

Now a cocktail that doesn't mask it—straight-up vinegar for acid. It's like a loose shrub, not fully incorporated; sip and swoosh it in your mouth and let the acidity wash over you.

DUCK DUCK BOOZE, FROM BRIAN MEANS, FORMERLY OF DIRTY HABIT, SAN FRANCISCO, CALIFORNIA MAKES 1 DRINK

7 RASPBERRIES

1½ ounces AYLESBURY DUCK VODKA

1 ounce LAVENDER HONEY

¼ ounce SHERRY VINEGAR

¼ ounce MOSCATEL

ICE

Gently muddle 4 of the raspberries in the mixing tin. Next, add the remaining ingredients and add ice to fill. Shake for about 15 seconds and then double strain into a cocktail coupe. Garnish with the remaining 3 raspberries on a garnish pick.

When I mention drinks with vinegars, people usually assume I'm referring to shrubs. But technically shrubs aren't vinegar—they are *made* with vinegar. I have nothing against shrubs (see recipes from Brian Means, above), as they're a great way of preserving and concentrating fresh fruit juice. But I thought it would be funny to poke fun at the shrub trend and make a vinegar of the fruit of a shrub/bush, or berries (e.g. raspberries, blueberries, and blackberries). In the end I decided to blend three separate berry vinegars together. The resulting flavor was reminiscent of Triple Berry Pie and is far more quaffable.

A bramble is a cocktail that uses berry-flavored liquor, traditionally crème de mûre, in the same way I use the vinegar here. Coincidentally, "bramble" is a British term for a shrub, specifically a blackberry bush, so it's all interconnected.

SHRUBS SHRUB BRAMBLE, **MY RECIPE** MAKES 1 DRINK

4 BLACKBERRIES

2 ounces GIN

1 ounce TRIPLE BERRY
  VINEGAR, *see recipe below*

½ ounce SIMPLE SYRUP,
  *1:1 ratio sugar to water,
  heated until reduced by half*

CRUSHED ICE

In a rocks glass, muddle 3 of the blackberries, then add the gin, vinegar, and simple syrup. Stir to combine and let sit for a minute or so. Add ice until spilling over the brim. Garnish with the remaining blackberry and sip through a short straw.

Shrubs Shrub Bramble   **281**

TRIPLE BERRY VINEGAR

¼ cup (60 ml) EACH
RASPBERRY,
BLUEBERRY,
BLACKBERRY
VINEGAR

¼ cup (50 g) SUGAR

¾ cup (75 ml) HONEY
VINEGAR

Mix all the ingredients together in a saucepan. Over medium-high heat, bring to a boil, then take off heat to let flavors combine, and allow to cool. Let sit for at least an hour, then strain.

POSCA SOUR, MY RECIPE   MAKES 1 DRINK

This is my twist on a drink that was popular in ancient Greece—water diluted with wine vinegar. Legionaries of the Roman Empire used to drink posca, which they believed would prevent scurvy and other diseases. This version has oregano-infused honey vinegar mixed with Metaxa (Greek brandy).

¾ ounce HONEY VINEGAR
INFUSED WITH
OREGANO, *muddle
oregano and steep for a
few hours*

2 ounces BRANDY
(METAXA BRAND) or
COGNAC

¾ ounce HONEY SYRUP,
*honey mixed 1:1 with water
by volume, heated until
reduced by half*

½ ounce LEMON JUICE

LEMON PEEL, *1 good pull*

ICE CUBES

SPRIG OREGANO,
to garnish

HONEYCOMB, *to garnish*

In a mixing tin, combine the vinegar, brandy, honey syrup, lemon juice, lemon peel, and ice and shake vigorously for 30 seconds. Strain into a glass small enough for sipping and refilling all day, and add an ice cube or two to keep it cold. Garnish with oregano and a small piece of honeycomb on a toothpick. The honey will drip into the drink, sweetening as you sip.

A traditional shandy is beer mixed with lemonade, usually in proportions of one to one. Eamon Rockey has a different take on the drink, and makes his with dark beer and malt vinegar. With smoky notes of honey and tobacco, it's like imbibing a cool haze, slowly sipped through a straw.

OLD DOG SHANDY, FROM EAMON ROCKEY, FORMERLY OF BETONY, NEW YORK CITY MAKES 1 DRINK

2/3 ounce HARDWOOD SMOKED HONEY, *see recipe below*

1/2 ounce DARK MALT VINEGAR

2 ounces DARK PORTER BEER

CRUSHED ICE

A MISTING OF TOBACCO TINCTURE, *see recipe below*

To make the smoked honey: Combine equal parts honey and water and place in a smoker until all the water is dissolved and the honey has been infused with the flavor of smoke.

To make the tobacco tincture: Steep Virginia pipe tobacco in unaged corn whiskey overnight, strain, and place in an atomizer.

To serve: Combine the honey, vinegar, and porter in a beer glass, then fill with crushed ice. Mist the top of the drink with tobacco tincture and sip through a straw.

Old Dog Shandy

Nick Fauchald is my neighbor and friend who has the best home bar in the 'hood. He helped write the book for Death & Company, a leading cocktail lounge in New York City, so he has a stockpile of weird and one-off bottles of booze and frequently challenges himself to use them in cocktails. So I had an invitation for him: Make a drink that uses vinegar in a classic and contemporary way. Fauchald was up for it, and came back with these two riffs on the sherry-based Bamboo cocktail. It made perfect sense to use sherry vinegar, mirroring the oxidized notes in the cocktail; the first version is refreshing and closer to the original, the second more savory and complex. Fino is recommended for both, but you can also try with amontillado for a bit more body.

TWO RIFFS ON THE BAMBOO, FROM NICK FAUCHALD, PUBLISHER OF SHORT STACK EDITIONS AND DOVETAIL PRESS

MAKES 1 DRINK

Version 1

2 ounces FINO SHERRY

2 ounces SWEET VERMOUTH

2 teaspoons AGED SHERRY VINEGAR

2 dashes ORANGE BITTERS

LEMON TWIST

Combine ingredients in a coupe, stir, and serve up with a twist.

Version 2

1½ ounces FINO SHERRY

¾ ounce SWEET VERMOUTH

¾ ounce DRY VERMOUTH

2 teaspoons AGED SHERRY VINEGAR

2 dashes ORANGE BITTERS

1 pinch SALT

LEMON TWIST

Combine ingredients in a coupe, stir, and serve up with a twist.

This is a nonalcoholic beverage from the team at EMP. Reduced maple syrup creates a round and smooth base, while the sherry vinegar helps bring out the tart traits in the apple juice. This one requires some specialty equipment, but it's well worth the effort.

MAPLE SODA, FROM DANIEL HUMM, ELEVEN MADISON PARK, NEW YORK CITY MAKES 4 SODAS, ABOUT 48 OUNCES (1.4 L)

2⅓ cups (555 ml) WATER

1⅔ cups (405 ml) MAPLE SYRUP

1⅔ cups (405 ml) APPLE JUICE, from about 4 apples

1⅔ tablespoons SHERRY VINEGAR

1⅔ tablespoons FRESH LEMON JUICE, about 1 lemon's worth

Prepare an ice bath.

In a small saucepan over low heat, warm 1⅔ cups (405 ml) of the water.

In a large saucepan, over high heat, cook the maple syrup, stirring frequently, until it reaches 300°F (150°C), about 10 minutes. Keep an eye on it; though it will reach a temperature that is hard-crack stage for sugar, the maple syrup will be foamy, and if you don't pay attention, it can overflow.

Be very, very careful for this part. Stand back, add the warm water in a small stream little by little, and stir to combine. The sugar may bubble and burst, so it's best to tilt the maple pan away from you when you do this. Slowly add the rest of the water, then remove the syrup from the heat and chill over the ice bath.

Once cooled, combine the maple syrup with the remaining water and the apple juice, sherry vinegar, and lemon juice.

To carbonate, transfer the mixture to a plastic 2-liter bottle. Squeeze the bottle to expel air from the top, screw on a carbonator-bottle adaptor, and seal. Attach the bottle adaptor to a ball lock joint connected to a CO_2 tank via a $5/16$-inch (8-mm) gas line assembly and a dual-gauge regulator. Make sure the CO_2 tank is

recipe continues on page 288

open and the regulator is pressurized to 40 psi (pounds per square inch). Press the ball lock straight down on the bottle; the bottle should inflate. Leaving the ball lock attached and locked, flip the bottle upside down and shake vigorously for 1 minute. Flip the bottle right side up and detach the ball lock. Keep cold, or transfer the soda to four 6-ounce (180-ml) glass bottles, capping each bottle with a crown cap, and continue to keep cold. Aside from two kinds of acid in the soda itself (vinegar and lemon juice), carbon dioxide is also a source of acid.

BAR SNACKS

I get hungry when I drink, so I had to put a few bar snacks in the book. The first is from my longtime friend Phillip Kirschen-Clark, a fellow three-name traveler in the world of food. We met in Boston years ago, when he and I were just starting in our respective fields. PKC had a brief run at what I think was a very progressive restaurant in the East Village called Vandaag, which offered an eclectic menu of Northern European cuisine focusing on Dutch and Danish traditions. *Droge worst*, or Dutch air-dried sausages, are similar to the smoked kielbasa that hang from the ceilings of many Polish butchers in Manhattan. Kirschen-Clark takes these sausages and lets them mature in brine for at least a week before serving, in a shot glass, so you get a pickleback to boot.

PICKLED SAUSAGES, FROM PHILLIP KIRSCHEN-CLARK
SERVES 6 TO 8

1 quart (960 ml) WATER

4 cups (800 g) SUGAR

2 quarts (2 L) CIDER VINEGAR

2 HEADS GARLIC, *split in half lengthwise*

10 FRESH BAY LEAVES, *torn in half*

1 tablespoon BLACK PEPPERCORNS, *toasted*

2½ pounds (1.2 kg) COOKED KIELBASA, *sliced ¼-inch thick on the bias*

In a large saucepan, combine everything except the kielbasa and bring to a simmer. Turn off the heat and allow to cool to room temperature. Place the kielbasa in a large container, pour the mixture over the sausages, and weight the sausages to submerge them. Place into the refrigerator and allow to mature for at least 1 week before using.

Dijon Beef Jerky, Pickled Sausages,
Salt and Vinegar Chicken Skins,   **291**
Pickled Grapes and Grape Tomatoes

PICKLED GRAPES AND GRAPE TOMATOES, MY RECIPE
MAKES ABOUT 2 QUARTS (2 L)

I'm an advocate of having an all-purpose pickling liquid, and this is mine. Pour it over most anything and wait a day or two. Now you've got yourself a dependable pickle routine.

1 cup (150 g) GREEN GRAPES

1 cup (135 g) GRAPE TOMATOES

1 teaspoon WHOLE BLACK PEPPERCORNS

1 teaspoon FENNEL SEEDS

2 STAR ANISE

2 BAY LEAVES

½ teaspoon CHILE FLAKES, OPTIONAL

2 cups (480 ml) CIDER VINEGAR

½ cup (120 ml) WATER

1 cup (200 g) SUGAR

1 teaspoon SALT

Pack the grapes, grape tomatoes, and all of the spices in a heat-proof jar, leaving one third free for the pickling liquid.

Put the vinegar, water, sugar, and salt in a medium sauce-pan and bring to a boil over medium-high heat, stirring so the sugar doesn't scorch, then pour the hot liquid over the grapes and grape tomatoes. You may have leftover pickling liquid, but that's okay—you can use it for future pickles! Let cool, jar, and refrigerate. The pickles will be ready in a few days; the pickles will keep for up to 1 month.

The pickles are great roasted too. Remove from the liquid, place in a ramekin, add enough olive oil to coat, and roast for about 10 minutes at 350°F (175°C).

SALT AND VINEGAR CHICKEN SKINS, MY RECIPE
SERVES 2 TO 4

As an Ashkenazi Jew, my idea of manna is schmaltz, or chicken fat. When you make it, there's the wonderful by-product of gribenes (bits of crispy chicken skin). Usually the skin is ground to best render out the fat, but I like baking big pieces of skin to make chips, because we all know that crispy skin's really the best part. Vinegar is used here as a flavoring agent, and it helps clarify the fat before you bake the skins.

½ pound (225 g) CHICKEN SKIN *(from 1 pound [455 g] chicken skin, with gribenes trimmed off; go to your local butcher and ask for nice big pieces of intact chicken skin, which they'll have trimmed off their skinless breasts)*

3 tablespoons VINEGAR

About 1 teaspoon SALT

Preheat the oven to 300°F (150°C).

Trim the chicken skins of extra fat into nice squarish pieces. Get a pot of water boiling and add 1 tablespoon of the vinegar. Blanch the skins for 2 to 3 seconds, just so they set and curl a bit. Drain the skins and toss with the remaining 2 tablespoons vinegar, and let marinate for 20 to 30 minutes. Spread the chicken skins out on a baking sheet lined with a silicone baking mat. Place another baking mat on top, then another baking sheet, and then a weight (a cast iron pan or two; try to distribute the weight evenly). Bake for 1 hour. Remove the skins from the baking sheet and place on paper towels to dry and drain. Sprinkle with salt.

DIJON BEEF JERKY, MY RECIPE
MAKES 1/2 TO 3/4 POUND (225 TO 340 G) JERKY

If there's one food I could eat for the rest of my life (aside from pizza and chicken wings), one food with which I am almost as obsessed as I am with vinegar, it might be beef jerky. And the shelf life of beef jerky is seemingly eternal, which would make it a wise choice if I were to only eat one food for the rest of my life. Made through drying top sirloin in a home oven, this jerky can also be finished by deep-frying it with rosemary sprigs. The result is so much more satisfying than what you get at the gas station.

1/4 cup (60 ml) DIJON
  MUSTARD

2 tablespoons CHAMPAGNE
  VINEGAR

1 tablespoon CHOPPED
  ROSEMARY

1 teaspoon FRESHLY
  GROUND BLACK
  PEPPER

1 pound (455 g) SIRLOIN,
  FAT CAP TRIMMED,
  cut lengthwise into 1/4-inch slices

Mix the mustard, vinegar, rosemary, and black pepper in bowl. Coat all the meat in the mixture, place in a plastic bag, and refrigerate for at least 8 hours, or overnight.

Preheat the oven to 200°F (90°C). Fit a baking sheet with a baking rack. Take the meat out of the marinade and blot some of the marinade off on a paper towel. Place the meat on the prepared baking sheets and bake for 3 to 4 hours, or until the meat is dried but not brittle. Cool to room temperature and eat right away or keep in an airtight container in a cool, dry place. It can be refrigerated and will last for months if free from moisture.

For an added dimension, try quickly deep-frying with a sprig of rosemary.

As a photographer with an interest in food, I've been in and out of the top kitchens around the world. In the basement of Daniel, Daniel Boulud's namesake restaurant in New York City, I met a six-foot, five-inch Italian guy from Yonkers whom I still believe to be the best bread baker in New York. Mark Fiorentino spent more than fifteen years as the in-house *boulanger* for Daniel, and with Boulud's ever-growing empire, the baking needs grew. When DBGB opened in 2009, a downtown location that riffed on Daniel's iconic dishes, Fiorentino was making hundreds of pretzel rolls for their burgers. I loved them so much that I would ask for a breadbasket just of pretzel rolls.

When I was married, Mark paid tribute to my love for my bride—and our mutual love for Brooklyn and Paris—by baking us pretzel baguettes to give out as wedding favors. He and I have bonded over grain builds in beer as well. We try to meet up for a pint every now and then, to talk hydration percentages in dough over a favorite new hoppy IPA. When searching for relevant ways to include bread baking in this book, we brainstormed and found a black bread reminiscent of pumpernickel, made with rye flour. It is fed a good amount of cider vinegar, and in the Baltic it is eaten with cured herring and maybe a side of Russian vinaigrette (which isn't vinaigrette at all, but instead a beet and carrot sauerkraut mixture). But in the end we decided to share a pretzel recipe, with all the flavors of mustard built into the dough. It's the perfect snack, and it goes perfectly with beer.

MUSTARD PRETZEL, FROM MARK FIORENTINO
MAKES 4 PRETZELS

Baker's percentages included below for greatest precision, but you can still make the pretzels following the traditional measurements.

235 grams ALL-PURPOSE FLOUR (1½ cups / 94 percent bakers percentage)

15 grams RYE FLOUR (2 tablespoons / 6 percent)

2.5 grams SALT (1 teaspoon / 1 percent)

13 grams SUGAR (3 tablespoons / 5.2 percent)

20 grams WATER (2 tablespoons / 8 percent)

10 grams YEAST (2 teaspoons / 4 percent)

150 grams MUSTARD, DELI or DIJON (⅔ cup or 165 ml / 60 percent)

4 grams, GROUND TURMERIC (1 teaspoon / 1.6 percent)

4 grams PAPRIKA (1 teaspoon / 1.6 percent)

FOOD-GRADE LYE

PRETZEL SALT, *to garnish*

Combine all the ingredients except the lye and pretzel salt in the bowl of a mixer fitted with the paddle attachment and mix for 5 minutes. Remove the dough from the bowl and knead by hand to form a smooth ball. Let rest for 30 minutes.

Cut the dough into 4 even strips. Tap out any large air bubbles. Roll into a tapered rope, about 2 feet (60 cm) in length. If the dough resists, stop rolling and wait for 2 to 3 minutes to let the gluten relax, then continue rolling. Twist each strip into a pretzel shape; place on a baking mat or parchment sheet–lined baking sheet and let rest for another hour or two, until they've noticeably risen.

Refrigerate for at least 1 hour. The pretzels may be frozen at this stage as well. It's almost easier to bake them directly from the freezer. Just thaw them lightly, but transfer to the oven while they are still firm. Once they have cooled thoroughly, dip them in a 4 percent lye* solution (follow manufacturer's instructions very carefully for this) for about 30 seconds. Remove from the lye and place on a baking sheet lined with a silicone baking mat or parchment paper. Score with a sharp knife (if desired) and top with pretzel salt. Bake for 10 to 12 minutes, until the skin is a nice even, rich brown.

*You can buy food-grade lye online or in a specialty market. Carefully read the instructions on how to use it, because it is a very caustic alkaline solution and can irritate the skin and be dangerous to use in a poorly ventilated space. That said, it's what makes a pretzel a pretzel to my mind, and I'm sure you will come to the same conclusion.

RICOTTA TOASTS WITH FENNEL JAM, MY RECIPE
SERVES 4 TO 8

This is a multidimensional recipe, one in which vinegar plays a role in cheese making as well as jamming. The ricotta ends up fluffy and fresh, the jam stewed and sapid, and the composite is better still, the acidity in each element complementing the other.

For the ricotta:

3 cups (720 ml) WHOLE MILK

1 cup (240 ml) HEAVY CREAM

1 teaspoon SALT

3 tablespoons WHITE WINE VINEGAR

Set up a sieve lined with cheesecloth over a large bowl. You can also use a kitchen towel over a colander.

Mix the milk, cream, and salt in a large saucepan (at least twice the height of the liquid, so it doesn't boil over) and bring to a near boil over medium-high heat. If you have a candy thermometer, take it off the heat once it reaches 200°F (93°C), then add the vinegar and whisk constantly for 2 to 3 minutes.

297

Pour the liquid into the cheesecloth-lined sieve. The liquid that comes out is whey, great to save for poaching fish and vegetables and to use as a hydrating liquid for baking. Let the cheese drain for 30 minutes, or until cool enough to handle. Remove the ricotta curds from the cheesecloth and put them in a container. Let cool.

For the fennel jam:

MAKES 1 QUART (1 L)

2 LARGE FENNEL BULBS, *sliced, or small dice,* about 3 cups

2 tablespoons OLIVE OIL

1 teaspoon SALT

1 teaspoon FENNEL SEEDS

½ cup (110 g) BROWN SUGAR

½ cup (120 ml) CIDER VINEGAR

½ cup (75 g) GOLDEN RAISINS

Trim the tops off the fennel. Cut in half lengthwise, remove the core, and slice the fennel into ¼-inch (6-mm) slices, or if you like a finer textured jam, dice the fennel.

Heat the olive oil in a saucepan on medium heat. Add the fennel and salt and let cook for 10 to 15 minutes, uncovered. It's okay if it browns a little, but don't let it burn.

Add the fennel seeds and brown sugar and stir to incorporate. Cook another 5 to 10 minutes, until the sugar is dissolved. Add the vinegar and raisins, drop the heat to medium-low, and cook for another 30 to 45 minutes, until everything gels together and there's little to no liquid left.

To assemble: Spread a good spoonful of ricotta on your favorite toast, then add a dollop of jam on top. Sprinkle with salt to finish. To make it more savory, add a glug of good olive oil.

*Ricotta Toasts with
Fennel Jam*

MAKING
VINEGAR

STARCH   SUGAR   ALCOHOL   ACETIC
ACID

Here we begin our journey into fermentation, highlighting the best methods to make honest vinegars, comprised of real ingredients, for inspired recipes. I've been lucky enough to travel the world to meet some of the top vinegar makers and chefs employing vinegar in their kitchen pantries. Please consider making your own vinegars with passion and care; they're living, breathing organisms that should be treated with the same respect you would any fruit tree or vegetable plant. Remember, the better the input, the better the output, so start with the utmost quality and you'll soon find great vinegars in your life.

As a novice vinegar maker, you're best off starting by taking a beer, a cider, and a wine and leaving them out. At first you won't notice much activity, but they're just moving slowly, adapting to the air, and beginning to transform. Kept on the counter (covered with cheesecloth—more on this later), it probably takes a couple of weeks for a noticeable change. Taste the developing flavors, and with a little luck you'll end up making vinegar without even trying (this is how I got started). The vinegar should take a month or two to fully acetify. It won't always work out, which is why I will go into much greater detail about making vinegar from start to finish with more reliable results, explaining some of the science and method behind the magical process of fermentation.

Vinegar may best be described as a study in restraint; you don't need much to achieve a noticeable effect. An elementary substance, vinegar is comprised of two things: H_2O and CH_3CO_2H, better known as water and acetic acid, which is an organic compound. In the non-culinary world, there exists undiluted acetic acid (sometimes known as glacial acetic acid, which is water-free) that must be combined with water before it can be used (e.g. it's diluted for treating invasive medical conditions). Vinegar can still be highly corrosive, which is one reason people associate it with cleaning (see page 319). In values of 10 to 25 percent of volume, acidity by weight, acetic acid is considered an irritant, though it can be found at that strength as a pickling agent in many Scandinavian countries. In the United States, we principally use vinegars in the 4 to 6 percent acidity range for culinary purposes.

If only a small amount is a required cooking component for a dish, why not use the finest stuff? In pickling, a preserving method that uses a greater volume of vinegar per recipe than a vinaigrette, you can reuse that valued liquid over and over; if anything, it gets better with age. On a microbial level, vinegar with real, live *Acetobacter*, the class of natural bacterium, of which *A. aceti* is the most common, undergoes fermentation (a type of chemical breakdown of one substance to form another, in this case, ethyl alcohol to acetic acid) and continues to evolve even as it denatures the food it affects. Its impression is enduring, so for an optimum outcome, you should begin with a great source.

Here's the simple biology: vinegar is a living organism that uses bacteria (the aforementioned acetobacter) to convert ethyl alcohol into acetic acid when oxygen is present. It generally calls for a two-part fermentation, meaning that to make vinegar you first have to make (or have) alcohol; that's why you see so many vinegars made from wine, beer, and rice (that is, from sake). What's seldom discussed in vinegar making is where the alcohol comes from in the first place. In the illustration above, you'll see there's a four-step sequence, and when read from left to right, one condition begets the next.

Let's take beer, for example: it's derived from cereal grains, to which heat is applied, transforming starch into sugar. Wheat, rice, and even potatoes are all starches that can be cooked with hot water (or steam) to form a sweetened starting liquid for vinegar making. (Hey, a lot of vodka comes from potatoes, so there's your starch starting point for eventual vinegar.) This process is called saccharification, whereby polysaccharides (starches) become soluble sugars.

Even if you're not a homebrewer, which I wasn't when I started making vinegar, understanding brewing, wine making, and distilling practices can help inform your vinegar-making decisions. The same set of principles are in place when converting sugar to alcohol, and even alcohol to acetic acid; some sort of heat needs to be applied, but at this stage a specialized type of fermentation must occur. In brewing, an introduction of yeast cells (which can be bought in homebrewing stores, or obtained naturally through the cultivation of wild yeasts) converts the sugars into CO_2 (carbon dioxide) and alcohol; this is similar to acetic fermentation, in which oxidation and the presence of acetoabacters turn alcohol into vinegar. But before we can go any further, have you considered what tools you will need and where you will store all this stuff?

EQUIPMENT

VESSELS

GLASS, PLASTIC, WOOD

To get started, you'll need some basic containers: glass jars or carboys, vessels to hold the vinegar in (eventually). Glass containers make for the least reactive vessels and don't really need to be an expensive proposition. Plastic works too but isn't preferred, as it sometimes dulls the overall impression of a finished vinegar, so if you have the option, start with glass, like a mason jar (or a carboy if you're going for a big batch); it creates a sharp, linear flavor and an acidity that develops quick and clean. Wood will give you a little more roundness in the end result, but starting with a barrel is a bit riskier than starting with glass because it's porous, breathable, and can let in unwanted microorganisms. Barrels are great for aging vinegar (which we'll get to later), but fermenting in the barrel takes a more adept understanding of potential issues and how to avoid them. So if you're just starting out, I recommend using wide-mouth mason jars.

It's important to make sure whatever vessel you're using is clean; the more sterile the environment, the better, so washing your jars in very hot water baths and drying them thoroughly before you start will help you avoid interference down the line. The challenge here is to make sure you don't contaminate your vinegar. Yes, bacteria are crucial to making vinegar, but there's such a thing as too much, and the wrong kind. Let your vinegar cultivate with its own inborn batch; this way, if there are any adjustments that need to be made along the way, you'll have a controlled environment.

ACCESSORIES

CHEESECLOTH, AIRLOCKS, WINE THIEF, RACKING TUBE

For the initial stages of making vinegar, you'll need a decent amount of exposure to oxygen. In a pinch, I've used paper towels and rubber bands to cover my jars, but you should invest in some cheesecloth. Cheesecloth will keep the fruit flies out and help regulate air flow. Be sure to cover the jar tightly with the cheesecloth, either by screwing the jar's ring on over the top or securing it with rubber bands.

Once your fermentation really gets going (after anywhere from a couple weeks to a couple months), which you'll be able to tell by a distinct change in smell and taste (and can check with a set of tools; see below), you're best off using an airlock, a small plastic device that keeps a relatively tight seal while regulating airflow through a pressure value. You don't want a completely anaerobic environment or your vinegar will asphyxiate.

A wine thief is kind of like a glorified straw. It you dip one open side into a liquid and plug up the other side, it will create a vacuum enabling you to remove a sample of your vinegar.

You'll also want to have a racking tube, which is a flexible plastic tube that's used to transfer samples from one vessel to another. You'll use gravity, by positioning whatever vessel you're drawing your sample from above whatever vessel you're transferring it to. You can suck on the non-submerged side of the tube to get the liquid going, but you'll risk getting a mouthful of vinegar

that way. I like using a turkey baster (which can double as a wine thief in a pinch) to build up enough pressure in the tube to get the liquid flowing.

MEASURING TOOLS
HYDROMETER, REFRACTOMETER, PH STRIPS, TITRATION KIT

Pick up a hydrometer, refractometer, pH strips, and a titration kit from a homebrewing and/or winemaking store or online from a medical supply website. All told, they'll cost you well under a hundred dollars (especially if you buy a cheaper refractometer). These tools will help you monitor and regulate the vinegar-making protocol that's outlined in the next pages by measuring potential alcohol, percentage alcohol, pH, and percentage acidity, respectively.

INGREDIENTS AND SOURCING

INPUT
STARCH, SUGAR, ALCOHOL, ACETIC ACID

The first order of business in making vinegar is figuring out your starting point; this is what I call an INPUT. Even before you choose a source (the more specific flavoring ingredient) you have to decide what kind of organic compound makes most sense in trying to achieve your desired OUTPUT.

Whether you start with a starch, sugar, or alcohol will determine the time and effort it takes to make a well-crafted vinegar.

SOURCE
MASH, JUICE, SYRUP, SPIRITS

A source is an ingredient that can be made up of starches, sugars, alcohol, and even vinegar in some cases. This is where vinegar making becomes less prescribed and more based on observation and experimentation. It's best to begin with *Alcohols* and then work your way to *Sugars*, then *Starches*. Not only will this force you to refine your craft step by step, but the tools of the trade are best calibrated for dealing with the readings for alcohol as a source ingredient. Eventually a combination of inputs, or source ingredients, can be used, just as long as you put together a mix that hits all the right marks for fermentation. While you're looking after your vinegar, you'll also want to make sure to work clean, similar to sterilizing your vessels, ensuring whatever tools come into contact with your vinegar are as aseptic as can be.

> Examples:
> *Starches*: Cereal grains, wheat, rice, tubers
> *Sugars*: Fruit and vegetable juices, sweeteners/syrups (e.g., honey, maple syrup), sodas
> *Alcohols*: Beer, wine, sake, spirits

If you're starting with a starch as your source, you'll have to make a mash first; this can be done by adding enough hot water to cook these starches into fermentable sugars. Some conversion processes are a little more complex and require steaming instead of submer-sion, but really what you're looking for is to make a sweet liquid from cooking your source ingredient in liquid. If you're making rice vinegar, for example, you can cook 1 cup of rice in 4 cups of water; this is a baseline recommendation for a good sugar solution and then alcohol outcome. If you use less water, you'll yield a lower amount of liquid, yet a more concentrated sugar solution, which would in turn be more alcoholic when fermented. From there you can strain the aforementioned mash, and you'll have a sugary solution similar to juiced fruit or vegetables or sweet syrups (e.g., honey, maple syrup) mixed with water. From here you have the base to make alcohol.

Brewing beer and making wine are areas of expertise in their own right, and a vinegar maker should be well aware that if not for those methods, vinegar couldn't be made. Joke all you want about how alcohol will turn into vinegar when it goes bad; while this is sometimes the case, it is not the best way to make great vinegars. Thankfully there are plenty of books available to help you produce quality alcohol, but you can also procure beer, wine, and spirits, which are more than suitable starting points. That said, vinegar itself is nonalcoholic; it's the complete conversion of alcohol to acetic acid. But rather than think of there being an absence, I like to think of vinegar as post-alcoholic, so again, you want to start with the best possible source.

The process is different for every source ingredient; in some cases, you'll pitch the yeast (add a starter) for fermentation, and in others, wild indigenous yeasts will occur and help with spontaneous fermentation (which happens in lambic beers, when the wort, the liquid extracted from the mashing process, is exposed to the air while still cooling). Because cloudy liquids are more likely to go sour (in a bad way)

in the fermentation process, I like to strain all my sources, unless otherwise indicated. It's best to ferment at room temperature. This creates the most livable environment for the largest latitude of bacteria to be present. Last, if you see something, sample something: that means if there's a color change, or something floating or growing on top, you should react to it, rather than simply let it transpire. You'll see below there are ways to adjust throughout vinegar making, and though it's not a highly active process, you still have to attend to it sooner than not.

VINEGAR MAKING INSTRUCTIONS

OUTPUT

SPECIFIC GRAVITY, BRIX, ABV

Sugars: 10 to 25 °Bx

Alcohol: 5 to 15 percent ABV

More sugar means a higher alcohol by volume (ABV), which has its advantages: faster fermentation times and less potential for error. However, it will yield more acidic vinegar. An expedited product has fewer of the natural characteristics of what it's made from because it's aerating or oxidizing too quickly. Using a slow and low technique increases your odds of producing a

vinegar that's resonant with flavor *and* acidity.

Once you have a sugar solution, use your hydrometer or refractometer to test the Brix (Bx) level of the liquid. Brix is the measurement unit for the sugar content in an aqueous solution. I aim for a range that's somewhere between 19 and 23 °Bx, which interestingly is the same sugar level that winemakers look for when making sparkling wines, and ends up yielding a solution of about 11 to 13.5 percent ABV. You can adjust the Brix level if you need to by adding a little sugar if the Bx is too low, or by adding water if the Bx is too high. I've found that when you keep your base sugar level in this range, you'll get nice body and structure in your resulting vinegar, rather than a lackluster, flavorless acid bomb. The lower the Brix, the slower your fermentation will be, yet the more aroma and flavor you'll retain; that said, if you go too low, there won't be enough sugar (and in turn, alcohol). If your sugars are too high, you'll produce too much alcohol and the acetobacters won't be able to survive.

As mentioned in the introduction (see page 11), measuring specific gravity will help give a sense of potential alcohol in a sugar solution, by comparing an initial reading pre-ferment to one post-ferment, indicating your ABV. Most of my vinegars are made from sources with 5 to 15 percent ABV. I tend to aim for the middle of that range because it gives me room to fine-tune along the way, and by that I mean you'll be able to readjust a source that's not going as planned.

ADJUSTMENTS

CHAPTALIZATION, DOSAGE, WATER BACK

Chaptalization is a process that's sometimes used in winemaking, through which sugar is added to unfermented grapes to increase the potential alcohol output. This is done when grapes don't get as ripe as desired, which means the wine will be too low in alcohol; it's a useful technique in making vinegar, too, when there's simply not enough sugar in the base. *Dosage*, another winemaking term adopted by vinegar makers, is often used in making champagne. A dosage is sugar that's added to the already fermented wine to influence the dryness of the ensuing beverage. In vinegar, adding a dosage will change the pH of the end result, softening the perception of acidity.

Should you have a source that's too sugary or alcoholic, it's easy enough to just add water to the liquid to get to a workable ABV. Alcohol normally converts to acetic acid at around a two-thirds rate. This means a liquid with 10 percent ABV would yield about 6.5 percent acidity, assuming all of the alcohol is converted to acetic acid. However, you'll usually lose about 10 to 15 percent volume thanks to evaporation throughout the fermentation process, which would readjust the final acidity to the 5.5 to 6 percent range, which is where I try to get mine to land. At this level of acidity, vinegars authoritatively show their stuff, and the ingredient you've worked so hard to make really shines.

MOTHER OF VINEGAR

MOV

Many vinegar makers rely on a mother, and I don't mean for familial support. Mothers, or MOV (mothers of vinegar), are large, creepy-looking cellulose substances. It's that mushroom-cloud SCOBY (symbiotic colony of bacteria and yeast) that we're used to seeing in kombucha or the bubbling starter used to make sourdough bread. With the aid of oxygen, MOVs create an efficient environment for the conversion of ethyl alcohol to acetic acid.

Contrary to popular belief, you don't have to add a mother to make a vinegar. They'll form naturally in the vinegar-making process. Like sourdough, it's best to cultivate your own. Mothers act as a means of speeding up the transformation of alcohol to vinegar, and adding one can hyper-accelerate a process that may otherwise occur naturally, compromising the depth of flavor that can only be attained through vinegar's slow and steady development. When a source just won't ferment, it's more than understandable to introduce a mother, but why be a helicopter parent, over-nurturing what could occur naturally? If a mother becomes too large and cumbersome, it can suffocate the active yeasts that feed on the sugars in the solution. Rule of thumb: if the mother grows deeper than the width of your finger, remove it and discard; on the other hand, not enough mother (it's inconsistent or in patches over the surface) is usually indicative of inactivity in fermentation. This, and only this, is a time when you might want to introduce a mother to get things going again.

ACETOBACTER

INDIGENOUS, SPONTANEOUS, LIVE BACTERIA

In my opinion, it's absolutely worth the wait to see if wild yeasts initiate spontaneous fermentation first; there are millions of indigenous microbes everywhere, live bacteria live all around us!

AERATION

STIR/SHAKE, FISH TANK BUBBLER, ACETATOR

Vinegars need a good supply of oxygen during fermentation so that the live yeasts can breathe, in turn feasting on the alcohol.

The simplest way to make sure your vinegar is getting proper aeration is by stirring or shaking the jar it's in. You can accelerate the process by adding a fish bubbler or an aerator to larger batches, but I prefer the slow and low method, stirring or shaking by hand as needed. This way you're more likely to be able to adjust if anything goes awry.

An interesting way to understand how sugar and alcohol interact with oxygen is to start the vinegar-making process in a zip-top bag. Fill a gallon plastic bag a third of the way with alcohol (such as beer or wine), and blow into the bag to fill the other two-thirds with air. Seal the bag, and you'll see that it will stay inflated for a few days to a week, until the oxygen has been used up, and then you can just unseal the bag and add more air until all the alcohol has been converted to acetic acid.

If you're starting with a sugar solution, you'll only want to fill up the bag a third of the way with liquid and a third with air, leaving the rest of the space for the CO_2 that will be released as sugars turn into alcohol, blowing up the bag like a balloon. When it's fully inflated, release the air, and repeat this process until the bag no longer inflates.

ENVIRONMENT

TEMPERATURE CONTROL,
HEAT JACKETS, IMMERSION
CIRCULATING WATER BATHS
You want to pick a nice dry, room-temperature spot to start making vinegar. You can mock an artificial setting to speed up the process by using heater belts or jackets (which can be found in homebrew stores, and look like heating pads), or even immersing the jars in an immersion circulating water bath to keep a consistent temperature, but I think that's going overboard. Like Parmesan and prosciutto, I've found the best vinegars are seasoned by their environmental conditions throughout the year, giving the final product unique nuances, just as in natural wines or farmhouse ales and saison beers.

In the summer, things will progress faster; in winter they'll go slower; even though most of the work is carried out by imperceptible acetobacter yeast, it's important to pay attention to the vinegar throughout the process. Taste it and smell it every week. If everything's going well, the liquid will lose some of its initial aromas and gain some acidity, but at no point should it start smelling or tasting like acetone (paint thinner) or ammonia or rotten eggs. Like wine, bad yeasts will make for a bad bouquet. Stir it up, and check it often. It's about finding an equilibrium that's fit for vinegar to thrive, and the right balance of sugar, alcohol, time, and temperature. Should you encounter any of those off-aromas or flavors, refer to MISSTEPS and CLARIFYING, below.

TESTING YOUR RESULTS

PH, PERCENT ACIDITY

Once all of the ethyl alcohol has been converted to acetic acid (easily checked with a hydrometer, it will read at a submerged volume near 1.05 g/cm^3 because vinegar is slightly denser than water, since there are acetic acid molecules dissolved in it), the next step is to taste your vinegar to see if you like it. What we feel on our tongues is different from what we taste; it's kind of like a boozy wine that's too alcoholic to sense its fruit. If vinegar is too acidic, it will disallow us from discerning flavors on the palate. The pH, or "power of hydrogen," is the concentration of acidity. This can also be measured using pH strips. All you do is dip one of the strips into your vinegar and it changes color to correspond to its pH value. Most vinegars are between 2.8 and 3.4—the lower the number, the higher the acidity. Lemons are actually more acidic than most vinegars, at around pH 2. Above 3.4, acidity is less perceptible; most wine is around pH 4, tomatoes are a bit higher, and milk is in the 6-plus range. At 7, pH is neutral (pure water is pH 7), and on the other side of the scale, pH increases in alkalinity, with ammonia around 11, lye at 13, and sodium hydroxide reaching the far end at 14.

While percentage acidity refers to vinegar's intensity or strength, it's something you feel more in your nose and chest than taste on your tongue. We all know those vinegars that make you cough because of their vapors and vibrancy. There's a litmus test called titration, a technique that adds controlled amounts of sodium hydroxide (NaOH) to vinegar, revealing itself through a visual cue. NaOH is slowly dripped into an acidic solution of an unknown concentration until it turns pink due to its reaction with phenolphthalein, a chemical compound added as an acetic acid indicator. It will eventually hold its color when agitated, and the amount of NaOH required to get to this stage will help you figure out the percentage acidity of the vinegar. You can double-check your samples by sending them to a lab to be titration tested.

MISSTEPS

KAHM, MOLD, VINEGAR EELS

Hiccups can happen in vinegar making, and I don't mean from acid reflux (which is not caused by vinegar consumption, by the way). A common problem is kahm yeast, which looks like a mold but is not. It appears as a white, wrinkled skin in the place of where a mother would form. This occurs when all the sugars are gone and there's a drop in pH, due to a number of conditions, like temperature fluctuations and/or humidity. You'll see kahm commonly happen in sauerkraut, as it has more to do with lactic fermentation than acetic, but if you do get kahm, be calm and carry on. You can skim off the film, and the sooner you can do so the better. Left to its own devices, this yeast will poorly flavor your vinegar.

Another hazard that can arise are little things called vinegar eels. These thread-thin, half-inch-long nematodes are not the next Sea Monkeys fad; rather, they're worms that feed off the yeast cultures that form on the surface of fermenting vinegar. To see if you have any, bring your vinegar into a dark room and shine a flashlight into it; you'll be able to see them, and they'll move toward the light. To avoid such microorganisms, I strongly encourage straining your base liquid before you even start. They're far less likely to appear in clean, clear vinegar. The truth is, these eels are harmless, if a bit unsightly. The good news is that you can easily strain them out if they do appear.

CLARIFYING

FINING, FREEZING, STRAINING
Another way to get rid of vinegar eels (and other unwanted detritus) is to pasteurize your vinegar at a low temperature, killing both the eels and their food source. That said, I am a big advocate for unpasteurized, live acetobacter vinegars, for many reasons (tradition, taste, health). I really avoid pasteurization as much as I can.

An alternative way to get rid of unwanted dregs is to use a fining agent. This can be achieved by inverting your vinegar through gelatin, which will pull all the bad proteins away from the solution and clarify your vinegar. You can even fine vinegar by freezing it and then letting it thaw slowly. The solids will separate and can be scooped out with a spoon. I'll usually strain my vinegars again through a cheesecloth or coffee filter, just to make sure they're as pure as possible.

STORING/AGING

BARRELS, BOTTLE CONDITIONING, CHAMPENOISE STYLE, A COOL DRY PLACE, REFRIGERATE ONCE OPEN
Storing your final product might be the last step of making vinegar, but knowing where to keep it is incredibly important, as is the understanding that vinegar has a shelf life. In general, you want to seal your vinegar in a bottle with just a little headspace. It's best stored in a cool, dry place—even refrigerated, if possible—to ensure you've stopped the fermentation

process. Unlike most supermarket vinegars, which are pasteurized and distilled for shelf stability (and lose much of their aroma and flavor in the process), good vinegars aren't meant to sit in a warm pantry; they should be used often after they're bought, or made fresh. Live vinegars, ones that haven't been pasteurized, are best kept in the fridge once they're opened.

You may have heard stories about vinegar crocks sitting on the counters of your European grandparents' kitchens, and this is actually a decent option, so long as you have a vessel that's nonreactive and not porous. Storing is also a question of aging; do you want to continue the evolution of the flavor of your vinegar? Barrels allow vinegar to breathe at a slow and steady rate. And while the vinegar will continue to ferment and reduce, it will also gain complexity from the barrel itself.

Lately I've been experimenting with conditioning vinegar in bottles, adding a little dose of sugar and champagne yeast before I cap or cork them, and letting them go through a secondary fermentation like a sparkling wine. This process is used in beer brewing too, as it allows yeasts to naturally carbonate a bottle. The reason this makes sense to me with vinegar is that the CO_2 created in the bottle keeps aerating the vinegar continuously. The bubbles create a wonderfully dry and vibrant mouthfeel as well! You'll want to find a cool, dark spot to hold your bottles during this process. When you open them, watch out, there will be some bubbling, so hold the bottles over a sink and point the cap/cork away from you and anything breakable.

MHT'S VINEGAR PANTRY

What follows is a loose guide on how to build flavorful vinegars, rather than a collection of actual recipes, because from apple to apple, ingredient to ingredient, sugar levels will vary. You may live in a different city or town than I do, and indigenous bacteria and yeasts differ from place to place. Conditions and environments aren't givens, but what's consistent is the way we can create our vinegars.

There are no exact equations for making live acetobacter vinegars, other than following the guidelines on pages 301 through 312. I'd love to say it's one gallon of this to one quart of that and add a tablespoon of whatever, but it's all about making it yours. For example, traditionally, *vinagre de piña* (pineapple vinegar) in Mexico uses the skins and cores of the fruit rather than the juice. A bit of fruit flesh stays intact, but the majority of the sugar comes from *pilon-cillo*, a native brown sugar also known as *panela*. I've made it a few times, and though it's good, I prefer making pineapple vinegar with straight pineapple juice; it has a full-bodied pineapple flavor as opposed to a vinegar that tastes like a combination of ingredients.

The way I think about it is to ask, "What am I hoping to use this vinegar for?" If it's for vinaigrettes, I want it strong, sharp, and singular. If it's meant for braising, maybe I want something a little broader, with interesting spice notes that develop over time. For a drinking vinegar, well, you want that a bit more balanced, rounder, maybe with the slightest bit of residual sugar.

It's all about thinking of the application before you start making vinegar. Below are a few flavor combinations I've made and enjoyed in the past. I'm constantly trying to find new profiles that not only taste great, but also put to use original combinations of ingredients that have reference points in the greater context of food and drink.

MHT'S VINEGAR FLAVORS

FOUR THIEVES VINEGAR
WHITE WINE, WATER, SAGE, ROSEMARY, AND GARLIC

Water back a high-alcohol (13 to 15 percent ABV) white wine by 15 percent (that would be about ½ cup [120 ml] of water to one 750-ml bottle of wine), and add herbs and aromatics. Allow all to ferment together, rather than just making an infusion.

MANISCHEWITZ CONCORD GRAPE WINE VINEGAR

This is a play on one of my favorite childhood flavors (not that I drank as a child). Instead of trying to ferment the fickle concord grape (skinning and de-seeding those suckers is no fun, either), you can make bright and tannic vinegar out of the bottled stuff purely by allowing it to re-ferment.

CHOCOLATE PORTER OR STOUT VINEGAR

This is a true malt vinegar that's great with fish and chips. Adding a pinch of malt powder to the beer rounds out the flavor and calls out the toasty grain build of the beer.

COCONUT RICE VINEGAR
COCONUT WATER, THAI STICKY RICE, WATER

Straight coconut water will ferment fast, so adding a bit of starch and water slows down the process and helps develop an almost creamy mouthfeel.

APPLE PIE VINEGAR
APPLE JUICE, WATER, CINNAMON STICK, BROWN SUGAR

The all-American vinegar. While store-bought cider vinegar is widely available, this version has a bit more depth and personality. Try out different apple varieties for distinctive outcomes.

TRIPLE BERRY VINEGAR
BLACKBERRY, BLUEBERRY, RASPBERRY

Another ode to pie, but this time rather than make a single varietal vinegar, I mix a few shrub berries and use them in my Shrubs Shrub drink (page 281). It's also great as a glaze on game meats.

MIREPOIX VINEGAR
CARROT JUICE, CELERY JUICE, ONION PEELS

Mirepoix is frequently used as the base flavoring agent for many stocks, and this vinegar version is great for deglazing a pan for a reinforced jus.

DRIED CHERRY AND CHERRY BLOSSOM VINEGAR

This one was inspired by my friend Adam Dulye's mignonette. Take dried cherries and heat them up in water, rehydrating the fruit and making a sugary solution. Add cherry blossoms (either fresh in springtime, or they can be bought dried) for the floral notes and allow to ferment. Pairs incredibly well with the sweet salinity of an oyster.

GINEGAR

HONEY, WATER, JUNIPER, CARDAMOM, CITRUS PEEL

You can add a little gin here too if you'd like, but rather than starting this off with booze, mock the flavor profile by incorporating some of the botanicals used in more floral and aromatic gins. If the vinegar needs a little push to ferment faster, of course, top with gin.

HOT TODDY VINEGAR

HONEY, WATER, WHISKEY, LEMON JUICE, CLOVES

One of my favorite vinegars I've ever made. I started with approximately 1 gallon of 5:1 water to honey, a 750-ml bottle of whiskey, the juice of two lemons, and a handful of cloves. This vinegar evolves into an aperitif that you can drink hot or on the rocks. It's also great for acidulating starches, like adding to a pot of beans or stewing with chili.

RED EYE VINEGAR

MAPLE SYRUP, WATER, COFFEE BEANS

Another great deglazer. Make sure the maple-to-water ratio is high enough to be like greasy-spoon diner syrup for pancakes. The coffee beans are cracked, not ground, and give the vinegar some tannin structure, making this "breakfast" vinegar a great addition to splash on a steak or fry with some eggs (see page 28).

ST-GERMAIN ELDERFLOWER LIQUEUR VINEGAR

I tried making an elderflower vinegar a few times, but the fresh flowers were so delicate that they didn't give the full-force elderflower flavor that I love in St-Germain. I just watered back the liqueur and found it makes a wonderfully potent vinegar for spritzing on top of a salad. Also nice stirred into a cocktail.

NEGRONI VINEGAR

CAMPARI, SWEET VERMOUTH, GIN, WATER, SUGAR

Yes, you're making a drink that is usually 1:1:1 aperitivo, vermouth, and gin, but here you water back and add a little more sugar to help this boozy cocktail ferment. What you're left with is a complex digestivo that also cleanses your palate.

In researching this book, I found that Christopher Kostow, the chef behind The Restaurant at Meadowood, an extraordinary fine dining experience in Napa, California, was also making vinegars. His kitchen is modern and experimental, but his food is viscerally rooted in the area surrounding the resort. In the thick of a well-known wine region, he forages the woodlands, considering the flora as more than garnish on a plate. Even with wine abundant in the area, Kostow makes his own red wine vinegar beginning with fresh grapes. The following recipe is a worthy foundation for making your own.

RED WINE VINEGAR, FROM CHRISTOPHER KOSTOW, THE RESTAURANT AT MEADOWOOD, NAPA VALLEY, CALIFORNIA
MAKES ABOUT 1 LITER

2 cups (480 ml) WATER, *distilled, room temperature*

½ cup (105 g) DEMERARA SUGAR

5 cups (750 g) RED WINE GRAPES, about 2 pounds (910 g)

Start by mixing the water and sugar in a bowl until the sugar is fully dissolved. Place the grapes into a glass or ceramic vessel and pour the sugar water over the grapes. Place the vessel in a warm room-temperature area and cover with cheesecloth or a clean kitchen towel. Twice a day, using a metal spoon, push the fruit down as it rises to the top, intentionally bruising, if not crushing, the fruit; though it may float back up, the fruit needs to be moistened to help prevent mold from forming. Continue this process for 6 to 9 days. After the first couple of days the mixture should be bubbling and alive; if not, add some more sugar, 1 tablespoon at a time, and repeat the agitation process for 2 to 3 more days. Strain the grapes and place the liquid back in the glass vessel and leave for another 2 weeks covered. Strain once more and you're done.

LEFTOVERS

TURNING DROSS INTO GOLD

Although the most basic form of vinegar involves the fermentation of wine, winemakers are notoriously wary of vinegar makers. Some fear that acetobacters from vinegar production, loose in the air or on the hands or clothing of a vinegar producer, might taint their wines, especially their younger vintages. Perhaps there's a cultural bias too—no winemaker wants their product *mistaken* for vinegar.

Roman Roth has long been the winemaker at Wölffer Estate on Long Island, and he has no such bias. He grew up in the Black Forest of Germany, home of sauerbraten and sour veal kidneys, and since 2012 he has been making 800 bottles a year . . . not of wine, but of rosé vinegar. "If you deal with wine, and you deal with juice, vinegar is not too far away," says Roth.

Wölffer Estate makes more than thirty-five thousand cases of rosé a year; add up all the sediment, or lees, that this produces, and you can easily get to one hundred fifty cases of settled rosé. Instead of using that toward the production of wine, which would be diluted anyway, Roth has found it's the perfect by-product for making vinegar. Many wineries will put the yeast back into wine or throw it away, but if you're patient and wait for it, you can still yield excellent, if somewhat oxidized, juice, the perfect base for vinegar.

Roth uses the Orléans method, filling decades-old barrels two-thirds of the way with the runoff of each year's harvest. The vinegar that results is round, fat, rich, as a real wine vinegar should be, in contrast to vinegar distilled from vodka or other high-proof spirits, which are all burn and no bite. Red wine vinegars should have tannins, and the nice thing about Long Island wines is that they already have nice acidity. Why would they deny their wine the right to its natural progeny?

SPENT GRAIN

Beer brewing yields a by-product that is viable for vinegar making as well. Madhouse Vinegar, a joint venture in Ohio from Justin Dean, a trained chef, and Richard Stewart, a farm manager, looked to produce a sustainable malt vinegar, made with excess batches of artisanal brews that would otherwise be wasted. Dean was picking up spent grains from MadTree Brewing Company in Cincinnati, Ohio, for hog feed, when he saw their routine of dumping excess wort down the drain, rather than looking for a potential outlet. Dean started picking up the surplus, adding back sugar and yeast for the beer to go into secondary fermentation and convert into vinegar. I like to think of it as a bad-beer recycling program. Next up for Dean and Stewart, looking for overripe fruits that they could cordially turn into vinegar.

KITCHEN SCRAPS

Lady Jayne's Alchemy sounds like a maker of the magic elixirs sold as a universal remedy, and in a way, it is. Jori Jayne Emde started making vinegars in 2006, and she's continually used them to cure her digestive problems, taking dried mother of vinegar and eating it like a fruit leather. She's cleared up poison ivy with a vinegar soak, and even rinsed her hair with vinegar to clarify it in lieu of shampoo. The majority of vinegars on the market have been pasteurized, zapped of their health benefits, so Emde suggests pureeing live mothers into a paste, which is great for many skin ailments and utilizes all their good bacteria.

She and husband, Zakary Pelaccio, run Fish & Game in Hudson, New York, a New American farm-to-table eatery. Natural wine is primarily what they use in the restaurant, featured as a beverage pairing option. During the winter months, bottles that are opened and unfinished on a Sunday could go to waste, as they don't have service again until Friday. Instead the wine goes into vinegar. Emde also ferments ribs of kale so they're softer and more palatable. Using open fermentation in an old barn, Emde tops off her vinegar tanks after service and softens them with hearty herbs (sage, summer savory, wild thyme, and a lot of carrot tops) and unattractive soft and bruised cherries. Any remains of kitchen prep are fair game to flavor her vinegars, with the goal of cleansing their kitchen of peels and scraps and filling it back up with something better.

CLEANING UP

Now, with all those dirty dishes, there's only one thing missing in this book, a way to clean them. Neil Kleinberg, who shared the joys of a model hollandaise sauce (page 187), can show you how to make your pans look revitalized, much like his groggy brunch-goers. Remember, a clean cook is a good cook.

COPPER POT CLEANER, FROM NEIL KLEINBERG, CLINTON STREET BAKING COMPANY, NEW YORK CITY MAKES 3 CUPS (720 ML)

1 cup (125 g) ALL-PURPOSE FLOUR

1 cup (132 g) KOSHER SALT

1 cup (240 ml) WHITE VINEGAR

Mix all the ingredients together until the mixture forms a thick paste. Rub on the copper side of pots and pans. Let stand for 10 minutes and then wipe off with a scrubby pad. Rinse and dry. Voilà! Copper will look shiny and clean.

ACKNOWLEDGMENTS

Megan, you are so dear to me. Thank you for indulging an interest that became an obsession, and for allowing a collection of vinegar to grow way too close to your wine. I promise to never let the good stuff go.

Mason, my noble companion and desk mate, who nosed every bottle, who kept me to task, and at play.

Turkells, for letting me find my own way, and giving me the courage to follow through on my eccentricities and infatuations.

Krigbaums, for listening to all the stories, and asking to hear them again. Your enthusiasm and support makes me want to do more.

Michael Sand, my editor, I came to Abrams because of your perspective. You were there when this all took form, and I knew you'd give it gravity.

Ashley Albert and Gabriel Levinson at Abrams, whose close reading and constructive criticism made the book stronger and sharper, like good vinegar.

Deb Wood at Abrams, who managed to map out many vignettes into one cohesive, graceful design.

Alison Fargis, my agent, a tireless advocate for my work and vision even prior to this process. With your gentle guidance, you gave this project integrity.

Rebekah Peppler, my brilliant stylist and esteemed colleague, your disposition radiates on set, and your intuition always puts food in its best light. Thank you for bringing Claire, Edouard, and Kelsey into the mix.

Dean Street Studios, Robert, and Deven, there's no place I'd rather photograph. Your kindness shines even after a day's shoot.

Patrick Watson, for opening your cheese shop (Stinky Bklyn) to a working theory, and allowing it time to mature (in barrel) with significance.

To all the chefs who cook with reverence and nurture artisans as the artists they are.

To all the vinegar makers, who have the passion and patience it takes to make things better.